Media, Anthropology and Public Engagement

Studies in Public and Applied Anthropology

General Editors: **Sarah Pink**, RMIT University,
and **Simone Abram**, Durham University

The value of anthropology to public policy, business and third sector initiatives is increasingly recognized, not least due to significant innovations in the discipline. The books published in this series offer important insight into these developments by examining the expanding role of anthropologists practicing their discipline outside academia as well as exploring the ethnographic, methodological and theoretical contribution of anthropology, within and outside academia, to issues of public concern.

Media, Anthropology and Public Engagement

Edited by

Sarah Pink and Simone Abram

berghahn
NEW YORK • OXFORD
www.berghahnbooks.com

First published in 2015 by

Berghahn Books

www.berghahnbooks.com

© 2015, 2017 Sarah Pink and Simone Abram
First paperback edition published in 2017

Library of Congress Cataloging-in-Publication Data

Media, anthropology and public engagement / edited by Sarah Pink and Simone
Abram.
        pages cm. — (Studies in public and applied anthropology)
    Includes bibliographical references and index.
    ISBN 978-1-78238-846-3 (hardback : alk. paper) — ISBN 978-1-78533-744-4
    (paperback) — ISBN 978-1-78238-847-0 (ebook)
    1. Applied anthropology—Philosophy. 2. Mass media and anthropology.
3. Applied anthropology—Methodology. I. Pink, Sarah. II. Abram, Simone.
    GN397.5.M385 2015
    301—dc23
                                                                    2015003133

British Library Cataloguing in Publication Data

A catalogue record for this book is available from the British Library

ISBN 978-1-78238-846-3 hardback
ISBN 978-1-78533-744-4 paperback
ISBN 978-1-78238-847-0 ebook

CONTENTS

———⚬⚬⚬———

PART II. PUBLIC ANTHROPOLOGY AND SOCIAL MEDIA

FIGURES

———◁◁◁◁◁———

ACKNOWLEDGEMENTS

Media, Anthropology and Public Engagement has been 5 years in the making. Our work over this time has brought us into contact with several Berghahn Books editors, all of whom we would like to thank for their support during this process. We also thank the anonymous reviewers of the book for their supportive and helpful comments.

INTRODUCTION

Mediating Publics and Anthropology

———— ⬬ ————

Simone Abram and Sarah Pink

Media, Anthropology and Public Engagement looks at how changing public media and arts practices are enabling the emergence of a new public anthropology. In doing so, we address a set of key questions about anthropology's public role. Each of the key terms in this phrase – public, anthropology, media, engagement – needs to be considered, since each has multiple referents and contested meanings. In this introduction, we set out the premises for understanding what an engaged anthropology can be, and how new media can be put to work to broad effect. The chapters in this collection demonstrate which questions must be asked, and how they can be addressed in practical terms as well as through intellectual argument, and illustrate how initiatives by a range of anthropologists in different (largely anglophone) countries have adopted media into their practices.

New media, and new ways of employing media, are developing all the time. In a book on the subject, we are necessarily committing ourselves to a discussion with longevity, in contrast to more ephemeral media. This brings with it the advantages of gathering together a set of chapters that mark a line in the sand about where we are today, to take stock of a number of innovative and rapidly changing scenarios, and to put them in a broader temporal and theoretical perspective. Behind the rapid change in the use of some media, in other words, there are issues that remain relatively constant, central debates about the discipline that require repeated assertion, and tensions and dilemmas that always need to be addressed. In a book on media, publics and anthropological engagement, we wish to remind our readers that there is a very wide range of media that do not necessarily replace one another, but offer different forms of communication, and create different kinds of public.

A challenge that we address in this volume is to bring together insights from media anthropology with questions about public engagement, and ask how or even whether these are compatible. What new opportunities arise from changing technologies to address long-standing problems for an engaged anthropology? While new technologies can open doors into new environments, and gather new audiences for anthropological communication, they also prompt us to question some basic assumptions about what anthropology is, what can and should be communicated, and what we actually mean by a public anthropology. The latter question has been increasingly debated in recent years, impelled by initiatives such as Borofsky's public anthropology programme (see Borofsky 2000, 2011; Vine 2011) and a revived *Anthropology in Action* journal,[1] as well as the series to which this book contributes, and other initiatives. One reason to shift the nomenclature from applied anthropology to public anthropology has been to break down the implied split between applied and 'pure' academic anthropology, and urge scholars also to engage in urgent and political issues faced by people subject to power imbalances around the world. It is interesting to note that all the contributors to this volume have scholarly appointments, as well as being engaged in various kinds of public activities. New forms of media might enable kinds of public engagement that were not previously available, but they require the time and effort in the same way as any other form of public engagement. Hence, in this book we address questions that integrate engagement, media and publics. We address these in this introduction by way of four questions, as follows:

– What is anthropological engagement?
– What are the publics of anthropology?
– What kinds of media are being used, and how do they affect the above?
– What kind of anthropology is implied by these questions?

What is Anthropological Engagement?

Various anthropologists bemoan the invisibility of the discipline in the public domain, including several contributors to this book. Eriksen (2012) is among those who claim that anthropology should have changed the world, yet remains almost invisible outside academia. In common with Peter Hervik (Chapter 2), he argues that anthropologists should have been at the forefront of public debate 'about multiculturalism and nationalism, the human aspects of information technology, poverty and economic globalisation, human rights issues and questions of collective and individual identification in the Western world', and yet they fail to get their message across (Eriksen 2012: 1).

Questions about anthropological engagement tend to fall into easy dichotomies. Despite contrary evidence, the idea persists that there is a pure, academic anthropology, which is a discussion between anthropologists, in contrast to an applied anthropology that is a discussion with people 'out there' beyond university departments of anthropology. The entrenchment of the idea of pure versus applied and the exclusion of active anthropology from academic departments is happily largely behind us, but the dichotomy tends to raise its head at regular intervals. But even within debates about engaged public or applied anthropology, there is a spread of approaches to consider. Fassin (2013) distinguishes between popularization and politicization, for example; and in a landmark volume, *Exotic No More,* MacClancy (2002) points out that throughout the history of the discipline, anthropologists have been engaged in both activities despite the unevenness of attention given to scholarly, popularizing and immediately politicized anthropological endeavours. It is this unevenness between what anthropologists do and what is reported that fuels a perception of disengaged academics, with no public profile, while, in fact, it is mainstream popular and broadcast media in anglophone Western countries that pay scant – or worse, sensationalist – attention to anthropological engagement in current issues.

This is not helped by an institutional entrenchment found in various countries. Francine Barone and Keith Hart (Chapter 9) point to debates about the AAA in the United States during a period when some of its members felt it was largely being run for the benefit of its employees rather than its membership, reinforcing a sense of an internal clique who disregarded the concerns of anthropologists and their research partners. Anthropological conferences, and sometimes departmental seminars, can also be alienating experiences for those not already steeped in their cultural practices, and the editors of this volume are hardly alone in bemoaning the tendency of anthropologists – and other academics – to wrap their work up in unintelligible jargon and dense texts, rather than communicating clear arguments about the real and exciting work of ethnography and anthropology to eager and fascinated audiences.[2] Conference presentations often reveal the way that anthropologists can be nervously wedded to text, and this remains a core challenge for the different kinds of communication that we discuss in this volume. While this book addresses questions about new media, the unappealing presentation that is so often to be found in anthropological conferences has no place in popular communication (we would argue it has no place at conferences either). Unfortunately, such practices also create an obstacle to communication in offering some kind of precedent for the style of published work, but at the same time they become a model against which many anthropologists seek to rebel.

On the other hand, there is a long and venerable history of public engagement by anthropologists, both in public debates, political campaigns, media worlds and local social movements. Beck (2009) points out that anthropological ethical codes have long included terms that require anthropologists to work in the interests of the people they study. Indeed, against the notion that public anthropology represents a response to anthropologists talking only to one another, Merill Singer (2000) has argued that the impression of an insular anthropology itself chooses to ignore the wide array of applied anthropology practised within and outside university academic departments around the world. In terms of presence in public consciousness, Eriksen reminds us that anthropologists like Ruth Benedict were best-selling authors, as were Margaret Mead, Anzia Yerzierska and Claude Levi-Strauss, while Edmund Leach, Bronislaw Malinowski and others wrote frequently for popular publications, and Leach was among UK scholars who gave televised lectures for national broadcast. Even earlier, Tyler's *Golden Bough* (1894) was a thoroughly genre-crossing publication, widely read and referred to, despite its multi-volume weight.

It is unfortunate that the public profile of earlier anthropologists is often recounted in parallel with the rejection of their work by academics who may have been unable to respect the work of public communication, or may have felt resentful of the attention that it garnered. Contributors to this book reject the notion that speaking outside academia, or translating ones arguments and messages for non-academic audiences, constitutes a betrayal of academic rigour. On the contrary, we hold that it is often academics who, secure in their knowledge and confident of their field, are able to speak in plain terms and communicate their message despite the compromises that engagement in public debates requires. Perhaps it is a lack of confidence that has prevented more anthropological scholars from putting themselves forward as public spokespersons in Western media debates.

In the 1950s, Vogt was reporting that anthropology was enjoying an improving profile in the 'public consciousness', but by the 1970s, Allen (1975) was identifying that 1969 had been the height of anthropologists' isolation, remarking that anthropologists were failing to communicate what was a subject of wide general interest, and one in which there was a demonstrable interest among newspaper readers. Since then, the difficulty of crossover from academia to journalism has become a persistent ache in anthropological debate. Divale complained in 1976 that anthropologists were failing to understand the working context of journalists, and that this explained their often hostile response to the idea of publishing their findings in newspapers, local and national. Despite Divale's patient outline of the everyday life of print and news journalists, and his clear suggestions as to how anthropologists and journalists could work together, Beema (1987) indicated that little had improved thus far in the 1980s, and Bird repeated the call for engagement as recently as 2010 (Bird 2010). In response to the ongoing saga of the absence of anthropology in mainstream media, Witteveen (2000) joked that the problem might lie in the discipline's overly long name compared to history or economics.

Despite this, we have occasional accounts of anthropologists' brushes with news media. McDonald (1987) provided what has become a classic horror story of finding her work publicized as a scandal despite her best intentions, a scenario that arises when journalists seize on and sometimes seek to sensationalize a topic that suddenly becomes a story, whether by dint of current affairs or journalistic imagination. Eriksen (2006) has drawn attention to how the speed of news media creates difficulties for scholars more used to leisurely reflection, and Gullestad (2002) has eloquently detailed the difficult position this creates for a situated author who needs time to consider his or her response to journalistic challenge, and to confer with colleagues in order to speak as a representative of their institution and for the discipline. Her critique is implied in Hervik's chapter, when he distinguishes between anthropologists presenting themselves as individual commentators, resting on the legitimacy that a position in a university and a record of publication offers them, and scholars who attempt to mediate anthropological scholarship rather than personal (if informed) opinion. Status or position is an issue, in other words, for news and other broadcast media, as it is often seen as shorthand for authority and legitimacy.

Fassin's recent (2013) article recounting his experience of being in the media spotlight as the attention of ministers and national news media focused upon him is a similar kind of story of sudden entry into a media debate, but Fassin had sought specifically to address an issue of public concern – the role of state police in the lives of residents of French housing estates – and had earlier been somewhat disappointed in the lack of policy response. Fassin was in a strong enough position to address journalists and ministers as an intellectual equal, not an option for post-graduate students (as McDonald was at the time of her encounter). Speaking, like Edmund Leach or more recently Adam Kuper, as a senior university professor is an entirely different experience to attempting to engage journalists as a junior scholar on an insecure contract. There are intermediate positions, however. Simone Abram hosted a BBC radio presenter at her home and field site for a summer special edition of an ongoing weekly social science magazine programme, 'Thinking Allowed', that various anthropologists have appeared on over the years. A magazine-style presentation offers a less sensational and more reflective opportunity to discuss research methods and findings, away from the hurly burly of newsrooms, but still within the short-article, wide-audience format that broadcast media offer.

Even this diverse engagement in broadcast media debates is only one form of engaged anthropology, and a term like 'public debate' has many meanings. While most anthropologists focus on text media, significant attention has been paid to the role of anthropologists in ethnographic film and indigenous media, and to the role of these forms for anthropology. Much attention was focused early on, on the potential for television as a medium of communication between and among indigenous people and minority groups (e.g. Eiselein and Marshall 1976), and ground-breaking projects such as 'Video in the Villages' became, or facilitated, significant social movements, particularly across Latin America (see Aufderheide 1993). A tradition of collaborative media has developed in which anthropologists have stepped back from the attempt to direct audiovisual production, instead participating in joint projects with professional directors and indigenous artists and producers (e.g. Deger 2013). In Chapter 5, Juan Salazar traces the ongoing history of engagement by media anthropologists in indigenous media practices, showing how various indigenous and workers' groups quickly took up the potential of video and audiovisual recording from well-intentioned anthropologists, and began to run with the technology according to their own priorities. In the process, anthropologists have had to learn how to decolonize indigenous media spaces, just as indigenous media have decolonized the methodologies of ethnographic film.

While early pioneers argued strongly for the use of audiovisual media to communicate anthropological research and ethnographic detail, other debates have been concerned with the apparent disappearance of an anthropological presence from mainstream television altogether (Henley 2005; Singer 2008). The imperative of finding a mass audience for anthropology remains an issue, but the focus often slips over towards calls for an anthropology of media, including mass media (e.g. Bird 2010, Coman 2005; Osorio 2005). This is not a criticism of media anthropology by any means, but an indication of the slipperiness of anthropological commitment to public engagement, and to broadcast and news media in particular, that receives the force of Barone and Hart's criticism in Chapter 9. Instead, however, new media channels mean that film with an ethnographic focus, and anthropological commentary can now appear through networked websites such as Vimeo and YouTube, as well as embedded in blogs and research websites. These further imply the creation of new audiences, new 'publics' for public engagement. In this book, we expand the focus from earlier discussions of news media and television to consider new digital media, and media mostly new (or persistently marginalized) to anthropology, such as verbatim theatre, art exhibitions and public-sector consultancy. In each of these, we ask not only what the medium offers in terms of collaboration and engagement, but what kinds of public they have the potential to create for discussions that build on anthropological knowledge.

If the public for this kind of public anthropology is users of media communications, there is another equally important public for anthropological research and practice in government and policy fields. Ironically, while Merill Singer (2011) argues that public anthropology ignores applied anthropology, he is comfortable in arguing that anthropologists are ineffective in influencing public policy, while ignoring the rich and plentiful evidence of policy influence from development anthropology – more invisible anthropology, in other words. Similar principles apply to the debate around publicizing anthropology, in that anthropologists have increasingly documented the worlds of public policy (Dyck and Waldram 1993; Shore and Wright 1997; Murdoch and Abram 2002) while being slower to document their own activities in engaging with policy practices (Stewart and Strathern 2004; Pink 2005). According to Shirley Fiske (2011), there has indeed been some effect from anthropology, but policy processes take some time, and effects are variable. More importantly, she points out that anthropologists are not alone in their engagements with policy, but work most effectively in collaboration with communities of activists and advocates, for whom anthropological methods and ideas can be inspiring, but whose support is needed to convince the dispersed actors in policy processes to admit insights that may be unfamiliar.

In this volume, Margaret Bullen sets out the practicalities of conducting policy consultancy, tying in with the earlier discussion by relating how her consultancy work used news media coverage to raise public engagement in the issues at stake. Bullen is hardly alone in this kind of work; the website antropologi.info lists a dozen anthropological consultancies in Norway and Denmark alone and prior to 2010.[3] Consultancies such as the Oslo-based 'Kulturell Dialog' were started up in the 1990s by enterprising master's students, some of whom have gone on to have long and very successful careers in anthropological consultancy. This point also highlights how widely debates vary internationally. The role of anthropologists in public policy is not the same in Norway, Spain and the United States, for instance, and although this volume by necessity addresses only selected countries, we remain alert to the particularities of anglophone debates, and to the effects of translation from other languages to the English of this volume.

What Public for Anthropology?

Arguments about going public, such as those discussed above, are challenged in this volume by Alex Golub and Kerim Friedman (Chapter 8). They see 'public anthropology' as only one of many ways of practising a publicly engaged anthropology, quite distinct from 'doing anthropology in public', which has been the aim of the well-respected blog Savage Minds. According to Golub and Friedman, proponents of a public anthropology (i.e. anthropologists communicating in public spheres) tend to imagine that anthropologists know something that the public would benefit from knowing, and should thus convey it accessibly. They see this as a misplaced self-confidence based on an idea of anthropologists as experts, and on the notion that publics are 'out there' as pre-existing audiences for the communications of anthropologists – as if to say, if only we could find the right language, we should reach that audience. In this, they build on the work of Gal and Woolard who apply a linguistic analysis to the notion of 'the public' to demonstrate that it operates rather like the term 'the field', to which a similar critique has been applied (Gupta and Ferguson 1997; Amit-Talai 2000).

In discussing public audiences for anthropology, we are seeking in each context to define an audience for our work that goes beyond academic debate, to share anthropological ideas and analysis across disciplinary boundaries, beyond the universities, and/or in local, regional or national contexts, or indeed internationally (see also Beck 2009). The public we seek for our ideas may also be defined through the medium of communication – students and audiences at lectures, television viewers, newspaper readers – or as we highlight here, social-media users, blog readers, and networked social acquaintances of various sorts. A public anthropology, in other words, may be an anthropology addressed to, created with, learning from and/or involving quite different constituencies, for whom the label 'public' merely indicates that they are not already our academic peers or graduates of studies in anthropology. Recent developments in media technology thus open up new publics. These developments obviously leave the potential audience wide open, and raise questions for every person seeking to achieve wider awareness of anthropological ideas about which groups of people they imagine their public to be (see also Abram 2012).

Golub and Friedman's criticism places the debates about anthropology and journalism into perspective as just one part of the debate about anthropological engagement, and one that is increasingly eclipsed by the new forms of mediation available to anthropologists. For the blogger, the internet provides a new means to create audiences, to gather new publics with shared interests that overlap with the anthropologist author. Blogging remains a one-to-many form of communication that allows a greater freedom of expression than journalism, with the latter's hierarchies of owners and editors. It also competes for attention with other kinds of media as well as with other blogs. This gives the blog a particular role. If anthropologists are to improve their public engagement, then it is valuable to have a forum where routes to engagement can be discussed, ideas played with, and possibilities explored. Blogs are equally open and accessible as other news media, within the limitations of internet access, language and time. Thus far, there is a lack of detailed information about the readers of anthropological blogs (however defined), and little to match Divale's 1976 survey of newspaper readership. Of the blogs discussed in this book and others, most attempt to open the subject to non-specialists, but all seem to attract readerships made up largely of anthropology students and scholars, even the avowedly open Open Anthropology Cooperative (OAC) (see Chapter 9).

The OAC is an important example of how point-to-point and mass-to-mass media (and combinations thereof) can be harnessed to create new forums for public debate. New media do not necessarily resolve old problems, though, and as Barone and Hart relay, in attempting to stage a revolution in anthropology, the OAC faced the difficulties that any revolutionary movement must face. In proposing an anarchic space, they soon had to consider how that anarchy should be organized, since media platforms are subject to organizational configurations that both enable and constrain communications. Freedom, as Mouffe (2000) has pointed out, cannot be complete if equality is also to be prized. The revolution may not have been televised, but it was compromised and remains partial, as Barone and Hart recount.

Which Media?

In creating diverse publics, anthropologists can now employ more interactive web-based media to engage particular interlocutors, as John Postill (Chapter 7) and others have demonstrated. The technologies that offer both autonomy and massification allow subversive or unofficial debates to spread rapidly beyond particular localities. Whereas resistance to policy or development was once fought through direct action, personal contacts and private channels of organizations, contemporary revolutions work around the increasingly penetrative surveillance by states of organizations by employing social media to communicate ideas and plans, and rapidly summoning and organizing crowds. Social media thus not only enable state surveillance but also resistance to it, and there are anthropologists who have not been slow to exploit the opportunities this offers.

Matthew Durrington and Samuel Gerald Collins (in Chapter 6) have employed the interactivity of web2.0 technology directly to challenge the dominant fictional representation of Baltimore that is broadcast on mainstream television around the world. Their audience is much smaller than that of 'The Wire', one of the most successful television shows produced, but they have the crucial task of offering alternative representations that can feed into the self-esteem of residents in neighbourhoods poorly portrayed, and, in turn, into neighbourhood relations and local development policy. To do that, they engaged students in a kind of action research, to make anthropological methodologies and ideas relevant to communities and institutions. Such work builds on a solid history of anthropological engagement in social conditions, but in hastening to chastise anthropologists for hiding in their academic offices, we should not deny that there have been many anthropologists, inside academia and outside, who have been thoroughly engaged in day-to-day struggles for the rights of oppressed people. Some, including Nancy Scheper-Hughes, have combined political action with a public media presence and representation in anthropological blogs and science media (see Scheper-Hughes 1993, 2004; Scheper-Hughes and Wacquant 2002; Bartoszko 2006; Watters 2014).

While engagement through fieldwork and through the methodologies of visual anthropology are now well recorded, perhaps less has been documented about the use of performance methodologies. Political theatre is world renowned, but there are relatively few anthropologists who have written about using it (even if some have used it in teaching research methods – such as Abram, pers. comm.). Debra Vidali, (Chapter 4), describes backing into political theatre through reinvention, attempting to address the same problems of articulating popular experience in a world dominated by unfair representations. Fed up of hearing reports blaming young people for political apathy, she used the methods of verbatim theatre to give voice to young people and their experience. With this in place, she went on to film the work, present it at conferences and other gatherings, and also distribute the work online.

Vidali confronts the prejudice about different forms of anthropological work that she encountered, occasionally explicitly, from scholars who object to academics working outside academia. Her theatrical work does not replace her scholarly work, she argues, but pushes conventional academic boundaries and concepts, blurring the line that others attempt to impose between public scholarship and social science scholarship, in the face of those who imagine these to be incompatible rather than complementary. Much of the pressure to produce strictly scholarly textual items comes from the institutional constraints that are tightening around academics today, referred to also by Barone and Hart in their chapter.[4] Yet such pressures can be resisted wherever it is possible to choose disciplinary solidarity over institutional solidarity – that is, as long as university hiring policy remains under some degree of local departmental control.[5] In encouraging respect for public scholarship as well as conventional academic production, Vidali pushes for experimentation in ethnographic methodologies, but she pushes the conventions of theatre too, and her theatre production challenged both sets of norms in order to build community with her audience, the people who participated in the production, the people who attended performances and joined discussions about it, and those who have seen film versions of the performance too. In each case, Vidali worked with different orders of knowledge production, negotiating participation, authorship and the established powers of media.

Paolo Favero (Chapter 3) has also used established media in new ways to provoke audiences into rethinking their common prejudices. Favero's work with middle-class Indian men generated images that explicitly play with clichés about India, and parody colonial imageries still circulating today. He used photography in contexts that are unusual for an anthropologist, creating exhibition spaces that confront Swedish and Italian audiences with their own presuppositions by combining conventional tropes with unexpected content. In an attempt to expand his audience beyond the visitors to an exhibition, he transposed the imagery into an audio-video installation that was played at nightclubs and bars, using aesthetic techniques to draw viewers into a visual world that challenged the preconceptions common in other media.

New media technologies thus also offer new ways to use old technologies, such as photography or theatre. But the 'newness' of new media is itself called into question by Deger (2013), who notes that the category 'new' tends to place everything before it into the category 'old'. Deger's work with Yolngu artists and professional media producers drew to her attention the shallowness of novelty in Australian modernity. In what she calls an 'ethnographic experiment' in digitally driven art, Yolngu collaborators worked with digital media and ritual aesthetics to adapt technologies to their own politics and aesthetics. Through their adherence to ancestral law, Yolngu participants incorporated digital video, photography and display into what Deger calls 'patterns laid down by ancestors', creating work that produced interplay between the old and the new, for recognition by an emerging Yolngu audience. Although Deger argues that this Yolngu 'ontological investment' in newness is different from that recorded by other anthropologists (ibid.: 356), particularly in their use of new media technologies to mediate between generations, it is perhaps less unusual that new media should be as likely to reproduce existing relations as to generate new ones. Despite the revolutionary hopes of Barone and Hart, for example, about the potential for a new balance of power for anthropology, the OAC seems to have become another, rather than a replacement, association for anthropology (Chapter 9).

Several of the chapters in this book point to the particular things that recent technological inventions enable. John Postill notes that email lists (e-lists) remain a mainstay of academic life, and that the EASA Media network, although open to non-members, is largely received by people with anthropological training or links. On the other hand, through social media posts, the discussions on the e-list are sometimes shared to diverse other networks, particularly by 'lurkers' who listen in to the e-seminars without making comments. Social media are becoming a means by which anthropologists and ethnographers try to publicize their research, as well as being a site for fieldwork. Postill refers to the Twitter storms around Spanish political activism in recent years, distinguishing between the relatively free-flowing and ephemeral trends and Twitter games, and the more personal networks of social media such as Facebook. Such nuances are essential both to the ethnography that is emerging from social media, and its interaction with face-to-face (or 'F2F') relations. Of note is a recent volume that attends to an uneven global networking form that specifically melds online and offline encounters, through 'couchsurfing', a form of hospitality heavily used by postgraduate students, offering them both accommodation and field sites (Picard and Buchberger 2013). Contributors to that volume are very much aware of the partiality of such networks, particularly in terms of the inequalities of gender accessibility and presence – an alarmingly stubborn issue that Golub and Friedman have struggled with over several years, and are concerned to address in their chapter (Chapter 8).

What Kind of Anthropology?

Each of these issues has implications for anthropology as a discipline and as a set of research practices. Firstly, we have yet to resolve – or some would argue even adequately address – what it means to talk of a public anthropology. Is it enough to publicize the results of our work; should we be doing anthropology in public that opens anthropological research to participants and brings less formal discussion to any audience that chooses to listen (or, more commonly, read)? Or is a public anthropology one that addresses issues of public concern, applying ethnographic methods and anthropological ideas and analyses to pressing social questions?

And does this mean working with public authorities (i.e. state authorities) to help them to improve their policies and their ways of serving citizens and clients, or facilitating protest and social movements by sharing extant knowledge and co-producing new knowledge? Clearly, these are not really alternatives, but facets of a more publicly engaged anthropology, one that builds on work from applied anthropology, from the eminent scholars of earlier generations who did much to bring their ideas to broadcast media, and from the very many anthropologists working outside traditional anthropology departments around the world, be that in government offices, aid agencies, interdisciplinary research departments, private businesses, community groups, or simply working in university departments that are not called 'Anthropology'.

One danger inherent in the talk of making a difference or improving the lives of others is always the potential for thinking one knows better, a danger that has been played out through many state projects and is well documented by anthropologists. Hence the discussion of co-production of knowledge and action is key to all the discussions in this book, following Ingold's emphasis on anthropology as not simply a description practice but 'an inquisitive mode of inhabiting the world, of being *with*' and 'a practice of *correspondence*', one which, like art, is a way of knowing 'that proceed[s] along the observational paths of being *with*' and explores 'the unfamiliar in the close at hand' (Ingold 2008: 87–88).

Another danger lies in presuming that all anthropologists share a political standpoint or a commitment to a particular kind of 'public good', a hotly disputed concept in its own right. We do not wish to enter into a discussion about infiltration into anthropology, but the debates played out in *Anthropology Today* (see Gusterson 2003; Moos, Fardon and Gusterson 2005; Price 2005, 2007, 2012; Gonzalez 2007, 2012) indicate quite clearly that the politics of actual anthropologists may not meet the expectations of the more idealistic claims for the discipline. Anthropologists are criticized for not being more aware of, or part of social movements, but should anthropology be imagined as a social movement itself with a shared political purpose? Certainly diversity is increasingly recognized as characteristic of the discipline, with Field and Fox agreeing that 'there is no singular, dominant anthropology that allows us to determine when and how to "engage" with "the public"' (Field and Fox 2007: 6).

Even so, it seems there are anthropologists who clamour for a sense of community, an idea that 'anthropology' exists in some coherent form as a discipline, a political project, and a distinct academic space. And it is also clear that being able to call oneself 'an anthropologist' is highly prized by many people, even if others consider it a false identity. In this book, we discuss the many ways in which 'anthropology' can give meaning to scholarly work, through effecting change in everyday life. The sport of defining anthropology remains popular, and the definition of the discipline has recently been discussed precisely with reference to applied (Pink 2005, 2007; Field and Fox 2007; Sillitoe 2007), public (Eriksen 2006; Borofsky 2007; Beck 2009) and interdisciplinary contexts of anthropology (Strathern 2006). The texts that generated these definitions might be defined as pertaining to a body of literature that was quite prolific during the first decade of the twenty-first century. Taken together these texts and their arguments constitute a set of commentaries that are concerned with the subject matter of anthropology, its boundaries, its claims to expertise and the unique characteristics of its practice. However, they do so with little reference to the audiovisual, digital or mediated element of public anthropology. For some, the expansion of anthropology as an increasingly applied and public discipline, suggests it defies any singular or universal definition. This is encapsulated by Keith Hart's argument that anthropology now has no common purpose and has thus lost its public profile. In making this point he is also tracing the progress of anthropology as an intellectual enquiry: its rejection of normative and colonial consensus about its purpose (or lack of purpose). Hart acknowledges that in outgrowing the narrow confines of anthropology's beginnings and escaping the old imperial centres, anthropology becomes eclectic. He has consistently called for an accessible kind of anthropology, championing the 'amateur anthropologist' (a title cheekily taken up by Gillian Tett, one of his former students), and one with the broadest of aims – 'the making of world society' (Hart 2013: 3).

The Book

In brief, then, the book sits at the intersection between three contemporary trends in anthropology: the shift towards a public anthropology; the increasing use of digital and social media in anthropological practice; and the growing interest in media practice amongst anthropologists. In the context of existing publications in the area of public, applied and engaged anthropology, it advances the focus through its attention to and recognition of this (changing) media(ted) context which is an inevitable part of the way anthropology is done in public. It invites anthropologists to consider not only the possibility of doing public anthropology (or anthropology in public), but also the dynamics of their potential engagements with different old and new media technologies, with media professionals, and with varied web platforms.

The book is organized into two sections. The first includes chapters exploring different ways that anthropologists are engaging new publics through journalistic, audiovisual and performative practices. The second looks at how social media platforms are forming part of a new digital public anthropology, with chapters offered by anthropologists who are leading the way in the use of social and collaborative online media. Through discussions about different projects, the chapters explore how different web platforms can become part of the practice of public anthropology.

In Chapter 1, Maggie Bullen discusses her experiences of 'doing anthropology in public' in the Basque Country. This chapter is set in a traditional media context, in that her work involved a series of press conferences and interviews with journalists, and included print and broadcast media. Moreover, like other anthropological studies that include engaging with media (e.g. Pink 1997) it is not only the ways in which broadcast media engage with research that is relevant, but also the ways in which existing and ongoing media content shape the very research questions and public environment in which the anthropologist is researching. Bullen's account makes clear that alongside the contemporary emphasis on digital participation and citizen journalism, a conventional broadcast media context can still frame anthropologists' modes of public engagement, and that anthropologists still need to be aware of how this contributes to the contexts in which they work and are represented. As Bullen puts it, '[p]ublic anthropology most certainly exposes us to the public eye, mediated by the journalists who are interested in our work and who ultimately represent us'. Revealing how her own projects have got caught up in the (mediated) local politics of the public sphere, Bullen shows how '[w]orking with institutions means that not only do we have to decode the context of our object of study but also be aware of certain hidden keys in the political discourse which belong to another context altogether'.

In Chapter 2, Peter Hervik calls for an 'offensive' approach to public anthropology. Engaging with the work of Marianne Gullestad and drawing on his own experiences of media and public anthropology in relation to ethnic and religious issues in Denmark, Hervik makes a powerful but controversial argument about the role of anthropologists in a mediated public sphere, detailing how anthropologists have been implicated in the Scandinavian press media. While this is a context in which anthropology and anthropologists certainly enjoy a privileged position in the public sphere, Hervik shows that there are a number of perils to such involvement. For Hervik, '[t]he issue of public anthropology involves difficult, broader questions about the self-understandings of institutional anthropology; the ability to do research when historical events take place; and, perhaps more importantly, the ideas and practices of anthropologists as citizens and publicly engaged intellectuals'. His chapter raises the question of the viability of taking a 'safe' approach to relating to the media as an anthropologist, and invites us to ask ourselves some very fundamental questions about the personal and institutional implications of bringing together anthropology, media and public engagement.

Chapter 3, by Paolo Favero, echoes Bullen's and Hervik's concerns about how anthropologists need to situate themselves in relation to the politics and priorities of representation through a reflection on how lens-based media might be engaged in the practice of public anthropology. Favero recounts how in his collaborative photographic practice with young men in Delhi he sought to contest existing mediated representations of India in Europe. By bringing to the fore 'metropolitan middle-class life' through his photography, he responded to the ways in which images of tradition, rurality and beggars had become key visual symbols for India in the popular press in Italy and Sweden. Through his subsequent photographic exhibition 'India Does Not Exist', and a large-screen video installation, Favero sought to break through conventional ways of representing India, inviting his audience to construct new meanings. As Favero's chapter shows, in a rather different way to Bullen and Hervik, a photographic anthropology has a role in making public alternative mediated routes to knowing and understanding. Importantly, it pulls visual anthropological and lens-based media practices out of the environments of ethnographic film festivals and the like, and into a public domain where they might be engaged to contest the dominant representational strategies of broadcast media.

In Chapter 4, Debra Spitulnik Vidali outlines an ongoing collaborative, performative and activist project called 're-generation'. She reiterates the questions over the division between 'applied' and 'pure' research, and argues that a clean division between public and non-public scholarship is not always tenable nor desirable. Beyond these now familiar critiques, Vidali shows how her theatrical project demonstrates that the fundamental dualities adopted in academic contexts rely on ideas of unitary selves, predetermined meanings and authorial authority, each of which is challenged by the project she relates. Vidali challenges the notion that research comes first, and turning it into audience fodder comes after. At the same time, she highlights the difficulties of being innovative in the increasingly rigid and narrow frames of media marketing. Books, plays or music, for that matter, that do not fit into a recognized shelf mark prove impossible to market. The question used to be where to display things in a bookshop – now the issue is that consumers apparently avoid cross-category products. Similarly, theatre professionals have conventional criteria by which to evaluate productions, and may be unenthusiastic about contrary approaches. Crossing boundaries (disciplinary, artistic, market) has never been more fêted, and rarely more difficult to achieve, but Vidali demonstrates that through careful audience feedback, the staging of ethnographic material is not only possible, but effective and powerful, and opens up anthropological insights for new kinds of publics using a mix of digital and direct media.

In Chapter 5, Juan Salazar describes a rupture of ethnographic engagement, through the history of the Latin American Council of Indigenous Film and Communication. In Latin America, he argues, indigenous media have been much more effective in decolonizing methodologies than anthropologists, and have achieved this in part by distancing themselves from anthropological knowledge practices. The emergence of indigenous nations and their struggle for rights has been defined in terms of 'recognition', and Salazar notes that anthropologists have been historically slow to recognise the theory and practice of either social movements or media and communication, although a significant body of anthropological knowledge does now exist on the role of embedded aesthetics in Indigenous media practices. Salazar shows how the Council's film festival has become a space of intercultural encounter, opening a new associative space. In the context of his own work, he explains how documentary video became a device for collaborative ethnographic research. Editing footage taken by his Mapuche collaborator, he entered into a new kind of ethnographic entanglement that offered an opportunity for deep engagement and activist anthropology, in Salazar's own version of Restrepo and Escobar's 'other anthropologies and anthropology otherwise' (2005: 99).

The chapters in Part I of this book therefore reveal the complexities, opportunities, problems and perils of anthropological engagement with the conventional media of newspapers, television, exhibitions and theatre. They show what happens when anthropologists become embedded in the face-to-face and increasingly digital materialities of public media, and impress on us the need to remain engaged with, or at least to acknowledge the relevance of, this domain of public-mediated activity for anthropological research, representation and potential intervention. In Part II of the book, the contributors reflect on the increasingly online dimensions of anthropologists' engagements with public media, and with doing anthropology in public. In some ways these contributors talk back to the concerns that have been raised about representation and participation in the chapters in Part I of the book. They do not necessarily offer 'solutions' (which is, of course, quite typical of anthropologists), but alternative ways of doing anthropology in public, with publics and for publics.

Part II of this book is opened in Chapter 6 by Matthew Durington and Samuel Gerald Collins, through a discussion of their 'Anthropology by the Wire' project, in which they 'are attempting to retool pedagogy toward an applied ethos and develop novel media based research methods while expanding the theoretical boundaries of a public anthropology'. Durington and Collins' project nicely bridges the concerns of both parts of the book, since they discuss using media anthropology methodologies to enable students to work alongside anthropologists and community residents in collaborative empirical research. In a context in which public media are saturated with aberrant perceptions of the community, Anthropology by the Wire uses Web 2.0 and participatory research processes to enable residents to disseminate their own versions of place, not only to each other but to 'other social actors in positions to help them: non-profit organizations, community organizers, city and state government'.

The final three chapters all address the ways in which anthropologists can engage more specifically with social media and different web platforms, as ways of doing public anthropology. In Chapter 7, John Postill, like other contributors, calls for an 'updated understanding of public anthropology' that will 'transcend the mass media channels of a previous era'. Postill discusses his own experiences of doing anthropology in public online. He reflects on the possibilities for engaging with the non-academic public and for constituting 'new forms of public engagement and democratic reform'. This includes a fruitful comparative discussion of the ways that different web platforms and social media activities (including blogging, Facebook and Twitter) have enabled him to participate in different ways and to different extents online, with multiple publics, including research participants and fellow anthropologists. Whereas Postill focuses on his work as an anthropologist who is actively engaged in online (as well as face-to-face) research that forms part of his own online activity, in the following two chapters contributors discuss their work in developing collaborative online public anthropology sites/projects.

In Chapter 8, Alex Golub and Kerim Friedman discuss the highly successful anthropology blog 'Savage Minds', which they situate as part of the growing anthropological blogosphere. Focusing on the blog as a medium for public anthropology, they 'argue that the goal of public anthropology is best served by the blog when it takes the form of "doing anthropology in public" – embodying the professional imaginary on a public platform'. In common with other contributors to this book, Golub and Friedman also call for a rethinking of public anthropology that moves away from the idea that 'that anthropologists know something that the public would benefit from knowing, if only anthropology were written in a style that suited the taste of the public', and overturns the privileging of the anthropologist as expert by highlighting how their audiences have defined them.

Chapter 9, by Francine Barone and Keith Hart, focuses on what has perhaps been one of the biggest online anthropology projects – the Open Anthropology Cooperative. Barone and Hart offer us a comprehensive report and analysis of the challenges and opportunities they were confronted with in developing this web-based collaborative project, hosted on a Ning platform. Their project rapidly became massive as huge numbers of anthropologists signed up, giving the team leading it a complex and demanding set of responsibilities and tasks. Barone and Hart's account offers a genuinely useful commentary for other anthropologists seeking ways to develop collective online forms of public anthropology. At the same time, in engaging reflexively and analytically with their own experiences, they provide us with an anthropological account of the processes and challenges that they confronted in their search for a 'genuine democracy' through online public anthropology.

Media, Anthropology and Public Engagement: Looking Ahead

Together, the contributors to this book convey to us some disquiet about the project of a public anthropology as it has evolved to date. Within the individual chapters there are frequent calls for a rethinking of public anthropology. Given the critical agenda of our discipline, this is not in itself surprising, yet in common the contributors here are calling for a rethinking of public anthropology in relation to media and the mediated environment of which it is a part. Indeed, with them, we would argue that any moves towards doing or rethinking public anthropology need to take into account the mediated nature of anthropological work and public engagement.

Simone Abram is currently reader at the University of Durham and at Leeds Beckett University in the UK, after a long period of working in interdisciplinary academic schools. Her work has explored the idea of governing and local forms of development, through studies of land-use planning, tourism, and more recently, energy. Her publications include: *Rationalities of Planning* and *Culture and Planning* (Ashgate), *Elusive Promises* (Berghahn Books), *Anthropological Perspectives on Local Development* (Routledge) and *Tourists and Tourism* (Berg). She has guest-blogged for Savage Minds and the Anthropology Project, and is founding-editor of ASAonline, an open-access, broad-ranging occasional journal of the ASA.

Sarah Pink is professor of Design and Media Ethnography at RMIT University, Australia, where she is Director of the Digital Ethnography Research Centre. She is also visiting professor a the Swedish Centre for Applied Cultural Analysis, Halmstad University, Sweden, and at Loughborough University UK in the Schools of Design and Civil and Building Engineering. Her research and scholarship is usually interdisciplinary and international, and has been funded by a range of research councils, industry and other stakeholders. She is co-series editor (with Simone Abram) of the Berghahn Books *Studies in Public and Applied Anthropology* series. Her most recent books include *Digital Ethnography: principles and practice* (co-authored in 2015) and *Doing Sensory Ethnography* (2nd edition, 2015).

Notes

1. See http://journals.berghahnbooks.com/aia/
2. Noting Ingold's distinction between anthropology and ethnography (2008).
3. http://www.antropologi.info/linker/konsulenter.html (accessed 23 July 2014).
4. See also Smart, Hockey and James 2014.
5. Debates on the blog 'Savage Minds' indicate how far the power of some academic departments to choose their own staff has been compromised, such that disciplinary solidarity is weakened by appointing people who are more loyal to the institution than the discipline.

References

Abram, S. 2012. *Culture and Planning.* Aldershot: Ashgate.

Allen, S. 1975. 'Predicting Reader Interest in Anthropology', *Journalism Quarterly* 521: 124–28.

Amit-Talai, V. 2000. *Constructing the Field: Ethnographic Fieldwork in the Contemporary World.* London, Routledge.

Aufderheide, P. 1993. 'Latin American Grassroots Video: Beyond Television', *Public Culture* 5: 519–92.

Darłuszko, A. 2006. 'Being Radical Critical without Being Leftist: Interview with Nancy Scheper-Hughes'. http://www.antropologi.info/blog/anthropology/2011/nancy-scheper-hughes.

Beck, S. 2009. 'Introduction: Public Anthropology', *Anthropology in Action* 162: 1–13.

Beema, W.O. 1987. 'Anthropology and the Print Media', *Anthropology Today* 3(3) (June): 2–4.

Bird, S.E. 2010. 'Anthropological Engagement with News Media: Why Now?', *Anthropology News* (April): 5–6.

Borofsky, R. 2000. 'To Laugh or Cry', *Anthropology News* 41(2): 9–10.

———. 2007. 'Defining Public Anthropology'. http://www.publicanthropology.org/public-anthropology/ (accessed 6 October 2010).

———. 2011. *Why a Public Anthropology?* Kailua, HI: Center for a Public Anthropology.

Coman, M. 2005. 'Cultural Anthropology and Mass Media: A Processual Approach', in E.W. Rothenbuhuler and M. Coman (eds), *Media Anthropology.* Thousand Oaks, CA: Sage, pp. 46–55.

Deger, J. 2013. 'The Jolt of the New: Making Video Art in Arnhem Land', *Culture, Theory and Critique* 54(3): 355–71.

Divale, W. 1976. 'Newspapers: Some Guidelines for Communicating Anthropology', *Human Organization* 352: 183–91.

Dyck, N., and J.B. Waldram (eds). 1993. *Anthropology, Public Policy and Native Peoples in Canada*. McGill-Queen's University Press.

Eiselein, E.B., and W. Marshall. 1976. 'Mexican-American Television: Applied Anthropology and Public Television', *Human Organization* 352: 147–56.

Eriksen, T.H. 2006. *Engaging Anthropology: The Case for a Public Presence*. Oxford: Berg.

———. 2012. *Engaging Anthropology: The Case for a Public Presence*. 2nd edn. London: Bloomsbury.

Fassin, D. 2013. 'Why Ethnography Matters: On Anthropology and Its Publics', *Cultural Anthropology* 284: 621–46.

Field, L., and R. Fox 2007. 'Introduction: How Does Anthropology Work Today?', in L. Field and R. Fox (eds), *Anthropology Put to Work*. Oxford: Berg.

Fiske, S.J. 2011. 'Anthropology's Voice in the Public Policy Process', *Anthropology News* 524: 17.

Frazer, J. G. 1894. *The Golden Bough: A Study in Comparative Religion*. London: Macmillan and Co.

Gal, S., and K.A. Woolard. 2001. *Languages and Publics: The Making of Authority*. Manchester: St Jerome Pub.

González, R.J. 2007. 'Towards Mercenary Anthropology? The New US Army Counterinsurgency Manual FM 3-24 and the Military–Anthropology Complex', *Anthropology Today* 233: 14–19.

———. 2012. 'Anthropology and the Covert: Methodological Notes on Researching Military and Intelligence Programmes', *Anthropology Today* 282: 21–25.

Gullestad, M. 2002. *Det Norske Sett med Nye Øyne*. Published in English as *Plausible Prejudice*. Oslo: Universitetsforlaget.

Gupta, A., and J. Ferguson. 1997. *Anthropological Locations: Boundaries and Grounds of a Field Science*. Berkeley, CA, and London: University of California Press.

Gusterson, H. 2003. 'Anthropology and the Military: 1968, 2003 and Beyond?', *Anthropology Today* 193: 25–26.

Hart, K. 2013. 'Why is Anthropology Not a Public Science'. https://www.academia.edu/5116140/Why_is_anthropology_not_a_public_science (accessed 16 November 2013).

Henley, P. 2005. 'Anthropologists in Television: A Disappearing World?', in S. Pink (ed.) *Applications of Anthropology*. Oxford: Berghahn Books, pp. 170–89.

Ingold, T. 2008. 'Anthropology is *not* Ethnography', *Proceedings of the British Academy* 154.

MacClancy, J. 2002. 'Introduction: Taking People Seriously', in J. MacClancy (ed.), *Exotic No More: Anthropology on the Front Lines*. Chicago: Chicago University Press, pp. 1–14.

McDonald, Maryon. 1987. 'The Politics of Fieldwork in Brittany', in A. Jackson (ed.), *Anthropology at Home*, ASA vol. 25. London and New York: Tavistock.

Moos, F., R. Fardon and H. Gusterson. 2005. 'Anthropologists as Spies', *Anthropology Today* 213: 25–26.

Mouffe, P. 2000. *The Democratic Paradox*. London and New York: Verso.

Murdoch, J., and S. Abram. 2002. *Rationalities of Planning*. Aldershot: Ashgate.

Osorio, F. 2005. 'Proposal for Mass Media Anthropology', in E.W. Rothenbuhler and M. Coman (eds), *Media Anthropology*. Thousand Oaks, CA: Sage, pp. 36–45.

Picard, D., and S. Buchberger (eds). 2013. *Couchsurfing Cosmopolitans: Can Tourism Make a Better World?* Bielefeld: Transcript Verlag.

Pink, S. 1997. *Women and Bullfighting: Gender, Sex and the Consumption of Tradition.* Oxford: Berg.

——— (ed.). 2005. *Applications of Anthropology.* Oxford: Berghahn Books.

——— (ed.). 2007. *Visual Interventions.* Oxford: Berg.

Price, D.H. 2005. 'America the Ambivalent: Quietly Selling Anthropology to the CIA', *Anthropology Today* 216: 1–2.

———. 2007. 'Buying a Piece of Anthropology Part 1: Human Ecology and Unwitting Anthropological Research for the CIA', *Anthropology Today* 233: 8–13.

———. 2012. 'Counterinsurgency and the M-VICO System: Human Relations Area Files and Anthropology's Dual-Use Legacy', *Anthropology Today* 281: 16–20.

Restrepo, E., and A. Escobar. 2005. 'Other Anthropologies and Anthropology Otherwise', *Critique of Anthropology* 25(2): 99–129.

Scheper-Hughes, N. 1993. *Death Without Weeping: The Violence of Everyday Life in Brazil.* Berkeley and London: University of California Press.

———. 2004. 'Parts Unknown: Undercover Ethnography of the Organs-Trafficking Underworld', *Ethnography* 51: 29–73.

Scheper-Hughes, N., and L. Wacquant (eds). 2002. *Commodifying Bodies.* London: Sage.

Shore, C., and S. Wright (eds). 1997. *Anthropology of Policy: Critical Perspectives on Governance and Power.* London: Routledge.

Sillitoe, P. 2007. 'Anthropologists Only Need Apply: Challenges of Applied Anthropology', *Journal of the Royal Anthropological Institute* 131: 147–65.

Singer, A. 2008. *Anthropology on Television.* Blogpost and responses: http://blog.theasa.org/?p=107

Singer, M. 2000. 'Why I Am Not a Public Anthropologist', *Anthropology News* 416: 6–7.

———. 2011. 'Anthropology as a Sustainability Science', *Anthropology News* 524: 5–10.

Smart, C., J. Hockey and A. James (eds). 2014. *The Craft of Knowledge: Experiences of Living with Data.* Basingstoke: Palgrave Macmillan.

Stewart, P., and A. Strathern (eds). 2004. *Anthropology and Consultancy: Issues and Debates.* Oxford: Berghahn Books.

Strathern, Marilyn. 2006. 'A Community of Critics? Thoughts on New Knowledge', *The Journal of the Royal Anthropological Institute* 121: 191–209.

Vine, D. 2011. '"Public Anthropology" in its Second Decade: Robert Borofsky's Center for a Public Anthropology', *American Anthropologist* 113(2): 336–49.

Vogt, Evon Z. 1955. Anthropology in the Public Consciousness. *Yearbook of Anthropology.* pp. 357–374.

Walters, E. 2014. 'The Organ Detective: A Career Spent Uncovering a Hidden Global Market in Human Flesh', *Pacific Standard: The Science of Society.* http://www.psmag.com/navigation/business-economics/nancy-scheper-hughes-black-market-trade-organ-detective-84351/

Witteveen, G. 2000. 'Anthro by Any Other Name…', *Anthropology News* 41(6): 4–5.

PART I

ANTHROPOLOGY IN THE PUBLIC MEDIA SPHERE

Chapter 1

DOING ANTHROPOLOGY IN PUBLIC
Examples from the Basque Country

———— ∞∞∞ ————

Margaret Bullen

This chapter sets out to examine the experience of doing anthropology in the public sphere of Spain's disputed Basque Country and the way in which the media record and represent the products of anthropological research. In the Basque context, a region fraught with sociopolitical conflict, yet forward looking, fast moving and an investor in innovation and change, anthropology has long enjoyed a public profile. Initially this profile was formed through the figures of ethnographers, archaeologists and only latterly social anthropologists, leading to an association of the discipline with caves and skulls rather than with the potential contribution of social anthropology to contemporary issues. At the same time, the concern with culture at the core of the contested Basque identity has meant that the anthropological community has not been invisible, but openly consulted by the media on sociocultural issues. The Basque media constitutes a significant arena where different versions of that identity vie with each other, and broadcast (mainly radio), print and digital media are players in that game. Finally, the 'entrepreneurial spirit' encouraged by modern Basque society and manifest in different initiatives promoted by public institutions, as well as the academy, has enabled the emergence of at least an incipient 'public' anthropology in the sense that it is institutionally instigated, usually commissioned by a public authority and directed at a particular topic of public interest or policy, which is thus of interest to the general public or a sector thereof, and as such is taken up by the media.

   Through the analysis of projects undertaken both academically and in conjunction with Farapi, a spin-off applied anthropology consultancy, this chapter examines the processes by which doing anthropology for public institutions or on issues of public concern makes us of interest not only to the entities who employ us but also to the media and to their audiences. However, the public projection of anthropology can be double edged: the media provide us with a platform to discuss our findings, but they compel us to take sides, give opinions and find solutions; they force us to be precise and articulate, but they can curtail our freedom to represent ourselves or the subjects of our research, use us for their own agendas and involve us in political issues. The margin for manoeuvre in doing anthropology in public is assessed from a dual perspective: firstly, from the point of view of working for the public administration in terms of their agendas and budgets, and secondly, from that of being in the public eye through the media attention our research draws.

Doing Anthropology in the Basque Country

Given the complexity of the region's geopolitical situation, I will begin with a brief description of its geographical, political and ideological make-up. The Basque Country, or Euskal Herria in Basque, is a stateless nation of 20.864 sq. km and 2.9 million people, located in south-western Europe and overlapping the state boundaries of France and Spain, reaching from the mountain slopes of the Western Pyrenees to the cliffs of the Bay of Biscay. The terms País Vasco (Spanish) and Pays Basque (French) are also used to refer to this portion of the political state of Spain and France respectively, but many Basques prefer to denominate the nation-state 'the state of Spain' or 'the state of France', indicating that their land is located within the political states of these two countries, but that they reject the nationhood of both. Euskal Herria is an imagined nation made up of seven provinces, summed up in the nationalist slogan 'zazpiak bat' ('Seven in One'). Those Basques who imagine their nation thus, conceive of their country as embracing the seven historical provinces of Bizkaia, Gipuzkoa, Araba and Nafarroa on the Spanish side, and Lapurdi, Nafarroa Beherea and Zuberoa on the French side. These provinces are in turn divided among three administrative structures. Two of them form part of the Spanish State: the Basque Autonomous Community (comprising Araba, Bizkaia and Gipuzkoa[1]); and the Autonomous Community of Navarre, made up of a single province of the same name.[2] The three Basque provinces which form part of the French State do not constitute a political entity in their own right but, along with Bearn, are part of the French department of Pyrénées Atlantiques (capital Pau), which itself belongs to the region of Aquitaine (capital Bordeaux).

The Basque identity is equally complex and continually under negotiation. One version is linked to the Basque language, Euskara, today spoken by over a third of the population of the Spanish side (around 750,000 of the population over 5 years of age qualify as bilingual in Spanish and Euskara and another 350,000 as passive bilinguals who understand Euskara but are not fluent speakers) in addition to some 70,000 speakers on the French side.[3] There is what I will call a 'classical' version of Basque identity associated not only with the language but also with a notion of mysterious origins and myths, the traditional rural way of life, music, dance and sport.[4] However, there are also many other representations that challenge the more romanticized and essentialist definitions of Basqueness, but before I discuss these, let us contemplate the significance of the classical discourses and practices for doing anthropology in the Basque context.

A classical representation of Basqueness was constructed in response to the Spanishness promoted by Francisco Franco's dictatorship, under the slogan 'Spain: one, free and great'.[5] The oneness of Franco's Spanish nation was to be achieved by outlawing the public use of all other languages and cultural expressions (dance, music, traditional dress and customs) to be found in Spain. The media were placed at the service of the regime, or subject to severe control and censorship (Deacon 1999: 309–17). The resistance of the Basques, both politically and culturally, led to an initially underground movement to rescue what was feared to be a disappearing language and culture, threatened as it was by Franco's dictatorship and decree against anything that diverged from Spanishness.

In anthropology, the mission to save the threatened Basque culture is personified in the figure and work of the Basque priest, José Miguel de Barandiarán (1889–1991) who went into exile just over the Spanish–French border into Biarritz and later Sara (1936–1953), and from there commenced an ethnographical project to salvage Basque myths and legends, folk beliefs and practices, at the same time as undertaking work with archaeologists to uncover cave paintings and unearth skulls and bones which he hoped would solve the enigma of the origins of the Basque people (Douglass and Zulaika 2007: 17–18). The political climate of protest against the dictator and what was perceived as the legitimate defence of the Basque culture consecrated the figure of 'Aita Barandiarán', hailed as a father in his role as priest, founder of Basque ethnography and object of people's affection. Thus it was that people who had little knowledge of anthropology came to associate the discipline with this man and his work, and although they had never met him, felt he was familiar to them.[6]

Whilst this set of circumstances has led to a public projection of anthropology in the Basque Country, it has also contributed to the distorted image of Basque anthropology – as in other parts of the world[7] – through the widely held image of anthropologists as archaeologists digging in caves or as ethnographers in search of stories from an idealized past. At the same time, the concern with culture as the backbone of the contested Basque identity has meant that the anthropological community is held in some repute by the Basque media, particularly those that use the Basque language, promote Basque culture or show sympathy towards Basque nationalist ideology, but also some of a Spanish socialist bent, such as *El País*.[8] Anthropologists are frequently sought out to give their opinion on sociocultural issues, participate in radio talk shows, discuss the revival of Basque stand-up poetry, explain the symbolism behind Carnival, pronounce themselves on the alleged existence of the Basque matriarchy, and provide arguments for changing hallowed traditions; but they are also consulted on other social issues such as equal rights and racism.

Anthropologists and the Transformation of Traditions

In the context of concern with cultural identity, together with a calendar replete with festivals, rituals and celebrations throughout the year, the evolution, modernization and modification of traditions is an area in which anthropologists have been implicated in the Basque Country. It is not of course unusual for anthropologists to work in relation to cultural heritage, whether in the area of material culture and museums or in performative and immaterial culture. Over the past twenty years my own research has led me to work on tradition and change, specifically the challenging or transforming of traditions in defence of gender or racial equality. Although my work in this area began as an anthropological and increasingly feminist interest in a specific social conflict arising from the refusal to allow women to participate freely in the annual *alardes* or parades[9] of the two Gipuzkoan towns of Irun and Hondarribia,[10] the dimensions of the controversy – unresolved even today – have made it a reference point for other studies with an applied rather than a merely analytical edge.[11] In fact, it was at the press conference to present our research in the co-authored book *Tristes Espectáculos* (Bullen and Egido 2003)[12] that I had my first encounter with the press. The conflict had raised considerable media interest (maintained, though to a lesser degree, over the nineteen years since it began), and the question on everyone's lips was the one I was least ready to answer: What is the solution to the conflict? I was unprepared. I was convinced my role was to describe, explain and interpret. I had carried out a thorough analysis of the situation but it was for 'the people', the social actors involved in the conflict, to work out what to do. For the journalists, this was not sufficient.[13]

Over the past two decades, I have continued to follow the polemic, and as public authorities have come under pressure to intervene in the breach of equal rights, I have become involved in other projects concerned with festivals and leisure activities from a gendered point of view and commissioned by the county council.[14] These projects are of an applied nature and carry a series of recommendations and proposals. They reveal the value attributed by the Basque public administration to anthropological knowledge in their willingness to consult us on problematic questions arising in the confrontation between the desire to preserve tradition and the need to respond to social change, particularly in the area of equal rights, dear to both institutions and media. This tension, intrinsic to the dynamic concept of culture, collides with a more static notion which has been influential in policy design, particularly in cultural and linguistic planning in the Basque Country.[15] The traditionalist discourse defends cultural relativity in the face of globalization, even when it confronts the defence of human rights related, in the case of the *alardes* of Irun and Hondarribia, to equality between women and men (Bullen 2006). Championing universal equal rights clashes with another aspect of the relativist discourse based on the widely held myth of the Basque matriarchy. This holds that women are powerful, but fails to address the domestic bounds of their authority and the limitation of their power and even presence in the public space (Del Valle et al. 1985; Bullen y Diez 2010).[16] This is another perennial problem which never ceases to fascinate the media. It has been the subject of more than one interview, most recently for a digital paper, *El Correo*, and a radio programme broadcast on Radio Euskadi.[17]

Another mythical notion that forms part of the Basque imaginary is egalitarianism (de Otazu y Llana 1986), carried over into an account of Basque society as neither class conscious nor racist. In the past two decades, non-European immigration has steadily increased in the region and this has confronted the population with the need to review some of their assumptions. In the same way as gender issues, the situation of the immigrant community is of concern both to the institutions and the media, and as a foreigner there is interest in this dimension of my anthropological self.[18] In 2006, I was called on to take part in a project in the small Gipuzkoan town of Antzuola. The town council had approached Eusko Ikaskuntza (the Society of Basque Studies) to collaborate in a project for the revitalization of the 'Alarde del Moro' or 'The Moor's Parade',[19] celebrated on the third Saturday in July. The stated concern of the local council and the organizers was the decline of the *alarde* and the ageing of the participants; they expressed their fear of losing the tradition if the young people did not take their place and their desire to protect, promote and publicize the historical value of the parade. To do this, their proposal was to invite representatives from other towns with similar parades to come and talk about their own *alarde,* in the hope that their enthusiasm might inspire the people of Antzuola to reconsider and revalue their own parade. According to the cultural agents and promoters of the Moor's Parade, the key to revitalization was historical knowledge which would lead to appreciation: once people knew what the origins of the parade where, they were bound to value it more.

It was not difficult to perceive that the encounter of *alardes* was not going to be the solution, that knowledge would not be equivalent to desire and that the people who wanted to know more were probably the ones who already supported and took part in their parade. So I proposed that before proceeding to such a grand gathering, it would be wise to talk to people in Antzuola to try to find out why they did not participate in the first place and involve them in the proposed revitalization process. Happily, the people responsible for the project welcomed the idea, and we designed a sociocultural study on 'The past, present and future of the Alarde of Antzuola'. As I began to interview people from the town's sociocultural network, I discovered an underlying motive for the study: it transpired that the organizers had been accused of racism because of the way the figure of the Moor was represented in the festival. The council had received letters of complaint, and these had been published in the press. The Moor was dressed in a plain white tunic with a red fez, a boot-polish-blackened face, and brought on in chains and riding a donkey. It was felt that this representation was racist and humiliating, especially as the Moor had to kneel before the Basque general and swear to never again invade Euskal Herria.

The concern with this negative image, however unintentional, met with the question of how far it was legitimate to change an ancestral tradition which had been handed down from generation to generation. Yet it was clear to the townspeople that it could not continue as it was. The younger generations, who already felt uncomfortable about the military style, did not want to be associated with a spectacle dubbed racist.[20] In this sense, the work of the historian who researched the origins and evolution of the festival was crucial in discovering that it was most unlikely that the events related in the *alarde* ever happened at all, that they were most probably invented to boost the status of Antzuola in relation to its neighbours and that the Moor was a representation of 'the Other'. This news was received by the people as the key to change: in Hobsbawm's terms, if the tradition had been invented to begin with, it could be reinvented.

Hence the anthropological method combined with historical study paved the way to solving the problem by involving the people in identifying what the problem actually was – that is, what was behind people's reluctance to take part in the parade – and deciding what the festival meant to them through thinking about the construction of history and tradition, which in turn freed them to make changes. The first round of individual in-depth interviews was followed up by a session of work groups in which the conclusions of the first interviews were discussed. This second phase of the study, plus participant observation of the festival and surveys conducted on the day of the parade, enabled us to make a series of recommendations which were presented at a public meeting and announced in the local press.[21]

However, an article published in the *Diario Vasco* just before our final report was submitted is worthy of note. The *Diario Vasco* is the most widely read daily paper in Gipuzkoa and is appreciated for its highly localized news, having special sections inserted for distribution in each borough. This means that local events are reported in detail for a reduced readership, and sometimes the news is caught up with personal interests and political wrangling. This was the case with our project. While we were hurrying to complete our report, I was contacted by an interviewee who had read in the *Diario Vasco* that everyone was waiting for our conclusions (we had agreed on 'the autumn', and it was early November) and that we were going to submit them to the parade organizers who would then communicate them to the local council (rather than the other way around). It would appear that the journalist, also an interviewee, wished to malign someone on the council, believing them to be giving preference to the parade's organization by concealing the report's findings until the organizers had had time to react.[22]

Once our report was duly submitted, committees worked over the following year to design a new version of the parade, which had been inaugurated in 2009, with a dignified Abd-ar-Rahman, dressed as a caliph, riding a horse and accompanied by his sequitur. As well as being significant for the traditional culture and Basque identity debates, the concern with racism and immigration made the modification of the festival worthy of interest to Radio San Sebastián, a local radio station belonging to one of the biggest Spanish commercial radio stations, 'La Ser', and the mayor of Antzuola and I were interviewed on a live magazine programme.

Basque Entrepreneurship and Innovation

Although the classical version of both Basque identity and Basque anthropology situates us in the realm of festivals, customs and traditions, I wish now to turn our attention away from the often romanticized and folkorized version of Basqueness, to the 'entrepreneurial spirit' that also constitutes part of the Basque identity and which can be exploited by anthropologists in the public sphere. This aspect is seen to belong not to the ancient and the rural, but to another two geo-cultural axes around which that identity is constructed: on the one hand, the coast and its maritime tradition; on the other, the city and its former steel-based industry. In contrast to the Basque rural culture, which concentrates the romantic core of Basqueness, modern Basque society projects itself beyond its borders and encourages innovation, no where better symbolized than in Bilbao's Guggenheim Museum.[23] This is the spirit – promoted by public institutions as well as the academy – that has enabled the emergence of an applied anthropology in the Basque public sphere and is beginning to make inroads into the world of business and industry.[24]

It was the existence of a business creation scheme, designed to capture talent and ideas from the university and enable newly fledged professionals to put their innovative ideas to work, that led to the creation in 2002 of Farapi, a consultancy in applied anthropology, working in the design and execution of qualitative projects. A spin-off from the University of the Basque Country, Farapi was founded by six social anthropologists (three Basque women, one Basque man, one German man, and my English self) with the aim of finding an application for our anthropology in Basque society. We started out as an association in November 2002, and in February 2003, Bic Berrilan, an organization supporting business and innovation, began to coach us through setting up the consultancy and gave us office space and facilities in the 'incubator' in San Sebastián (or in Basque, Donostia). In August 2004 we became Farapi Ltd., and in April 2005 we moved out of the incubator into our own office in the Technological Park of Miramón where we were protected by a soft rent for three years, after which we moved out into our own office in town.

Farapi aims its services at institutions, organizations and businesses of all types, though most of its work is public anthropology for local authorities, especially Gipuzkoa's county council, but also for town councils and the Basque autonomous government.[25] It is not unusual for other bigger or better known consultancies to subcontract our services or for us to be invited to collaborate with university departments.[26] Since the crisis set in, we have been trying to attract more work from businesses and have joined with a design group, Evidentis, who combine the hallmarks of Farapi's work – a qualitative methodology and a gendered perspective – with their own 'creative social approach'. Some of the themes that have been analysed are: attitudes towards innovation, science and technology; coeducation and schooling; space and urban planning; gender and employment in the rural sector and in the immigrant community; mobility, transport, driving and masculinity; gender violence; attitudes towards sexual diversity; single-parent families; and youth, gender, health and drug abuse.[27]

One of the projects I would like to comment on here concerns baby feeding in public places, which was commissioned by the Department of Social Policy of Gipuzkoa's county council. The first part, entitled 'Study of the Viability of Baby-Feeding Points in Public Buildings in Gipuzkoa', consisted of an evaluation of the council's proposal to implement baby-feeding points in public buildings. The proposal was based on the hypothesis that it is problematic for mothers and fathers of small children to attend to their children in public spaces, whether it be breast or bottle feeding, warming baby food or nappy changing. Farapi carried out a study based on observations and interviews to try to identify specific problems and to find out parents' wishes and expectations. In this first phase, observations were carried out in town squares and parks. Taking into account hygiene and other factors, it was concluded that public buildings and spaces were inadequately prepared for the care of babies and small children. Interviews conducted with families of small children confirmed the conclusion and also identified certain issues that had not previously been considered in the council's proposal, and which were to change the course of the investigation. In this case, the experiences of both women and men and the opinions of an expert in feminist anthropology and care were decisive in developing a new feminist and inclusive approach to the problematic.

In this case, baby and child care was construed as being far more than breast feeding as had first been intimated, and was extended to refer also to milk extraction, bottle feeding and baby hygiene, as well as rest and relaxation for the mother, father or other carers. The mention of the father is especially important as breast feeding focuses on women, whereas we proposed a gender equal approach where spaces would be made available for men to bottle feed babies as well as change or rest them. The aim was to include fathers, not as mere figures of support to aid and assist the feeding mother, but as independent carers who could bottle feed and attend to their babies without requiring the presence of the mother. To go one step further, 'carers' would include anyone who participates in the caring process (grandparents, other family members, professional carers). Moreover, this approach was aimed at including bottle as well as breast feeding, providing facilities for both with a non-judgmental attitude that refuses to naturalize breast feeding or prioritize it over other options. At the same time, there was a concern for not contributing to the invisibility of baby and child care in public spaces by shutting parents and children away in closed-off corners, but rather trying to provide adequate and comfortable spaces connected with the rest of the building or public space, in which intimacy was prioritized without leading to isolation, and without giving preference to breast feeding over bottle feeding.

The second phase involved Ithaka, an innovation and design group, and an architect in the analysis of public buildings and spaces and the development of proposals for the modification of both interior and exterior spaces for baby and child care. First, the needs identified in the viability study were taken together with the observation and analysis of eight selected public spaces, and used to draw up different designs. Secondly, the proposals were used to lay down a set of criteria for intervention in public spaces and buildings which could facilitate child care, and these were used to compose a decalogue of good practice.[28]

Epistemological Considerations of Public Anthropology

The experiences related here allow me to make some observations about doing anthropology of a public nature, involving the public administration and, potentially, the media. That institutions approach anthropologists or take up their applications for research can be seen as an opportunity to effect change, or at least to make a contribution which affects the decisions of those in a position to make changes. I would like to argue that the anthropological method, coupled with a predisposition to value anthropological knowledge in the realm of cultural identities and certain social issues such as gender and racial equality, allows us to contribute to processes of social transformation in the Basque Country, which are at the same time assisted by the media's interest in at least some of our work. I would also like to consider the effects of this social engagement and mediatized projection of our work on the methodological choices we make in doing anthropology publicly.

One of the issues which Mercedes Jabardo (1999: 156) has signalled is the difficulty of doing anthropology outside the academy unless a relationship is established with institutions so that there are personal contacts with people on the inside. This is my privileged experience of being at the same time a member of an anthropology department and a partner of a consultancy. The relationships between political and academic institutions mean that the public administration often prefers to deal with a fellow institution such as a university, both as a source of prestige and a guarantor of quality. This can make it difficult for the private consultancies to secure contracts, and when they do they may then sacrifice their own profile to that of the institutions, often taking a back seat and forced to remain behind the scenes in the publication of the findings. Nevertheless, the very fact that public money is being spent exposes the projects to public scrutiny and prompts media interest.

As anthropologists in the public sphere we must consider the nature of applied anthropology, which determines that our research arises around a question, problem or conflict and thus demands an answer, recommendation or solution. This problematic can be approached as a laboratory, not that in social science we can introduce a slice of life into the laboratory, manipulate it or perform an experiment on it. But once in a while there occur certain 'revelatory incidents' or 'ethnographical manifestations' that, according to James Fernández MacClintock (1986), test our anthropological understanding and 'allow us to situate ourselves as in a laboratory, not as manipulators of social stuff, but as privileged observers' (Bullen and Díez 2002). Thus, the crisis sparked by the request of women to parade in the *alardes* has prompted a broader enquiry into equal rights, gender and change in Basque festivals and traditions. Both this and the placing on the political agenda of certain social issues such as baby-feeding points have led to anthropologists being commissioned to propose solutions, providing special opportunities to analyse aspects of society which demand a practical response.

In terms of the subjects of our studies, doing anthropology for public authorities necessarily influences the relationship between anthropologist, informants and client. Anthropology, as we well know, offers that all-round, holistic and contextualized vision that brings into the research process the very people amongst whom an effect is desired. If we work for the public administration with people in political posts who need the approval of their voters, or if we work in private enterprise where the client has to reach the greatest number of consumers, we can be seen – and can act – as facilitators of that contact and access to people. Adam Drazin (2006: 102) has observed that anthropologists invariably have greater empathy with their informants than with their clients, and while this may be awkward, it is not necessarily a disadvantage, and can be used as a tool. By allying oneself with the people who are the object of study, the client might be forced to rethink their strategy, with better results for both parties. In terms of what we can offer, there is the possibility of modifying the initial focus of the investigation and identifying something extra that improves on or complements our client's proposal (both the project in Antzuola and the baby-feeding study are examples of this). This is something we can 'sell' to the client, but at the same time it allows us to place ourselves on the side of those with whom we best identify (Bullen and Pecharromán 2006).

Working in public anthropology means not only discovering possible strategies of intervention, but also motivating people to participate in their own decision-making processes. This can be facilitated by the public nature of the research: for example, in Antzuola, the identification of and contact with possible informants was accelerated by the information placed at my disposal by the municipal department of culture and the fact that people already knew about the project and recognized the official backing I had. However, whilst access to a public database can be one of the advantages of working with public institutions, a negative side can be the element of control in influencing with whom we should talk, and the complications of internal political interests interfering with our own agenda.[29] In Antzuola, the first phase of interviews was directed by the client, but the discussion groups organized in the second phase were planned to try to increase the number of participants in the decision-making process and advance the proposal of possible change. Here the idea was to implement a popular consultation, carrying over into anthropology a democratic way of testing public opinion and encouraging participation in community decisions, with an attractive ethical edge (working from grass roots) of theoretical and epistemological interest.

Maria Jesús Buxó maintains that applied anthropology is about discerning 'the reconstruction of social phenomena through finding out how people want to give meaning to their world and how they decide to act in consequence' (2002: 159, my translation). Both the problem and the solution should be seen as a human and subjective construction. Rather than focusing on the end product, the emphasis is on the process that occurs when people see that something is wrong and needs putting right: 'the applied task is not to predict, plan nor provoke change following a prior definition of the problem, but rather to design ways of sharing ethnographical narratives and means for social learning' (ibid., my translation). The idea of promoting 'interactive communication' in the formulation of problems and possible scenarios of change has been used by anthropologists, such as Greenwood and Levin (1998), who have promoted participative action-based research. In the Basque Country, where there is an emphasis on the concept of citizenship, it is a propitious time and context for such a participatory approach (Buxó 1996: 419).

There is substantial debate over the difficulties of applying anthropology (in the public sense we have been using here) with regard to the need to fit our methods into the timescales and demands of the institutions for which we work; and here we must add the dimension of working in the public eye of the media. By way of conclusion, I will point to four issues which have arisen in the cases I have described: the duration of the projects; the mistrust of qualitative methods; the problems of political agendas; and the publicity given to our work by the media.

The first issue is time. One limitation of public anthropology is usually the little time we have in which to produce the results; but if we conceive of the job to be done within the metaphorical laboratory, it can help to reduce the scope of our work. We do not have to understand a whole cultural system, but following James Clifford (1991: 118) with regard to the evolution of fieldwork, we could 'claim to get to the heart of a culture more quickly, grasping the essential institutions and structures', thanks to our training and the ability to identify a 'problem' spatially or temporarily, thus circumscribing the situations or events to be examined. The fact that we work in or near our own communities reduces the amount of time we need, and although we must not lose sight of the concept of the 'Other', however near to home we are, we do not usually have to learn a new language or the basic norms and values of the society.

In this kind of study, participant observation tends to be limited to no more than a few short sessions, but its potential should not be underestimated as it is a hallmark which is absent from most other kinds of social research. It is a theoretically informed technique that we have learned, which grants us insight in order to make a more accurate interpretation of what our informants describe to us. We do not need to produce a 'thorough inventory of customs and beliefs' but should rather 'go after selected data that would yield a central armature of structure to the cultural whole' (Clifford 1991:119). It is important to choose well the scenarios we observe: for example, in Antzuola, as well as observing the main fiesta itself, we observed other festivals during the year and in other parts of the region where there were points of comparison, as well as the preparations and rehearsals for the parade, and for the activities organized after it. In the baby-feeding project, we selected eight different types of indoor and outdoor spaces to observe. In addition, it must be pointed out that nowadays we have a variety of technologies at our disposal to complement our descriptions and aid our observations (recordings, photographs, information and images from the internet).

The second question is the qualitative method, ideally suited to the analysis of phenomena related to sociocultural change, but mistrusted by the institutions. We are often faced with a request for 'hard facts and figures', which means that sometimes we are obliged to include more quantitative methods such as questionnaires (in Antzuola it was seen as a way of reaching more people, just as the council placed a 'suggestion box' and e-mail address at people's disposal). We might not always be convinced of their efficiency, but the effect of some statistics nicely arranged in brightly coloured graphs cannot be underestimated in the public sphere.[30] This may be an advantage of working in multidisciplinary groups with others better trained in such techniques (the Farapi–Evidentis partnership is an example of this), which is fashionable in Basque social research and fits with the holistic proposal. For example, on the *alardes* we worked with sociologists, in Antzuola with a historian, and in the baby-feeding project with designers and architects. The very mistrust of the qualitative method can also be good training for us, forcing us to refine our answers and be prepared for the media's questions on specific, straight to the point 'information bullets' – for the solution to, and not just the explanation of, the problem explored.

The third issue regards the political implications involved in doing public anthropology. My experience reveals the tension that exists between the explicit and the latent, a tension which is always present in our anthropological undertaking of interpretation and cultural code-cracking. Working with institutions means that not only do we have to decode the context of our object of study but also be aware of certain hidden keys in the political discourse which belong to another context altogether. In the case of Antzuola, there was a tension between the first expressed intention to revitalize the parade and the anthropological interest in uncovering the problematic surrounding the celebration of the parade, or people's reluctance to do so. The council agreed, probably in good faith as well as being politically and strategically motivated, but they risked having to face a bigger change than they had initially anticipated. At the same time, I experienced a sense of unease at what was *not* being said, at the possibility of another code that needed to be deciphered. As I discovered the need to add another objective to the original one of reviving and promoting the parade – that is, updating it to a politically correct twentieth-century version – I was better able to identify with the task in hand, but found it unsettling that this issue had been 'covered up' by my clients. This led to reflection on our double responsibility to the client and to the people affected by our work (in this case, not only the participants but also those who were being represented), and the need to transform traditions in keeping with social change. As Pilar Monreal (1999: 80) has pointed out, 'within critical anthropology, one of the central issues for discussion is the relation between theory, politics and its applicability, and the awareness that our findings can be used to implement actions when the political implications are contrary to our preferences' (my translation).

Fourthly, in the diffusion of results in the media, I found this to be positive in making work visible as it responded to a concern for transparency from the institutions involved, wanting to make it clear to everyone what was being done stage by stage, and how public money was being spent. In Antzuola, this was done by the publication of an explanatory leaflet, press conferences and the involvement of local radio and television. At the same time, media interest brings an added responsibility to represent a project adequately and politically correctly, but also an added danger of misrepresentation and of being caught up in the airing of personal complaints against the people responsible.

Finally, I would like to return to my initial questions of how far applied anthropology in the public sphere is successful in achieving change, and to what extent the media attention we attract can aid or abet our work.

In general terms, I would advocate the evaluation of success in terms of results rather than academic achievement, taking into account the satisfaction of clients with our product; quality in relation to resources invested (the time–money equation); the implication for the target community in search of a solution; and the contribution to social change. Public anthropology most certainly exposes us to the public eye, mediated by the journalists who are interested in our work and who ultimately represent us. This means that in addition to our conclusions we have to draw up recommendations and be prepared to commit ourselves, give an opinion and play the role of experts. This requires that we are confident in what we are doing, carve out our professional personality, and develop a public profile that can properly represent ourselves, those we study and our discipline to the institutions who employ us and the media who publicize us.

Margaret Bullen is a social anthropologist who has lived in the Basque Country since 1991 and has lectured at the University of the Basque Country since 2005. She graduated in Modern Languages (Bristol, 1987) and went on to do a Ph.D. (Liverpool, 1991) on cultural and social economic change amongst Andean migrants in the shanty towns of Arequipa, Peru. Her interests in migration, identity, language and change have remained a constant, strengthened by a gendered perspective and a commitment to applied anthropology. She is a founding member of the Consultancy of Applied Anthropology, Farapi, and continues to collaborate in different projects related to gender, ritual, conflict and violence in the Basque Country. Representative of this work is the co-authored book, *Tristes espectáculos: las mujeres y los Alardes de Irun y Hondarribia* (2003). She is also the author of *Basque Gender Studies* (2003), which was produced in conjunction with her teaching activity in Basque Culture and Gender Studies with the University Studies Abroad Consortium (USAC) in Donostia-San Sebastián.

Notes

1. My work is based largely in the province of Gipuzkoa, especially in the provincial capital Donostia-San Sebastián.
2. I have used the Basque spellings for the seven provinces, but opted for the English 'Navarre' in translating the name of the autonomous community. For a description of the geopolitical make-up, see Douglass and Zulaika (2007: 21–30).
3. Data recorded in EUSTAT, the Basque statistical agency (2006), published in Euskal Jaurlaritza-Gobierno Vasco, *IV. Mapa Sociolingüístico* (2009).

4. There is abundant literature on the Basque identity, but for a summary and bibliography in English, see Douglass and Zulaika 2007: 380–90, 402–9.
5. For an account in English of the rise of Basque nationalism under Franco, see Heiberg (1989); on the slogan 'España una, libre y grande', see pp. 90–103.
6. When I arrived in the Basque Country at the end of 1991, on hearing I was an anthropologist, a new acquaintance, with no links to the centenarian, exclaimed: 'Oh what a shame! We could have introduced you to Aita Barandiarán!' He had died on 21 December 1991 and I landed on the 28th.
7. A similar observation is made by Veronica Strang (2009: 1): '[P]eople's ideas about anthropology are often gleaned from portrayals in literature, film and television, which tend to favour rather dramatic stereotypes'. She mentions 'colonial adventurers' living with jungle tribes, forensic anthropologists cracking murder mysteries, and bearded, sandals-with-socks hippies in the outback.
8. It must be stressed that we are here referring to the Spanish Basque media, loosely defined as the printed and broadcast media consumed in the Autonomous Basque Community and Navarre. According to data published by *El Correo* (http://www.elcorreo .com/vizcaya/interactivo/comun/tarifas-ELCORREO-2012.pdf), the most widely read newspaper is a centre-right non-nationalist paper, *El Correo* in Araba and Bizkaia and its equivalent, *El Diario Vasco* in Gipuzkoa and *El Diario de Navarra* in Nafarroa (mostly in Spanish, with the occasional article in Basque); the conservative nationalist paper, *Deia* has the next largest readership after the sports paper *Marca*, followed by the biggest Spanish national paper, *El País*, which takes a socialist position, and has a section for each of the autonomous communities, and then *Noticias de Gipuzkoa* and *Noticias de Alava*. The one entirely Basque-language paper is *Berria*, and one weekly magazine, *Argia*. *Gara* is a left-wing pro-nationalist paper written in Spanish with some Basque. With regard to the broadcast media, mention must be made of the Basque public television and radio network, EITB (Euskal Irrati Telebista), and particularly the radios Euskadi Irratia (broadcasting in Basque) and Radio Euskadi (in Spanish).
9. '*Alarde*' refers to a military march past or parade, also meaning a show (of strength, wealth, knowledge, etc.). The *alardes* enacted in different parts of the Basque Country today commemorate the militias which, up until the nineteenth century, called on all men between the ages of 16 and 60 to assemble in case of invasion and defend the border until Spanish reinforcements arrived. To that end, they were to take part in an annual review to show themselves ready to fight and that their firearms were in working order.
10. The *Alarde* of Hondarribia comes under scrutiny in David Greenwood's chapter in *Hosts and Guests*, 'Culture by the Pound' (1989: 171–85).
11. On 18 January 2012, Emakunde, the Basque Institute of Women's Affairs, awarded its annual prize for Equality to the organizers of the mixed sex *Alardes* for their fight for equal rights for women and men in their towns' festivals. In addition to applauding their efforts to achieve unconditional access for women to the parade, the jury stressed the repercussions of their cause in other comparable festivals and in the academic and social studies of such cases. The award received widespread coverage in the printed and digital press, as well as on local television and radio.
12. The title is taken from Shakespeare's *Twelfth Night's*, reference to '*woeful pageants*'. Much has been written on the conflict over the *alardes*, but for an English account, see Bullen (1999, 2003).
13. I had to improvise answers which appeared in the articles published, such as E:\Tristes Espectáculos\Artículos prensa\ DIARIOVASCO_COM AL DÍA – Tiempo, diálogo e

implicación institucional, soluciones para los Alardes, según un estudio.htm, Javier Peñalba, 1-06-2004.

14. Initially, Emakunde pledged support if we could engage the municipal councils in the project. As this was and has remained impossible, the work was done without funding, and so Emakunde financed the publication of our research with the university press. Later, however, two studies expanding on tradition, gender and change were carried out by Farapi: 'Análisis de las fiestas del Territorio Histórico de Gipuzkoa desde una perspectiva de género' (2009) Dpto. de Cooperación y Derechos Humanos, Diputación Foral de Gipuzkoa: http://www.gizaeskubideak.net/upload/documentos/es/analisis .pdf 'Relevancia e impacto social de las sociedades gastronómicas' (2010) Defensoría para la Igualdad de Mujeres y Hombres: http://www.euskadi.net/r332288/es/conteni dos/informacion/publicaciones_informes_ext/es_publis/adjuntos/OK%20CASTEL LANO.pdf

15. This was particularly so under the Basque nationalist party, leading the autonomous community from the 1978 transition until the pro-Spanish socialists took over in March 2009.

16. This myth has been debunked by feminist anthropologists in the 1985 book *Mujer vasca, imagen y realidad* [Basque woman, image and reality]. For a critical account in English, see Bullen and Diez (2010).

17. *El Correo,* '¿Matriarcado vasco?' by Itsaso Álvarez http://www.elcorreo.com/viz caya/20130205/mas-actualidad/sociedad/matriarcado-vasco-201302041913.html. Radio Euskadi, 25 December 2011, 'Más que palabras' by Almudena Cacho, http://www.eitb .com/es/radio/radio-euskadi/detalle/800585/almudena-cacho-repasa-clave-musical-ano-2011-roberto-moso/

18. In 2006, I was interviewed by Juan Antonio Hernandez for the 'Nuevos Vascos' (New Basques) section of *El País's* local section: http://elpais.com/diario/2006/11/27/pais vasco/1164660015_850215.html

19. The Moor in question is said to be Abd-ar-Rahman III, emir and caliph of Cordoba from 912 to 961, supposedly defeated by a Basque army in Valdejunquera (Navarre) and brought back in chains to Antzuola where the story says he was forced to kneel and swear submission to the triumphant militia.

20. When obligatory military service was still enforced, the men were given leave from the army to come back and take part in their town's parade. This was an incentive to the men and ensured participation. Nowadays there is no military service, and even when there was, Antzuola was one of the towns with the highest percentage of *insum- isos* – those refusing, even at risk of imprisonment, to serve. Military service was to the Spanish army and so was seen as an obligation imposed by an occupying force.

21. *El Diario Vasco,* 6 May 2007, 'Un alarde vivo en Antzuola' by Cristina Limia: http://www .diariovasco.com/prensa/20070506/gipuzkoa/alarde-vivo-antzuola_20070506.html

22. *El Diario Vasco,* 7 November 2007, 'Herriko arduradunak, Eusko Ikaskuntzak Mairu- aren Alardeari buruz egingo dituen proposamenen zain' by Joseba Lezeta: http://www .diariovasco.com/20071107/alto-deba/herriko-arduradunak-eusko-ikaskuntzak-2007 1107.html

23. Joseba Zulaika has written extensively on the Guggenheim Museum and its contribu- tion to Bilbao's postindustrial revival (Douglass and Zulaika 2007: 340–46).

24. Fagor Hometek S. Coop., a company belonging to the Mondragon Cooperative Group, has commissioned studies such as 'Estudio sobre los usos y conceptos de la lavadora desde la antropología social' (2008), and employed an anthropologist until the compa- ny's closure in 2013.

25. Contracts from the county council have come from the following departments: Human Rights, Employment and Social Reinsertion; Urban and Regional Planning; Innovation and Knowledge Society; and Social Policy. From town councils, work has been commissioned by departments of Equality and Welfare, and other work by the Observatory of Youth and a local development agency.
26. Farapi has worked in conjunction with: Dept. of Philosophy of Values and Social Anthropology, University of the Basque Country; Dept. of Geography, University of Alcalá; Faculty of Business Studies, University of Mondragón; Technical University of Iasi, Romania; Dept. for Sociology, Loughborough University, UK; Dept. of Social Anthropology, University Vytautas Magnus, Lithuania; and Bremer institut fuer kulturforschung, Universitaet Bremen, Germany.
27. Examples of Farapi's work are available in digital form: 'Sinestralidad vial y género' (2009), http://www.berdingune.euskadi.net/u89congizon/es/contenidos/informacion/material/es_gizonduz/adjuntos/9_siniestralidad_vial_y_genero.pdf; 'Diagnóstico urbano desde la perspectiva de género en Arrigorriaga' (2008), http://www.arrigorriaga.net/eu-ES/Udala/Sailak/Ikerketak%20eta%20lanak/MEMORIA-CONCLUSIONES.pdf; 'Investigación cualitativa documental: abuso de drogas y violencia de género' (2007), http://umaantelasdrogas.files.wordpress.com/2012/03/drogas-y-violencia de-genero.pdf
28. 'Estudio de viabilidad sobre la implantación de centros lactarios en edificios públicos del Territorio Histórico de Gipuzkoa' (2008); 'Decálogo para la adaptación de espacios a las necesidades de las labores relacionadas con la lactancia y el cuidado de bebés' (2009), FARAPI S.L., Dpto. Política Social, Diputación Foral de Gipuzkoa. The plan to implement the study's findings are mentioned in the press: http://www.diariovasco.com/20090216/local/san-sebastian/sebastian-tendra-cinco-puntos-200902161335.html
29. In Antzuola, as I carried out the interviews agreed with the council, I discovered that the village's so-called 'sociocultural network' was totally endogamic: my informants were almost all related to each other in one way or another. This in itself would have been an object of analysis in a classical study, but it was not analysed in the applied investigation.
30. Hacking (1990) provides an analysis of the increasing reliance on statistics in the modern industrial state.

References

Bullen, M. 1999. 'Gender and Identity in the Alardes of Two Basque Towns', in William A. Douglass et al. (eds), *Basque Cultural Studies*, Basque Studies Program. Reno: University of Nevada, pp. 149–77.

———. 2003. *Basque Gender Studies*. Reno: University of Nevada Press.

———. 2006. 'Derechos universales o especificad cultural: una perspectiva antropológica', in G. Moreno and X. Kerexeta (eds), *Los Alardes del Bidasoa: Pueblos versus ciudadanía*. Lasarte: Antza, pp. 21–47.

Bullen, M., and C. Diez. 2002. 'Violencia y cambio de culturas androcéntricas', IX Congreso de Antropología de la FAAEE, Barcelona, 4–7 September.

———. 2010. 'Matriarchy versus Equality: From Mari to Feminist Demands', in M.L. Esteban and M. Amurrio (eds), *Feminist Challenges in the Social Sciences: Gender Studies in the Basque Country*. Reno: Center for Basque Studies, pp. 113–26.

Bullen, M., and J.A. Egido. 2003. *Tristes espectáculos: las mujeres y los Alardes de Irun y Hondarribia*. Bilbao: Servicio Editorial de la UPV-EHU.

Bullen, M., and B. Pecharromán. 2006. 'La profesionalización de la antropología ¿ficción o realidad?', VII Congreso Internacional de la Sociedad Española de Antropología Aplicada, Santander.

Buxó, M.J. 1996. 'Antropología, prospectiva y nuevas tecnologías', in J. Prat and A. Martínez (eds), *Ensayos de antropología cultural: Homenaje a Claudio Esteva-Fabregat*. Barcelona: Ariel, pp. 417–22.

———. 2002. 'Antropología Aplicada: razón critica y razones prácticas', ANKULEGI 6, pp. 145–62.

Clifford, J. 1991. 'On Ethnographic Authority', *Representations* 2: 118–46.

Deacon, P. 1999. 'The Media in Modern Spanish Culture', in David T. Gies, *Modern Spanish Culture*. Cambridge: Cambridge University Press, pp. 309–17.

Del Valle, T., et al. 1985. *Mujer vasca, imagen y realidad*. Barcelona: Anthropos.

Douglass, W., and J. Zulaika. 2007. *Basque Culture: Anthropological Perspectives*. Reno: Center for Basque Studies.

Drazin, A. 2006. 'The Need to Engage with Non-ethnographic Methods: A Personal View', in S. Pink (ed.), *Applications of Anthropology: Professional Anthropology in the Twenty-First Century*. New York and Oxford: Berghahn Books, pp. 90–107.

Euskal Jaularitza-Gobierno Vasco, Kultur Saila-Dpto. de Cultura, 2009, *IV. Mapa Sociolingüística*, Vitoria-Gasteiz, Euskal Jaurlaritzaren Argitalpen Zerbitzu Nagusia.

Fernández MacClintock, J.W. 1986. *Persuasions and Performances: The Play of Tropes in Culture*. Bloomington: Indiana University Press.

Greenwood, D.J. 1989. 'Culture by the Pound: An Anthropological Perspective on Tourism as Cultural Commoditization', in Valene L. Smith (ed.), *Hosts and Guests: The Anthropology of Tourism*, Second Edition. Philadelphia: University of Pennsylvania Press, pp. 171–85.

Greenwood, D.J., and M. Levin. 1998. *Introduction to Action Research*. Thousand Oaks, CA: Sage Publications.

Hacking, I. 1990. *The Taming of Chance*. Cambridge: Cambridge University Press.

Heiberg, M. 1989. *The Making of the Basque Nation*. Cambridge: Cambridge University Press.

Jabardo Velasco, M. 1999. 'Entre la academia y la sociedad: reflexiones entre la teoría y la práctica de la intervención social con inmigrantes', in C. Giménez (ed.), *Antropología más allá de la academia*, Donostia-San Sebastián: Ankulegi, pp. 155–64.

Monreal Requena, P. 1999. 'La perspectiva de género en las políticas públicas', in C. Giménez (ed.), *Antropología más allá de la academia*, Donostia-San Sebastián:Ankulegi, pp. 81–85.

Otazu y Llana, A. de (1972) 1986. *El 'igualitarismo' vasco: mito y realidad*. San Sebastián: Txertoa.

Strang, V. 2009. *What Anthropologists Do*. Oxford and New York: Berg.

Chapter 2

THE PERILS OF PUBLIC ANTHROPOLOGY?
Quiescent Anthropology in Neo-Nationalist Scandinavia

──────❦❦❦──────

Peter Hervik

When the Muhammad cartoon crisis in 2005/6 dominated the Danish news media, political discussions, and popular exchanges, no anthropologists were to be found taking part in the intense public debate. With Denmark's mostly negative dialogue approach to the country's vulnerable Muslim minority and the harsh reactions of non-Western people to stories about the cartoons, the crisis had at its centre claims about cultural issues, social dilemmas and global responses that are central to anthropological interest, inquiry and understanding. There was the vulnerable minority with large internal differences and conflicts; Muslim agency; Muslims being approached as 'good' and 'democratic' as well as Muslims being perceived as 'bad', 'undemocratic' and 'too different' to stay in Denmark; the largest national newspaper going far to insult, mock and ridicule Muslims – for being Muslims; 'Western' vs. 'Non-Western' relations of all sorts (neo-nationalist, post-colonialist, eurocentric, orientalist, racist – as well as denials of all); and local responses from around the world, where anthropologists would be expert witnesses and commentators, emphasizing the complexity of reactions. Yet, during the Muhammad cartoon crisis, Danish anthropologists, for various reasons, were largely invisible in the public debate. This raises a number of questions, such as: What does 'public visibility' mean and entail? Should public anthropology be practised as an individual moral responsibility, or supported in the programmes and policies of anthropological institutions as the discipline's public intellectual responsibility in society? How does this vary from one institution to another? Is the visibility of anthropologists changing? In sum, what are the perils of engagement in events like the Muhammad cartoon conflict, and in more general issues of anti-migration?

Thomas Hylland Eriksen, Norwegian anthropologist and prominent cultural personality in the Scandinavian public sphere, has noted a general lack of visibility of anthropologists and anthropology in the Anglophone world (Eriksen 2006), whereas he and others (Gullestad 2006a; Howell 2010) have found anthropology to be much more publicly visible in Norway. On the other hand, anthropologists Setha M. Low and Sally Engle Merry have noted that anthropology 'has increased its public visibility in recent years with its growing focus on engagement' (Low and Merry 2010: 203). These observations provide an entrance into what should be an ongoing, never-ending discussion of anthropology's engagement in public issues and its contribution to society, even at the risk of what Borofsky called 'subverting the narrow niched conversations of specialization' (Borofsky 2002).

Low and Merry, Eriksen and Howell do not provide criteria or references for their observation of anthropologists' visibility or lack of visibility in the public sphere. However, the divergent personal observations may point to an absolute increase in visibility but a relative drop. In line with the drastic decline in newspaper sales in the last fifteen years in most countries, IT news sites proliferate and compete for public attention. This requires explicit communication strategies to bring points of anthropology to well-defined specific target groups or even individuals. Accordingly, the relative decline may suggest a shift of medium for expressing anthropological views publicly, which is due to the explosive growth of public and semi-public sites and platforms for anthropological appearances.

Based on the premise that professors can be regarded as signposts of and for the field of anthropology, I decided to do a small unscientific survey. I simply wanted to find the media appearances of the four Danish anthropology professors with more than five years in the job and within the last decade. The finding confirmed the lack of visibility beyond the confines of the academic world.[1] The only hits were a few academic references to publications by Professor Kirsten Hastrup. This lack of presence in the news media may be surprising given the large transformation in Danish society related to the integration policies, the media coverage of minorities and the dire consequences for the country's most socially vulnerable groups. Such groups are usually of primary interest to social anthropology in a double sense, as ethnic minorities in their own right and as minorities in vulnerable situations.[2] (In researching the media coverage since the mid-1990s, I encountered Norwegian anthropology professors participating in the debate. The same cursory search in the Danish database, Infomedia, showed that two Norwegian social anthropology professors, Thomas Hylland Eriksen and Unni Wikan, have appeared in the Danish written press on different occasions.)

Danish anthropology professors, or anthropologists more generally, were not present as sources for news stories or proactively writing opinion pieces or op-eds during the Muhammad cartoon conflict in 2005/6, which ranks as one of the most comprehensively covered media events in Denmark (Hervik 2011, 2012). Scholars of other disciplines were present and being heard (Rothstein and Rothstein 2006), and especially political scientists appeared via academic articles (Eriksen and Stjernfelt 2008; Klausen 2009; Stage 2011). In addition, scholars from media studies and journalism research were among the first to publish research-based publications (Kunelius et al., 2007; Eide, Kunelius and Philips 2008).[3]

Norway is one country where anthropologists do play a significant role in popular media. However, writings on the practice of Norwegian public anthropology are not clear as to what extent presence in the public 'qualifies' as 'public anthropology', since the criteria are vague. Thus, it is not clear whether all these anthropologists are known purely because of anthropology or if, for some of them, it is because of their personal wit and personality (Howell 2010). Indeed, Howell notes that while social anthropologists at Norwegian universities 'have, from time to time, stepped down from the ivory towers of academia' (ibid.: 269), Eriksen finds that Norwegian social anthropology 'has enjoyed a reputation as an anti-elitist kind of activity – an unruly, anarchist science of great coated, ruffled men with unpolished shoes and strange views' (Eriksen 2006: 27).

The issue of public anthropology involves difficult, broader questions about the self-understandings of institutional anthropology; the ability to do research when historical events take place; and, perhaps more importantly, the ideas and practices of anthropologists as citizens and publicly engaged intellectuals. In this I will argue for a narrower conception of the term than mere visibility in the public; one that focuses on anthropological engagement in pressing contemporary social issues and the construction of society's core values, developed through my experiences in the media coverage of ethnic and religious issues for the last two decades, including the Muhammad cartoon crisis of 2005/6.

By discussing these cases I will identify a number of perils of public anthropology and will list some features that may characterize a more offensive, biting and critical kind of public anthropology. One of these perils is the quiescent anthropologists who refrain from engaging proactively as public intellectuals in debates and activities concerning the representation of ethnic and religious minorities in the Danish news media. Another peril in public anthropology is the position of competing anthropologists in public with widely different viewpoints, preferences and motivations that may for instance be reproducing majoritarian stereotypes. Then I will turn to the Muhammad cartoon story and discuss the issues and conditions for doing public anthropology in this story, where society's minorities found themselves in the most vulnerable situation – potentially a situation in which anthropology could be expected to be fully engaged.

The Peril of Quiescent Anthropology

Changing Media Landscape

In European anthropology, few have worked as much on the theme of public anthropology and the changing circumstances for practising public anthropology as the late Marianne Gullestad. Gullestad emphasized two general interrelated premises of public anthropology: a loss of scholarly authority in the public realm, and a decline in social status for scholarship as a whole. She felt that disciplines like anthropology risked falling from grace and sliding into oblivion (Gullestad 2006a).

In the late 1990s, Fredrik Barth noted the relative weakness of American cultural anthropology within the academic community and in American society, which he found to be paradoxical given the rich and diverse anthropological tradition (Barth 1997: 60), yet he placed the responsibility at the individual level. Barth argued that the reason for this weakness lies with senior anthropologists in the 'mood or withdrawal among anthropologists today – and perhaps, a failure of nerve. Too many American anthropologists choose to speak only to a narrow audience of fellow anthropologists' (ibid.). On the other hand, he found smaller traditions of anthropology in Scandinavia and elsewhere to be far more influential in the public arena.

The limited presence of public anthropology in Denmark must be held up against the restructuring of news journalism, with the decline of printed newspapers and the explosion of electronic news sources as well as the drastic expansion of political news management. Within these changes the news stream editors may find detailed anthropological material and thinking attractive, but the fact is that in Denmark this is hardly the case. Despite the many new outlets, anthropologists have had difficulties communicating their research-based experiences and are often relegated to the bottom of the news triangle, where experts can easily be edited out as the least relevant material.

Academics' desire to appear as experts took a serious blow in 2001, when a new right-wing government came into power on 20 November with support from the radical right-wing party, the Danish People's Party.

Beginning with the Institute for Human Rights and extending to the universities, funding for these institutions was questioned whenever critical voices were raised about the new government's politics (Hervik 2011), leading to a withdrawal from speaking to the press.

Likewise the explosive growth of strategic (spin) communication by media-trained professionals created a hostile atmosphere for public intellectuals, who were not media-trained and had to rely on their 'natural' talents. One example of what experts were up against can be seen in the case where spin doctors from three ministries, lawyers and officials started preparing a coordinated spin attack on a report from the European Commission against Racism and Intolerance (ECRI) on racism and discrimination in Denmark, twenty-seven days before it was published on 16 May 2006. The government was quick to deny, trivialize, individualize and explain away racism and discourses about racism and anyone with dissenting voices. In addition, the government used its international diplomatic network to convince nine European ECRI member countries to support its criticism of ECRI's report. On 16 May, the prime minister noted at his weekly meeting with the press that the report would be thrown straight into the wastebasket (Pihl 2006).

Scholarly experts who were critical of the news media itself also risked bad press and personal attacks through one of the many radical websites mushrooming in the 2000s. A statement about non-Western migrants in the public media was then followed by much antagonistic rhetoric on these websites, which then was reflected in the search engines. Most reacted according to the negative coverage. Surveys have shown that fourteen out of fifteen media researchers do not speak to the press for the same reason. Those who do are known among the rest of us to be nourishing a safe, uncritical relationship with the press (*Mandag Morgen Monitor* 2002).

Anthropologists rarely appear as sources or objects of news stories. Some universities responded to the changing circumstances and academic experts' role in the press by adopting an explicit communication strategy for media exposure. For example, my own university, Aalborg University, rewards scholars for public visibility. This is also a proactive strategy to strengthen its position in the Danish university system, since Aalborg is located in the northern region and is an object of some stereotypification, which of course also goes from this region to the capital. This strategy has contributed to Aalborg University now having the highest number of quoted social scientists among the country's universities (Uglen 2011).[4]

The mediatization of news, politics, networks and social relations gave rise to a new area of interest, namely media anthropology. As Faye Ginsburg says in the introduction to media anthropology:

Anthropologists at last are coming to terms with the inescapable presence of media as a contemporary cultural force engaged with the mediation of hegemonic forms and resistance to them; the growth and transnational circulation of public culture; the creation of national and activists' social imaginaries, with the development of media as new arenas for political expression and the production of identity. (Ginsburg 2005: 21)

This would seem to promise a special slot for public anthropology, but many other media anthropologists see the field more as an important contact field of academic exchange between anthropologists of sorts, media studies, communication studies and others (Coman and Rothenbuhler 2005), with their diverse intellectual trajectories and interests, without devoting attention to the issue of public anthropology. Ultimately, the edited volumes, the emerging courses, programmes and network exchanges do not reveal much in terms of a public, engaged, critical anthropology that stands apart from the rest of anthropology.[5] In this way I agree with Marianne Gullestad when she argues that the lack of visibility of anthropology is not specific to anthropology, or even to media anthropology (Gullestad 2006a). Instead, transdisciplinary objectives can be found in the shape of statements about working for a better society; enlarging the public sphere; broadening our understanding; introducing more nuances; or the more noble, humanistic objective of working for greater human solidarity by turning the wildly different people into the range of 'us' (Rorty 1989).

Quiescent Anthropology as a Peril to Public Anthropology?

In the research for this chapter, I came across what I see as two clusters of approaches to public anthropology, in the broadest meaning of the term: a North European 'Engaged Anthropology' and a more institutionalized and narrow North American 'Public Anthropology', or even 'Public Interest Anthropology'. These clusters seldom refer to each other or show signs of identifying themselves explicitly as exponents of the other cluster.

One illustration of the difference can be seen in the way Margaret Mead is being talked about. Thomas Hylland Eriksen describes Mead's work as contributing to a cultural auto critique, but continues:

Mead's books never became classics within anthropology. She was perceived as too superficial in her ethnography, too quick to make sweeping generalizations and, arguably, too *engaged* to be properly scientific. Her uncomplicated, often overtly sentimental prose also had its detractors … In Europe at least, Mead is scarcely read by students, unlike her contemporaries Malinowski and Evans-Pritchard. (Eriksen 2006: 3)

Where Eriksen alludes to her role as a cultural critique, this is seen as affecting her academic work; Setha M. Low and Sally Engle Merry explain:

> Margaret Mead was a pioneer of engaged anthropology. She was active as a writer and public speaker on all facets of people living in the contemporary world … But her celebrity and success in translating anthropological insights from non-Western cultures to critiques of American society were not necessarily received positively within the academy. In more recent years, her efforts were scrutinized for their scientific merit. (Low and Merry 2010: 205)

Thus the three authors recognize her impact, but Eriksen seems to suggest that it lies outside of anthropology, while Low and Merry identify her work as part and parcel of anthropology.

Eriksen argues at the end of his book that anthropological institutions need a PR strategy to communicate the findings, the insights and the experiences of anthropology, especially in the areas of making sense of other people's worlds, translating other people's meanings, and explaining what they do and how societies work to a broader public. Such a strategy would enlighten the world – if the world wants it (Eriksen 2006: 131).

Signe Howell, another Norwegian anthropology professor writing on engaged anthropology, is similarly not blind to the importance of anthropological visibility in the public sphere. She emphasizes the contribution of research-based anthropological insights to a more nuanced understanding of questions debated in the public (Howell 2010: 269). She sees the fact that her two colleagues, Thomas Hylland Eriksen and Unni Wikan, are among the ten best-known intellectuals in Norway as a reflection of the Norwegian public's openness to anthropology, even though there is no evidence that this is actually the case. In fact this may be as much an image that anthropologists have created for themselves than the image of anthropology that is widespread in public discourse. The two public intellectuals are also strong cultural personalities who appear in the media for various motivations and with different ways of practicing anthropology, but we do not know if they are known as 'anthropologists' or as 'strong personalities' who happen to be anthropologists. Perhaps they would have ended up as well-known personalities regardless of which discipline they had chosen. Howell's interlocutors did point out that one needs a special personality and skill set to get oneself into the public sphere.

> [Anthropologists] see their task as one of education and instilling tolerance; they also face the personal and ethical challenge of taking a normative stance and, more disturbing personally, of having to come to terms with their disapproval of some of the cultural practices that they try to defend. (Howell 2010: 272)

Eriksen's and Howell's engaged anthropology seems to be tied to the individual efforts of anthropologists, through opinions, politics and personality, rather than by promoting research results produced within academic institutions. The two authors do not speak about the engaged anthropology within anthropology courses, programmes, or institutional strategies. This is the peril of a quiescent anthropology devoid of institution-based support and agreement in the shape of policies, training and education.

Whereas quiescent anthropology seems to stay clear of issues of power, normative positions, critical discourse analysis and such, and relies on personal initiatives, the North American public anthropology addresses these issues directly and incorporates them as integral aspects of anthropological inquiry. James Peacock has stressed that public anthropology is an obligation not to be confused with the publication of research findings, but to be engaged in seriously as individuals and departments through research projects and investing expertise in public issues, such as combating discrimination, deprivation, intolerance, political manipulation, and inequalities, by using the special strengths and creativities of anthropology that may enlarge the public sphere (Peacock 1997). This *second* approach to public interest anthropology can be seen in the United States, where it forms a notable contrast to the non-normative stance of surveyed Norwegian anthropologists. Public interest anthropology can be distinguished from public anthropology in its provision of a coordinated conceptual framework for engaged research and theory development (Sanday 2004).

PIA (public interest anthropology) can be seen as an attempt to move away from the academic climate of the late 1960s and the 1970s that was not receptive to using anthropology to research or speak on public issues. Scientism and social disengagement were trendy (Sanday 2004). Peacock believes that anthropological voices should be heard along with politicians, philosophers, religionists and economists, who have no qualms about creating normative formulations. So, PIA should also examine, for instance, 'the degree to which foundational rights are breached in legally sanctioned behavior in their own country' (Peacock 1997: 27). In fact anthropologists should engage more in public issues and, instead of merely analysing problems, engage in the creation of core values (ibid.). Beyond the statements and practices to encourage anthropologists to 'go public or perish' (Peacock 1997), Peggy Reeves Sanday has been a key figure in establishing a programme in PIA at the University of Pennsylvania. In addition, the Center for a Public Anthropology was launched in 2001 by Robert Borofsky as a non-profit centre that 'encourage[s] academics to move beyond the traditional "do no harm" ethos of funded research to one that strives to do good, to one that focuses on helping others' (Center for a Public Anthropology n.d.). Various American anthropologists have

argued consistently for anthropology: 'to engage critically with the urgent crises faced by the socially vulnerable under the lie of democracy
and neoliberal prosperity in the 2000s' (Bourgois 2008: ix); to tackle issues
of 'social justice, inequality, subaltern challenges, impact of globalization, our ethical position' (Warren 2008: 213); to get beyond 'textual angst'
(Bourgois 2008: x); and to 'engage with political stakes that matter to the
people who bear a disproportionate toll of the suffering caused by the
inequalities that power empowers' where 'writing against inequality is
imperative' (ibid.). 'Denouncing injustice and oppression is not a naive,
old-fashioned, anti-intellectual concern or a superannuated totalizing vision of Marxism' (ibid.). Common to these calls for publicly engaged anthropology and public interest anthropology is the critical engagement
that includes also the normative engagement into the creation of core values in society, grounded in 'principles of inclusion, equal rights, and equal
access' (Davis 2008: 233).

How would these two clusters of approaches deal with competition
from other public anthropologists in charged political circumstances, such
as neo-nationalist Nordic countries – circumstances in which public interest anthropology could prove to be especially important but risk having
its impact contained?

The Peril of Public Anthropologists
with Opposing Messages

In the spirit of Marianne Gullestad's invitation to further dialogue upon
her 'explorative' reflections, I will draw attention to some challenges, perils if you wish, to both her scheme and to the recent public interest anthropology that is growing stronger in North American anthropology. While
I agree with Gullestad that our research needs to be based on 'truthful',
reflexive, multiperspective scholarly authority, and that anthropologists
need to take a more offensive approach to the dissemination of findings
and experiences to wider audiences, I do not see this as a solution to the
decline of scholarly authority. The fact is that there are competing scholars in the neo-liberal free media market who may not be as articulate or
reflexive as Gullestad, but are still scholarly authorities in the public domain with a large audience, working intentionally for change, even if this
change goes in a different – perhaps controversial – direction.

Marianne Gullestad has done research on public intellectuals, including fellow anthropologists, several of whom found her interest and analysis disturbing. In 2002 she published a new book about the debate on
racism in Norway, which triggered heated public debate, with Gullestad

now both object and participant. One of the public anthropologists she discussed is Professor Unni Wikan. The quick search in Infomedia that I referred to earlier showed that she was one of the two Norwegian anthropologists quoted in the Danish news media with eighteen exposures.

Immigrants are at risk of becoming a new Norwegian underclass was Wikan's point of departure in a book that was meant to be provocative (Wikan 1995). Most of it is included in the English language book *Generous Betrayal* (Wikan 2002); see also Hervik 2002b. On the one hand, she described what she saw as foreigners coming to take advantage of the Norwegian welfare system while maintaining practices, especially in dealing with women and children, that are not welcome in Norway. She especially focused on domestic violence by Muslim men, and effectively put the plight of Muslim women and children in conflict-ridden families on the political agenda.

Wikan finds anthropology's outdated concept of culture 'loose in the streets' of Norway, and criticizes the Norwegian authorities, who encourage the creation of an ethnically based underclass by offering overly generous welfare payments and by excusing the male immigrants' violence against their women and children out of 'respect for their culture' and out of fear of being called racists. The thrust of her argument is that Norwegians who try to treat immigrants 'fairly' practise a 'foolish generosity' based on a misguided notion of culture. Wikan calls these practices 'racism', 'cultural fundamentalism' and 'welfare colonization'. Culture is a new concept of race, she argues, and the Norwegian government instead needs to be more restrictive and make more demands on 'immigrants', otherwise its generosity will be misused and racism will go on. At the same time, Wikan has contributed to the stigmatization of large groups of innocent people, in particular Muslim men, and thus contributed negatively to the dramatic change in the political climate in relation to immigrants in Norway in the 1990s (Gullestad 2006).

While 'we' (the Norwegians) represent ourselves as people with different character traits and with the ability and the will to think for ourselves, immigrants are by and large treated as products of their culture – as if they (the immigrants) are powerless in relation to their culture, and have no independent judgment. But by doing this we participate in taking motivation and intention away from them. This shows a lack of respect, which is degrading (Wikan 1995: 18), 'We' regard ourselves as thinking, reasoning, acting human beings with the ability to reflect and respond to changing circumstances; 'they' are portrayed as caught in the web of culture and propelled to do as culture bids (Wikan 1999: 58).

Is Wikan's work outside the academy an example of public interest anthropology? If so, then this is one of the perils that are ignored in discussions about public, engaged or public interest anthropology. Based on her own words it seems so: 'I am hoping thus to capture the attention not only of Norwegians but also of members of other plural societies – politicians and public of diverse origins – who are concerned with social justice and the future of an increasingly shared world' (Wikan 2002: 1).

However, Wikan's public engagement is not anchored in the anthropological institution in Oslo, but is driven by herself as an individual effort. But what is more important and relevant here is that in the public engagement she uses her position as professor of anthropology as symbolic capital for her engagement. She goes public as an anthropologist, and in the name of anthropology seeks to engage in the creation of core values. At the same time she speaks as a Norwegian observer, a Norwegian commoner, and so on (see Wikan 2000). Yet, this is what public anthropologists do. Sanday tells us that anthropology must learn to play by the rules of public sphere discourse and be prepared to make discursive moves that catch the public's attention. This means entering the public sphere with an argument – and, in Wikan's case, with outstanding communication skills.

In 2002 the Danish prime minister proudly declared that Denmark now had the strictest immigration policy in the world (Hervik and Rytter 2004), while the minister of integration, Bertel Haarder, praised his Norwegian anthropology acquaintance for teaching him to make demands on immigration. Haarder went as far as to call *Generous Betrayal* one of the best books he has ever read (ibid. 148; see also Ellegaard 2002). In this way, Wikan became part of the academic legitimacy behind a discriminatory anti-migrant government practice and philosophy (see ECRI 2006; Hervik 2011).

Sanday has argued that public interest anthropology involves four types of activities: speaking to broad public audiences including proactive work in this regard; being involved with the media as well as getting the media involved; consulting with lawyers on legal issues; and acting as an expert witness. Broadly conceived, these activities would include Wikan's activities and do not provide a disapproval or exclusion from public anthropology of those who supply controversial anthropological support to radical right-wing governments' anti-migration policies and practices. Obviously, the role of colleagues as competing public anthropologists is a sensitive affair to deal with.

In my view anthropology is inherently public, and public interest should ideally be an integral aspect of anthropological practice. In Peacock's words, anthropology should engage more in public interest issues and even 'engage in the creation of core values' (Peacock 1997). Waiting around for the journalists to call and express a genuine interest in your research is a misperception of how the news is working, although this may happen in some cases. More than anything, journalists call to get opinion statement rather than learning about your research. At the same time, I recognize the diversity of opinions on this and the immense variation in terms of themes and issues dealt with by anthropologists that are not of equal public interest concern. Accordingly, I do not see a general solution to the issue or think that anthropologists should agree among themselves before they go public. Instead, it has become increasingly clear to me that public anthropology is best seen as being of a group of anthropologists who are united in at least three areas of concerns, as outlined below. This view is shared by those who have explicitly articulated themselves as public anthropologists and worked to institutionalize their public anthropology.

First, there is concern about the character of news and popular media coverage of the groups of people we study and know about. The level of popular knowledge about immigration and the integration of immigrants may be so loaded with factual errors and anti-migrant ideology that it does not live up to the level of knowledge necessary to make informed choices in a modern democracy. Corporate ownership of the news media, for instance, implies that audiences are approached as consumers rather than as citizens, and competition serves to satisfy audience tastes (lowest common denominator) rather than public needs. The loyalty is to advertisers, sponsors and governments rather than public interest, so some themes and stories are suppressed, and critical journalism limited. This concern is to be dealt with through some form of critical thinking (Sanday 2004), not least since private companies may not be the most reliable to look out for public interest or take on the role of the fourth estate. Can a democracy rely on the press to fulfil a public information service that has little chance of economic gain for the company's investors? Obviously not, and public anthropology has an obligation to deconstruct these relations, and contribute to the forming of popular knowledge and core values.

Secondly, we need an approach that merges problem solving with theory development and analysis in the interest of change; one that is motivated by a commitment to social justice, ethnic harmony, equality, human rights, and well-being (ibid.). Public anthropology's commitment to such issues must also include a commitment to relevant theory and comparative experiences.

Thirdly, public anthropology embodies a critique of the state of affairs in mainstream institutional anthropology, that in a world of crisis anthropology is not playing much of a role – at least this is the case in Northern Europe and North America – but is often relegated to the role of conveyers of curious knowledge, regional experts, or narrow yet important niches in the world of news and popular programmes.

These three concerns I see are shared in public anthropology, as a community of critical-minded anthropologists working for change do not

yield anthropologists as either 'within or without' but in terms of holding these concerns to 'larger or smaller degrees'. From this perspective, I
argue that versions of public anthropology represented by Unni Wikan's
practice are not showing concern with the character of news as such, but
are making Wikan herself a frequent source and object of news. Likewise,
in spite of saying that Norwegians are committing 'racism' in the name of
good, Wikan is not drawing on theories or comparative experiences of racism. She is working for change, although her publications and activities
show little, if any, critical concern about the role of public anthropology
within the institutional anthropology. In other words, Wikan's example
may not be the type of public anthropology that the public interest anthropologists had in mind, yet she is visible as an anthropologist in the public.
The other side of this argument is the question of to what extent Wikan's
work is good or bad public anthropology, which I will not discuss further
here (see Gullestad 2006).

The Perilous Relationship between the
Muhammad Cartoon Conflict and Public Anthropology

The Muhammad cartoon conflict would seem to be the kind of unfolding event at which anthropologists could be expected to be present, not
only with their insights into various dimensions of the conflict and stories
about the conflict, but also from the perspectives of social justice, grossly
distorting news coverage, misinformed publics and social memory out of
tune with fact-based history. Public anthropology or public interest anthropology was not seen during or after the Muhammad cartoons episode.
Numerous books were published on the cartoons directly; later there were
hundreds of articles, mostly by political scientists, and thousands of news
media articles (Hervik 2008, 2011, 2012), but anthropologists and the anthropological institutions did not make themselves visible.

The structural organization and routine practices of the news media
may of course in themselves be an obstacle to public intellectuals in general and public anthropology in particular. Some were blacklisted and denied a voice, particularly Muslims (Hervik 2011: 242–68), but generally
I have no evidence that anthropologists tried to influence the debate in
Denmark. We can therefore turn the question around and ask whether
the philosophy of the anthropological community concerning when to go
public has something to do with the lack of visibility of direct engagement.

Most people remember the cartoon conflict through the violent reactions in cities around the world in early 2006. They did not follow the first
publication of the cartoons in September 2005, but only learned about the

cartoon story later, after strong narratives had been circulated. One narrative insisted that the conflict was an issue of free speech; another blamed the Danish imams for stirring up trouble in the Middle East, thus causing violent reactions in many countries. A third weaker narrative blamed the Danish daily *Morgenavisen Jyllands-Posten* and the government's anti-Islamic stance for creating the conflict that eventually led to the publication of the provocative cartoons.

In September 2005, *Jyllands-Posten* initiated a project about self-censorship that ended up with twelve cartoonists willing to have their Muhammad cartoons published in the opinion pages of the Sunday edition. *Jyllands-Posten* officially endorsed the product by dedicating its editorial on 30 September, the day of publication, to the cartoon project (Hervik 2008, 2011, 2012). The initiative spearheaded by cultural editor Flemming Rose and best seen as the result of *Jyllands-Posten*'s 'Cultural-war-of-values' strategy in 2003, which prioritizes critical stances towards Denmark's radio (public service television), communism, and Islam.[6] Rose was called home from his foreign correspondence job in Russia to lead the strategy for *Jyllands-Posten* (Hervik 2014).

As criticism mounted, eleven ambassadors from Muslim countries asked for a meeting with the Danish prime minister, Anders Fogh Rasmussen, to discuss *Jyllands-Posten*'s initiative and other worrisome incidents in Denmark. Rasmussen rejected the invitation, making one of the biggest mistakes of his political career (Wæver 2006; Hervik 2011, 2012). When the criticism kept growing, Rasmussen launched a spin campaign via an interview with *Jyllands-Posten* on 30 October 2005, in which he framed the issue as being about free speech, which 'good countries' have and 'bad countries' do not. From a spin perspective, any criticisms of the government from non-Westerners were to be countered by the argument that the critic had not understood what democracy and freedom of speech were about (Hervik 2011). Government critics such as the daily newspaper *Politiken* found it obvious that the ambassadors had to consult with their home governments about what to do, since the Danish government was refusing to have a dialogue with them. They went on to argue that if the prime minister had not refused a dialogue with the ambassadors or had shown an interest in their concern it is highly unlikely that the Danish imams and businessmen would have travelled to the Middle East (Larsen and Seidenfaden 2006; Hervik 2011, 2012).

In late March 2006, Rasmussen scolded organizations, companies and personalities for not standing up for freedom of speech when the country needed it the most. Without mentioning the names of individuals or companies, his media initiative presented him as standing strong and firm in the fight for Denmark and freedom of speech. This initiative helped to control how history will remember this as a free speech issue rather than an issue of a country with anti-Islamic sentiments and practices.

Two and a half years later (in the autumn of 2008), focus group participants in our research project declared that they remembered the cartoon conflict as being all about freedom of speech (Hervik 2011, 2012). Two participants were particularly upset about people not standing up for freedom of speech when it was most necessary. Their collective memory confirms what we, as researchers, had already experienced outside of the focus group gatherings (Hervik 2012). The free speech strategy has become so hegemonic today in the Danish news media that claiming that the Muhammad cartoon conflict was not, at least in the beginning, about freedom of speech may seem utterly absurd to most Danes.

What, then, would a public anthropology engagement with the cartoon issue be? Among many other themes, an anthropological response might be concerned that Muslims' right to free speech was never emphasized, although the issue from a political and a spin communication perspective was approached as a free speech issue. Secondly, a neo-conservative network dominated the media coverage calling for zero tolerance and confrontation with Islamists. Their rhetoric and ideology were much more aggressive and confrontational than the act of publishing the cartoons (Berg and Hervik 2007). Thirdly, the use of free speech, as noted by a few lawyers (Koch 2006), was institutionalized in the mid nineteenth century. The founding fathers of the Danish democracy introduced freedom of speech as a protection device for vulnerable minorities. During the Muhammad cartoon conflict the government and the largest national newspaper used freedom of speech to lever a negative dialogue project, which is the belief that certain conflicts are impossible to resolve, thus legitimizing zero tolerance and confrontation as the only valid responses (Hervik 2012). Fourthly, public anthropologists could counter the claim that two imam delegations travelling to the Middle East were the sole cause of the violent outbursts around the world. This myth ignores the fact that the delegations would most likely not have travelled to the Middle East if the ambassadors had not been denied a meeting. On such occasions embassies have no choice but to inform and consult their home government (Larsen and Seidenfaden 2006; Wæver 2006; Hervik 2011). Furthermore, Al Jazeera had, through its coverage on 10, 12 and 15 October 2005, already given the event a global reach. This is not of course to say that the delegations did not have a catalytic effect on the explosion of the conflict into violence in Africa and Asia. Fifthly, the very gap between research findings on what actually promoted the cartoon conflict and the social memory of it is a crucial illustration of what public anthropology must address.

My own role as a public anthropologist in this regard was shaped by my research on the news media coverage of Islam in 2001, prior to 9/11. The research found *Jyllands-Posten* presenting the most articles on Islam, and the most antagonistic ones. Therefore, this newspaper's coverage played an important role in my research, to the extent that I devoted an entire chapter to it in my book-length report (Hervik 2002a). My analysis included at least one relevant drawing by a cartoonist with *Jyllands-Posten*, Kurt Westergaard, whose drawing in 2001 included the association of a Danish politician with Pakistani background as a hidden Taliban warrior or terrorist. The report was critical of *Jyllands-Posten*'s coverage, as well as of the public service station, Denmark's radio. In a public meeting, three news leaders attacked my work for being 'tendentious and therefore not research'. They were not happy about my criticism of the lopsided coverage of Islam in the news media, but when I checked their specific criticism it turned out that their assertions were not supported by fact. I concluded that they had not read the report (see Hervik 2011: xi).

In the follow years I heard little from the news media. But my surprise was great when the Muhammad cartoon story ran and the Danish press showed no interest in the history of *Jyllands-Posten*'s Islam coverage.

During the Muhammad cartoon crisis of 2005/6, I was working at Malmö University in Sweden, which is a short train journey away from Copenhagen. There I took part in the Swedish news media's coverage of *Morgenavisen Jyllands-Posten*'s long-term coverage of Islam and Kurt Westergaard's drawings with associations to the prophet Muhammad and terrorism since 1997, which were never taken up by the Danish news media. Swedish interest continued as I published my book *The Danish Muhammad Cartoon Conflict* in 2012.

Incidentally, my new research on the Muhammad cartoon coverage, which included large international projects on global news coverage, revealed that ordinary and concerned Muslims were unable to get *their* voices heard in such coverage. As one Danish Muslim with ethnic minority background, Ahmed, explained:

> It is as if we were told that this is how we have decided to deal with it. We have decided to ridicule, mock, and insult all of you because you are Muslims. We have no intention of changing this. We do exactly what we want to do. There was no debate. There was no discussion. When you tried to say something, the door was shut by journalists sitting there babbling about free speech. (Hervik 2012: 263–64)

My own experiences with the Danish, Swedish and international press, as well as Ahmed's and other Muslims' experience, suggest that public anthropologists also face an increasingly commercialist and corporatist news media that has little interest in making space for certain stories, regardless of how relevant they may be.

Public Anthropology in Neo-Nationalist Scandinavia

One of the most difficult general challenges for anthropologists is to accept that they need to adapt their message and simplify (Gullestad 2006). It seems, as James Ferguson (2006) noted, that anthropologists' main general contribution is to state that the world is more complicated than how it is represented by others. Much of the media often does not really want to hear what we have to say about, for example, freedom of speech, Muslims, *Jyllands-Posten*'s prioritizing of Islam critical stories, or Kurt Westergaard's earlier drawings associating Islam with terrorism.

Another obstacle for public anthropologists to cope with is the professionalization of news management associated mostly with the drastic growth of political spin communication. This raises the ethical and analytical issue of whether public anthropologists should let themselves be absorbed by spin strategies or insist on using proper analytical vocabulary, experience and theories, even though dark shadows are cast on to the words we use for our research.

In 1994, Newt Gingrich distributed a memo 'Language: A Key Mechanism of Control' (GOPAC memo) to Republican members of Congress and others. The short text includes two sets of words. Republicans were to use the positive words when talking about Republicans and the negative words when speaking about Democrats, Liberals and everything associated with Liberals (FAIR 1995). Republican leaders learned it by heart or kept it close to their telephone (Press 2002 85–86):

Republican	Democrat
peace	crisis
liberty	greed, self-serving
hard work	corruption
family	threaten
prosperity	decay, collapse
success	failure
pioneers, passionate	traitors
truth	lie

The idea was that if you are associated with positively loaded words you will – in the end – attract far more voters. These ideas about 'plus' words and 'minus' words are now textbook knowledge in communication studies.

How are we to deal with this as public anthropologists? I am thinking about those analytic categories from our theoretical vocabulary that are used in everyday conversations and in the media, which are loaded with negative values and at times with diverging meanings. Some words, events and personalities are so negatively loaded that you do not want to use them, because they are associated with negativity, which again may deflect attention from your core arguments and push potential supporters away. Thus, for example, communication experts in the Nordic countries will today advise you to avoid association with the Muhammad cartoon conflict (Hervik 2012).

For some research applications and official reports you are advised not to use certain words, or at least to be keenly aware of the values of key words. Currently, in Denmark and the Nordic countries more generally, the local words for nationalism, neo-nationalism, neo-racism, racism, integration, immigrant, ethnic, ethnicity, multiculturalism, non-Westerner, second generation, and Muslim all carry negative associations and are to be used accordingly. Instead you can use social cohesion, citizens, populism, hyphenated identity categories, and our friends (see also Aidt and Hervik 2009).

In the last five years, I have given lectures and held seminars in a number of countries about the emergence of neo-nationalism and neo-racism. Much of this has revolved around the Muhammad cartoon conflict. Norwegian listeners have said things like 'I don't think it is racism' and 'I don't think it is nationalism either', and in Denmark I have heard that the so-called celebration of 'Danishness' is associated with Europeanness and not racism. A Danish colleague asked, 'Why do you insist on using "neo-nationalism" or "neo-racism" when people get upset with this usage? Why don't you avoid it?'

In response I asked directly (and checked subsequently) if these potential deniers or deflectors of racism had read literature on 'racism', 'neo-racism' and 'neo-nationalism', and the result was a predictable negative. The same thing could even be argued for anthropologists who talked about Norwegian racism and political correctness: Unni Wikan (2002), Inger-Lise Lien (1997) and Jonathan Friedman (1999). Obviously not relying on research-based findings and experiences of these phenomena increases the risk of reproducing mainstream populism.

When I did the same lectures in Sweden, the United Kingdom, the United States and Japan, anthropologists agreed with my use of these terms; in several cases I was in fact encouraged to use the terms and apply them more explicitly to these other countries. Those anthropologists who commented were also considered to be experts in anthropology or sociology on racism and ethnicity.

By avoiding negatively loaded everyday concepts, such as racism and nationalism, anthropologists risk falling into convenience and complacency while reproducing mainstream-biased opinions and losing sight of the aim of showing the inherent biases and asymmetries between the minorities and the power holders. But we now know that the conditions for maintaining this ideal are not necessarily conducive to public anthropology. We do need a communication strategy to break into the public space and make a difference.

It raises the question of to what extent the premise for doing public anthropology is to adjust our concepts and avoid the empirically negative words.

Final Remarks

Anthropologists need a more offensive approach, as Marianne Gullestad called for. When facts give way to moral logics, and rights are given to certain people and not to others because we like the former and not the latter (Schneider and Ingram 1993), we are in need of an offensive approach. In this lies a criticism that lurks behind what I feel the EASA session preceding this book was about: colleagues and institutions that are absent on the public scene. While it may be the easiest and most comfortable position for anthropologists to take, the absence of public anthropology means a worsening of conditions for those minorities we otherwise like to study and fight for; democracy will suffer if society is unable to supply the credible information we need to make informed choices. To reach the same audience as the news media, public anthropology must also be present while the debates are going on, and not just return to the topic years later when research has finished, seminars have been held, and anthropologists are ready to set the record straight – although this is also part of what public anthropology should do.

With the decline in the authority of scholarship, simple visibility in the public domain runs the risk of being entertainment – short-lived and maybe in some cases irrelevant. And since, as Laura Nader pointed out, teaching needs to include whatever students are upset by, puzzled by, feel strongly about, and are indignant about (Nader 1972, 1997), then we need an engaged dialectical relationship with research and practice, and some dose of activism. Everything else is bad for students, bad for minorities and bad for the discipline.

One of the practical ways to get started is to work on a communication policy and strategy at the level of individual universities and institutions. When we have results, strong viewpoints that can be translated, or reduced to simpler formulations, could follow the strategy, but more importantly this work must include breaking down the target groups we want to influence, which is the first step of substituting crossed-armed attitudes with some active postures and building society's core values.

Peter Hervik holds a Ph.D. in Social Anthropology from the University of Copenhagen, and is currently professor at the Centre for the Study of Migration and Diversity (CoMID) at Aalborg University, Denmark. Hervik has conducted research among the Yucatec Maya of Mexico and in Denmark on issues of identity, categorization, neo-racism, neo-nationalism, ethnicity, multiculturalism, tolerance, and the news media. His books include *Mayan Lives Within and Beyond Boundaries: Social Categories and Lived Identity in Yucatan* (Harwood Academic Publishers, 1999; Routledge, 2001); *The Annoying Difference: The Emergence of Danish Neonationalism, Neoracism, and Populism in the Post-1989 World* (Berghahn Books, 2011); and *The Danish Muhammad Cartoon Conflict* (Malmö University, 2012). Recent articles include 'Erostratus Unbound: Norway's 22/7 Converging Frames of War' (with Susi Meret) and 'Danish Media Coverage of 22/7' (with Sophie Boisen), both in the *Nordic Journal for Migration Research* 3(4); and 'Ending Tolerance as a Solution to Incompatibility: The Danish "Crisis of Multiculturalism"', *European Journal of Cultural Studies* 15(2).

Notes

1. The search on Kirsten Hastrup, Karen Fog Olwig, Susan Whyte and Ton Otto was done in the database Infomedia, where national and regional Danish newspaper articles are included. The five year criteria was chosen to separate 'old' 'full professors' in the Danish system from a newer promotion of temporarily named 'professors with special responsibility'. At the level of Ph.D. researchers and master's students, research was initiated with the Cartoon conflict either as the focus or the backdrop of ongoing studies of minorities in Denmark (see, for instance, Kublitz 2010).
2. For a likewise unimpressive news media appearance of American Anthropology, see the website www.publicanthropology.com and Borofsky 2002.
3. We were two anthropologists engaged in these projects committed to combining anthropology with certain forms of activism (Boe and Hervik 2008; Hervik 2011, 2012).
4. Aalborg University is built on strong interdisciplinary research groups that are well geared to direct research and respond to current issues, regionally and nationally. Teaching builds on strong principles of project- and problem-oriented learning, with resemblances to the pedagogical strategies known in the Danish Grundtvig and Kold tradition of the nineteenth century (Kolmos, Fink and Grogh 2004).

5. The epitome could be a session at the meeting of the Media Anthropology Network held in Maynooth, Ireland, in August 2010. A presenter talked about a certain computer game and the online communities of practice. He mentioned the notorious politically incorrect language used by the players during the game, but never permitted space for information about whether such language relates to the language used outside of the game scenario.

6. *Jyllands-Posten's* initiave echoes the Danish government's strategy of 'cultural war of values', launched in 2001 (see Hervik 2014).

References

Aidt, M., and P. Hervik. 2009. 'Sprogbrug. Kulturel mangfoldighed, interkultur, flerkultur, multikultur, etnisk, 2G'er, indvandrer, integration, nydansker', *Cultures* 1: 21–23 (August–September). http://www.kunstoginterkultur.dk/assets/files/Artikler/Cultures-nr-1_Sprogbrug-artikel.pdf

Barth, F. 1997. 'How Others See Us: An Interview with Fredrik Barth', *Anthropological Newsletter* (February): 60.

Berg, C., and P. Hervik. 2007. 'Muhammad krisen. En politisk kamp i dansk journalistik'. Aalborg: AMID Working Paper Series 62/2007.

Boe, C.S., and P. Hervik. 2008. 'Integration through Insult', in *Transnational Media Events: The Mohammed Cartoons and the Imagined Clash of Civilizations,* Elizabeth Eide, Risto Kunelius and Angela Phillips (eds). Gothenburg: Nordicom, pp. 213–34.

Borofsky, R. 2002. 'A Structural Contradiction: Public and Public Interest Anthropology'. Introduction to AAA Panel session, New Orleans (unpublished manuscript).

Bourgois, P. 2008. 'Foreword', in *Engaged Observer: Anthropology, Advocacy, and Activism,* ed. Victoria Sanford and Asale Angel-Ajani. New Brunswick, NJ, and London: Ruthers University Press, pp. ix–xii.

Center for a Public Anthropology. n.d. No title. http://www.publicanthropology.org/about (accessed 10 June 2013).

Coman, M., and E.W. Rothenbuhler. 2005. 'The Promise of Media Anthropology', in *Media Anthropology,* Eric W. Rothenbuhler and Mihai Coman (eds). Thousand Oaks, CA: Sage, pp. 1–11.

Davis, D.-A. 2008. 'Knowledge in the Service of a Vision: Politically Engaged Anthropology', in *Engaged Observer: Anthropology, Advocay, and Activism,* ed. Victoria Sanford and Asale Angel-Ajani. New Brunswick, NJ, and London: Ruthers University Press, pp. 228–38.

ECRI (European Commission against Racism and Intolerance). 2006. 'Third Report on Denmark'. Strasbourg, 16 May. http://hudoc.ecri.coe.int/XMLEcri/ENGLISH/Cycle_03/03_CbC_eng/DNK-CbC-III-2006-18-ENG.pdf (accessed 9 April 2012).

Eide, E., R. Kunelius and A. Phillips (eds). 2008. *Transnational Media Events: The Mohammed Cartoons and the Imagined Clash of Civilizations.* Gothenburg: Nordicom.

Ellegaard, M. 2002. 'Undskyld – men jeg er så engageret!', *Socialrådgiveren* 26.

Eriksen, J.-M., and F. Stjernfelt. 2008. *Adskillelsens politik. Multikulturalisme – ideology og virkelighed.* Copenhagen: Lindhardt og Ringhof.

Eriksen, T.H. 2006. *Engaged Anthropology: The Case for a Public Presence.* Oxford and New York: Berg.

FAIR (Fairness and Accuracy in Reporting). 1995. 'Language: A Key Mechanism of Control'. http://www.fair.org/index.php?page=1276 (accessed 9 April 2012).

Ferguson, J. 2006. *Global Shadows: Africa in the Neoliberal World Order.* Durham, NC: Duke University Press.

Friedman, J. 1999. 'Rhinoceros 2', *Current Anthropology* 40(5): 679–94.

Ginsburg, F. 2005. 'Media Anthropology: An Introduction', in *Media Anthropology,* ed. Eric W. Rothernbuhler and Mihai Coman. Thousand Oaks, CA: Sage, pp. 17–25.

Gullestad, M. 1992. *Det norske set med nye oejne: Kritisk analyse af norsk innvandringsdebatt.* Oslo: Universitetsforlaget.

———. 2006a. 'Reconfiguring Scholarly Authority: Reflections based on Anthropological Studies in Norway', *Current Anthropology* 47(6): 915–32.

———. 2006b. *Plausible Prejudice: Everyday Experiences and Social Images of Nation, Culture and Race.* Oslo: Universitetsforlaget.

Hastrup. K. 2005. *A Passage to Anthropology.* New York and London: Routledge.

Hervik, P. 2002a. *Mediernes muslimer. En antropologisk undersøgelse af mediernes dækning af religioner i Danmark.* Copenhagen: The Board for Ethnic Equality.

———. 2002b. 'Unni Wikan *Generous Betrayal*: Politics of Culture in the New Europe', *Norsk Antropologisk Tidsskrift* 13(4): 252–55.

———. 2008. 'The Original Spin and its Side Effects: Freedom Speech as Danish News Management', in *The Mohammed Cartoons and the Imagined Clash of Civilizations,* ed. Elisabeth Eide, Risto Kunelius and Angela Phillips. Gothenburg: Nordicom, pp. 59–80.

———. 2011. *The Annoying Difference: The Emergence of Danish Neonationalism, Neoracism, and Populism in the Post-1989 World.* New York and Oxford: Berghahn Books.

———. 2012. *The Danish Muhammad Cartoon Conflict.* Current Themes in IMER Research 13, Malmö Institute for Studies of Migration, Diversity and Welfare (MIM), Malmö University.

———. 2014. 'Cultural War of Values: The Proliferation of Moral Identities in the Danish Public Sphere', in *Becoming Minority: How Discourses and Policies Produce Minorities in Europe and India,* Jyotirmaya Tripathy Sudarsan Padmanabhan (eds.). New Delhi: Sage Publications, India, pp. 154–173.

Hervik, P., and M. Rytter. 2004. 'Med ägteskab i focus', in *Ægtefællesammenføring i Danmark.* Udredning nr 1, kapitel 6. Copenhagen: The Danish Institute for Human Rights, pp. 131–60.

Howell, S. 2010. 'Norwegian Academic Anthropologists in Public Spaces', *Current Anthropology* 51(S2): 269–78.

Klausen, J. 2009. *The Cartoons that Shook the World.* Connecticut and London: Yale University Press.

Koch, H. 2006. 'Ytringsfrihed og tro', in *Gudebilleder. Ytringsfrihed og religion I en globaliseret verden,* ed. Lisbet Christoffersen. Copenhagen: Tiderne Skifter, pp. 72–88.

Kolmos, A., F.K. Fink and L. Grogh (eds). 2004. *The Aalborg PBL Model: Progress, Diversity and Challenges.* Aalborg: Aalborg Universitetsforlag.

Kublitz, A. 2010. 'The Mutable Conflict: A Study of How the Palestinian–Israeli Conflict is Actualized among Palestinians in Denmark'. Ph.D., Department of Anthropology, University of Copenhagen.

Kunelius, R., et al. (eds). 2007. *Reading the Mohammed Cartoons Controversy: An International Analysis of Press Discourses on Free Speech and Political Spin.* Working Papers in International Journalism. Bochum: Projektverlag.

Larsen, R.E., and T. Seidenfaden. 2006. *Karikaturkristen. En undersøgelse af baggrund og ansvar.* Copenhagen: Gyldendal.

Lien, I.-L. 1997. *Ordet som stempler djevlene: holdninger blant pakistanere og nordmenn*. Oslo: Aventura.

Low, S.M., and S. Engle Merry. 2010. 'Engaged Anthropology: Diversity and Dilemmas. An Introduction to Supplement 2', *Current Anthropology* 51(S2): 203–26.

Mandag Morgen Monitor. 2002. 'Danske samfundsforskere vender ryggen til medierne'. Månedens tema (6 May), pp. 6–11.

Nader, L. 1972. 'Up the Anthropologist: Perspectives Gained from Studying Up', in *Reinventing Anthropology*, ed. Hymes, Dell. New York: Pantheon, pp. 284–311.

———. 1997. 'Controlling Processes: Tracing the Dynamic Components of Power', *Current Anthropology* 38(5): 711–37.

Peacock, J.L. 1997. 'The Future of Anthropology', *American Anthropologist* 99(1): 9–29.

Pihl, M. 2006. 'Racisme-rapport: Operation ECRI', *Morgenavisen Jyllands-Posten*, Indblik (23 July), p. 5.

Press, B. 2002. *Spin This! All the Ways We Don't Tell the Truth*. New York: Pocket Books.

Rorty, R. 1989. *Contingency, Irony, and Solidarity*. Cambridge: Cambridge University Press.

Rothstein, K., and M. Rothstein. 2006. *Bomben i Turbanen*. Copenhagen: Tiderne Skifter.

Sanday, P.R. 2004. 'Public Interest Anthropology: A Model for Engaged Social Science'. Paper prepared for the SAR Workshop, AAA Meetings Chicago. Unpublished manuscript, http://www.sas.upenn.edu/~psanday/PIE.05.htm (accessed 10 June 2013).

Schneider, A., and H. Ingram. 1993. 'Social Construction of Target Populations: Implications for Politics and Policy', *American Political Science Review* 87(2) (June): 334–47.

Stage, C. 2011. *Tegningskrisen – som mediebegivenhed og danskhedskamp*. Aarhus: Aarhus Universitetsforlag.

Uglen. 2011. Vol. 3. Aalborg University, p. 29.

Warren, K.B. 2008. 'Perils and Promises of Engaged Anthropology: Historical Transitions and Ethnographic Dilemmas', in *Engaged Observer: Anthropology, Advocacy, and Activism*, ed. Victoria Sanford and Asale Angel-Ajani. New Brunswick, NJ, and London: Ruthers University Press, pp. 213–27.

Wæver, O. 2006. 'Aviser og Religioner i en Globaliseret Verden', in *Gudebilleder. Ytringsfrihed og Religion i en Globaliseret Verden*. Copenhagen: Tiderne Skifter.

Wikan, U. 1995. *Mot en ny norsk underklasse: innvandrere, kultur og integrasjon*. Oslo: Gyldendal.

———. 1999. 'Culture: A New Concept of Race', *Social Anthropology* 7(1): 57–64.

———. 2000. 'Kampen mot barneranerne'. Feature article, *Aftenposten*, 20 March, Oslo.

———. 2002. *Generous Betrayal*. Chicago and London: The University of Chicago Press.

Chapter 3

FOR A CREATIVE
ANTHROPOLOGICAL IMAGE-MAKING
Reflections on Aesthetics, Relationality, Spectatorship
and Knowledge in the Context of
Visual Ethnographic Work in New Delhi, India

―――――∞∞∞――――――

Paolo Favero

This chapter explores the potentialities of audiovisual experimentation
for engaging with wider audiences and for addressing issues and debates
that may surround the anthropologist in the field as well as at 'home'. In
other words this chapter is about image-based practices for intervening in
the public realm. Based on examples gathered from my own practice as an
image-maker, and in particular on the work that I have conducted over the
years for communicating my research in and on New Delhi, this chapter
will move in the border zone between anthropology, visual arts, and the
new possibilities for conducting and communicating our researches (and
for teaching too) made possible by contemporary digital technologies.
Reflecting on what creative image-making[1] can give to anthropologists
(and anthropology), I will here challenge the (ruling) scepticism towards
any attempts at allowing anthropology to 'flirt' with art and aesthetics (cf.
Ruby 1975; Banks 1992). Schneider and Wright (2010: 3) suggest that what
dominates the scene of contemporary anthropology is a 'blanket condem-
nation of formally experimental visual and audio work'.

Anthropologists have long been overly dismissive of formal experimentation, not only in terms of expanding the range of methodologies
and forms of presentation involved in exhibiting anthropological work,

but also in the sense of 'policing' the kinds of work produced by research students (Schneider and Wright 2010). Taking such critique further I will show how a creative audiovisual experimentation is a vital resource for generating a more processual and participative kind of knowledge, one able to close the gap not only with new potential audiences but with our field interlocutors and students too. I will also suggest how art-inspired image-making practices attentive to questions of 'relationality' (Bourriaud 1998),[2] participation and new forms of spectatorship can today allow anthropologists to rethink some of the silent assumptions that inform their engagement with visual work.

I will open this chapter with a few introductory reflections on the assumptions that have informed my practice as an image-making anthropologist and on the role of images in our discipline. Such reflections will be useful for allowing the reader to locate the position from which I write. They may also help to present some key debates on the role of the visual in anthropology to those readers who have not explicitly engaged in the subject before. I will then proceed to offer some background notions on the research that I have conducted in Delhi, given that this research constitutes the ethnographic base on which the visual projects that I will discuss here were built. In this section I will also offer some glimpses into the politics of representation that surrounded my fieldwork and into the methodologies that informed my practice in the field. I will then proceed to discuss three examples. Through the first one, a single field photograph, I will share some reflections regarding how a creative and relational approach to photography can offer anthropologists a new entry into the stories of their interlocutors. Such practices can generate new insights about the people we engage with our researches, and give birth to participated forms of knowledge-making. With the second example, a photographic exhibition that I produced in 2001, I will discuss, reawakening perhaps the ghosts of the 1980s 'writing culture' debate, the importance of aesthetical choices and stratagems in communicating ethnographic knowledge. Finally, with the last example (a video installation), I will address the role of the spectator in the construction of meaning in the context of display of anthropological work. All together, these examples will allow me to suggest that a creative experimentation with audiovisuals is fundamental not only for reaching out to wider audiences but also for allowing us to update our notions of images and image-making, and for renewing the practices that characterize our practice. This is, I will suggest in the conclusions, particularly important in the present context. New image-making practices and technologies have, in fact, extensively changed conventional meanings regarding images and communication. They are also increasingly interpellating the spectators, transforming them into skilled and active producers of image-work and hence into more authoritative and critical consumers of our works.

Background

Like many students who trained in anthropology in the early 1990s, I was urged to think that anthropology could and should occupy a public role – one going beyond the boundaries of academia. The discipline, we believed, should have engaged more extensively in the critical issues that characterized the habitats where we conducted research, lived and taught. We envisioned engagement and participation as a kind of 'pay back' for the privilege of being able to 'live' other individuals' lives and for the 'epistemic violence' that anthropology had historically exercised through its engagement with, and representations of, the 'Other' (Talal Asad 1995; Said 1995; Tobing Rony 2001). We believed that communicating across the academic boundary was a useful therapeutic exercise for us, and for the discipline at large. However, in order to engage the 'outer world' (i.e. wider generalized audiences), we needed to find a language able to convey the insights gathered through ethnographic research to individuals who were not socialized into academic (or, for that matter, anthropological) discourse. While some of my colleagues took to writing for newspapers and magazines, images became my own answer to this search. Images' intrinsic polysemy[3] and open-endedness (Berger 1972; Barthes 1977), and their capacity to open us up to the sensorial and emotional dimension of everyday life (MacDougall 1997; Edwards 2006; Pink 2006) attracted me. Images did appear as MacDougall (1998) had suggested – a powerful medium for transcultural communication. Starting to test the potentialities of visual media for anthropological work, I became progressively interested also in the approaches to image-work coming from the fields of art and communication. I was, in particular, inspired by art historian Achille Bonito Oliva's notion of art as 'accident',[4] of art as a kind of generator of insecurity regarding our conventional assumptions about the world we live in. Offering a notion that resonates very strongly with the anthropological questioning of the (culturally) 'taken-for-granted', this made me curious about the extent to which anthropologists could actually push their communication practices beyond conventional notions of 'explanation' and 'description'. What would happen if we started to produce and communicate our research work armed with ideas of incompleteness, suspension, counterpoint and relationality?

Inspired by such ideas, I progressively started using images as instruments for 'provoking' viewers rather than as items 'conveying' an objective piece of information. This I believed could be a useful strategy for reaching out to the public, entering a new terrain where notions gathered through scholarly work could be shared with wide varieties of people. Envisioning the public as a political arena (Chatterjee 2006), my ideas about experimenting with more open-ended and accessible languages merged with my need to also challenge conventional representations of India and 'other' postcolonial societies. With my work I wanted to unleash in my viewers a desire to participate in the 'world of others', and to close, through a number of provocations and inversions, the perceived gap between 'us' and 'them', between the so-called First and Third World. In more specific terms, I took off in my work with the idea of playfully challenging the hegemonic notions portraying India as the locus of prototypical alterity. The dominating notions of India as a place of 'tradition' and 'contrasts', of 'spiritual purity and physical filth' (Khilnani 1997) were prolongations into the present of colonial tropes and divides. My interlocutors – young, upcoming, educated Delhi-based middle-class men – were strongly reacting against such stereotypes. Incorporating their views, I decided to attempt to break such associations and 'force' the viewer, through the combined adoption of specific aesthetical stratagems and choices of content and through a strategic use of the spaces in which I exhibited my work, to see India from a different angle. This approach gave birth across the years to a number of different projects (a couple of photographic exhibitions, two video installations and a film), all aiming at offering such critique while simultaneously also giving insights into the life of young middle-class men in Delhi.

With the years, my work also led me to reflect on anthropology's ambivalent relation to images. I do not intend to go into any greater depth with this issue here, but it should be remembered that the roots of this problematic relationship are probably to be found in the intimate connection that the discipline had, from its very birth, with camera technologies. As is well known, taking off for the Torres Straits expedition in 1895, Sir Thomas Haddon described the camera as an 'indispensable piece of anthropological apparatus' (Grimshaw 1997: 41). For many decades after that, visual technologies were granted status as fundamental tools for scientific research. They were pivotal in transforming anthropology into a proper science. In an environment obsessed by notions of positivism and objectivity, the camera was in fact a precious instrument capable of 'capturing', and bringing back home, distant cultures to the metropolitan centra (as samples brought back to the laboratory, Grimshaw 2001). A (metaphorical) cage substituting the one that missionaries and colonial administrators had used for bringing living natives to the studio of the 'armchair anthropologist', the camera however also had something new to offer. It could reproduce the contexts in which the natives lived, the landscapes surrounding them, their material culture. The camera quickly proved, to quote Spivak, to be 'the most versatile tool for "worlding" the world' (quoted in McQuire 1998: 193). It was pivotal to the (colonial, imperialist) cataloguing of human kind and hence also for the critical distancing of cultures outside Europe and North America (MacDougall 1997 and Tobing Rony 2001).[5] With the turn of the century, however, signs of what Jay (1989) called the 'crisis of ocularcentrism' became visible. Scientists progressively shifted away from the ideas of positivism and objectivity that had characterized the Victorian era. This led to the inevitable marginalization of the practices of photography and filmmaking (that were so tightly coupled to such attempts), and to the development of what some scholars have defined as a proper form of 'iconophobia' (Taylor 1996).

For many decades, such marginalization has kept growing. The increasing awareness regarding visual media's hidden power agendas (Herman and Chomsky 1994), combined with suspicions regarding images' intrinsic superficiality and sexiness (Banks 1990) and the imputed technical difficulties required for exploiting their potentialities, have all contributed to this marginalization. As a celebration of such distancing, in 1997 Kirsten Hastrup defined photography and film as perfect examples of 'thin descriptions' (in MacDougall 1997: 282). However, today's growing interest in sensoriality, corporality, affectivity, and so on (Edwards 2006; Pink 2006; Pinney 2009; Taussig 2009), and the growing amount of research conducted on digital technologies and platforms (Wesch 2009; Horst and Miller 2012; Pink and Hjorth 2012; Favero 2013) are opening up the space for a renewal of our understanding of the meaning of images (and of the 'sensible' at large too, Rancière 2004) and image-making. This may progressively contribute to bringing the visual back to the centre of the discipline, and the recent boom in courses and programmes in visual culture can perhaps be seen as a sign of this change. Notwithstanding this, the lack of a creative exploration of the potential of film, photography and multimedia can still be traced at many different levels: from, to give some banal examples, the absence of full-page photographs in major peer-reviewed academic journals of anthropology (online journals are indeed offering a critical questioning of this), to the problematic status of films and exhibitions in international academic CVs (Jackson 2011). As I will suggest in the conclusions, I believe that the ruling scepticism for the exploitation of the aesthetical, sensorial, emotional and relational potential of visual media depends on anthropology's incapacity to move beyond the notion of images as 'documents' and beyond the logic of 'realism'. Creative experimentation, I believe, can function as an antidote to this tendency.

The Context

The visual material that I will discuss in this chapter was generated during the fieldwork I conducted in Delhi on young middle-class men, globalization, and cultural identity between 1997 and roughly 2001.[6] My original research aim was to focus on the cultural changes that followed the opening of India's economy to the global market, an entry officially sanctioned in 1991 with the economic reforms designed by the then finance minister, Manmohan Singh.[7] I was interested to understand how the generation that epitomized this entry experienced and constructed their identities vis-à-vis the growing number of messages and images reaching the country (at high speed) from all over the world. I created a network of interlocutors among English-speaking, educated, Delhi-based men between twenty and thirty years of age, who were enthusiastically 'using' the opening up of India for both career and leisure purposes. Tourism, the internet, journalism, sports, multinationals and such like were the work arenas in which I initially met my interlocutors, and then I let myself get pulled by them into their circles of friends and colleagues, and became involved in a web of relations characterized by a high degree of heterogeneity. The stories of my interlocutors were a window onto the new India – a country that, with all its compromises and difficulties, was dreaming of a new phase bringing it back to the centre of world affairs. My fieldwork, in other words, gave birth to an early description of the enthusiasm for a future 'Tiger India'.[8] This was a period of intense pride in the country, and my interlocutors were among the most vivid signs of such a historic phase. In their lifeworld, being 'cool', 'cosmopolitan' and 'modern' (terms adopted by them) was not synonymous with copying the 'West' but rather with being proudly 'Indian'. Playfully inverting the meaning of the so-called 'colonial dichotomies' (i.e. India vs. West, tradition vs. modernity, spirituality vs. science – Gupta 1998), my interlocutors contributed to renew the discourse that had historically functioned as the foundation for debating change in India. Their creative use of 'India', 'West', 'modern', 'traditional' (which given their changing, fluctuating and emotional connotations, I chose in my writings to label as 'phantasms')[9] and their growing faith in India's future intrigued me and became the main focus of my study.

My interest in such issues was further enhanced when, hanging around with these young men in Delhi, I observed how their stories mirrored those expressed in the visual culture of the spaces of the city to which they gradually introduced me. These places too seemed to be characterized by the production of novel forms of merging between the Indian and the foreign. Here too I could notice how the conventional significance of

'India', 'West', 'modernity' and 'tradition' was being twisted, and how 'Indianness' (even though from within a cover of cosmopolitanism) was always being brought to the fore. With my interlocutors I became a frequenter of *kabab*[10] restaurants, outwardly resembling an elegant version of McDonald's but offering experiences of 'authentic' Indian cuisine and culture. I attended 'cosmopolitan' parties culminating in collective *bhangra*[11] dances (rather than to the tunes of Kylie Minogue or Madonna). I also noticed how advertisements, films and television programmes addressing young people progressively started to promote 'Indianness', expressing the 'coolness' of Indian things and traditional symbols, as did the latest architectural trends that I would study and photograph during my walks and rides around Delhi. 'India' was indeed in fashion.

This was indeed a different 'India' to the one that had been portrayed in Sweden and Italy, the countries where I was living and working at the time. A few photos, gathered from Italian and Swedish dailies and weeklies of the late 1990s, will help to express the content and aesthetics of this exotica (see Figure 3.1).

In these images, 'India' is visually marked out to the viewer through the conventional exhibition of crowds, of poor people sleeping or bathing in the streets, and of picturesque holy men (the sadhus). In the second picture, from the left, above, for instance, the choice of the editors of the Swedish daily *Dagens Nyheter* is to let a photo of a 'Holy Man' illustrate an article discussing the tensions between Hindus and Muslims in relation to Gandhi's heritage. Being unrelated to the content of the article itself, the use of the image of the sadhu seems to fulfil the purpose of allowing the viewer to rapidly identify the India-related content of these pages. A deeper look at the other images, however, and in particular the way in which they display elements of what a European viewer would associate with the idea of 'the modern', also reveals something else. One of the images, for instance, (third from the left) focuses on nuclear reactors – obvious indicators of 'modernity'. Their appearance is, however, 'Indianized' by the photographer through the presence, in the foreground, of peasants carrying baskets and buckets on their heads. As obvious indicators of 'tradition' and 'rurality', and therefore, according to the logic of the colonial dichotomies, evident markers of 'Indianness', such peasants allow the photographer to give birth to a composition that reproduces the idea of contrast. The same logic can also be detected in the third photograph from the left, where a contrast is generated between a street dweller and the rich clothes of a woman passing by. The notion of India as a 'land of contrasts' has been fundamental to European representations of India. With its roots in the colonial fascination for the couple Maharajas vs. beggars/fakirs,[12] this is a resilient notion in European popular culture and it keeps

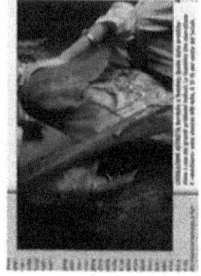

Figure 3.1 Composite of images relating to India taken from Swedish and Italian daily newspapers. Collage by Paolo Favero.

reappearing today in a variety of contemporary fields ranging from tourism, to journalism, to academic research and cinema. Playing with such rhetoric, the photographs that I have just described here allow the viewer, who has been historically socialized into these codes, to easily identify the geographical area under discussion. 'India' is therefore 'produced' not only through the display of a specific content able to epitomize the character of the country (i.e. poor peasants, holy men, etc.), but also by acting on the formal structure of the images, through the visual reproduction of the notion of contrast.

My research in and on India was indeed informed by these representations. The choice of focusing on metropolitan middle-class life, I believed, could give me an opportunity to address such notions critically. Inspired by Partha Chatterjee (1993), I wanted to address India as a producer of a mundane 'modernity' (rather than just as a consumer of it). By 'studying sideways' (Hannerz 1998) – fieldworking among individuals occupying more or less a similar role in their home societies as I was occupying in mine – I was aiming to avoid falling into the logic of the contrast. And, by addressing Delhi as a 'starry' point of convergence of influences crossing the borders of space and time (Favero 2003), rather than as a given 'symbol of India', I was hoping to be able to challenge the imperialistic and colonial notions that informed such hegemonic representations of India that allowed/upheld/generated a gap between the so-called 'First' and 'Third World'.

Relational Ethnographic Photography

My engagement with visual ethnography emerged progressively in Delhi in response to the needs of the field. Given my research interest, described above, for the 'phantasms' (i.e. for materializations in everyday life of abstract notions of 'India' and 'West', 'modernity' and 'tradition'), I devoted attention during fieldwork not only to the stories, actions and choices of my interlocutors but also to the material and visual culture that characterized the spaces they inhabited. I constructed my observations in a continuous bouncing between outer environments and my interlocutors' intimate experiences. Photography proved to be a valuable instrument for exploring this dialectic, and the visual material produced with such an approach was of great value in analysing my material and writing up. Besides illustrating the life context of my interlocutors, my photographs were also able to 'evoke' (in a Barthesian sense) a series of memories and associations, providing my written notes with an additional sensorial and emotional dimension. In tune with the experiments conducted by many anthropologists (Caldarola 1985; Prosser 1998; Ruby 2000; Banks 2001; Loescher 2005; Pink 2007), I also handed cameras over to them, asking them to take pictures of their lives, and we spent time discussing with them the material we all had produced regarding the hangouts where they used to spend their time. Through such practices I developed a deeper understanding of the relation between these young men's life trajectories and the larger cultural narratives expressed in the urban texture of the city. I noticed, to give an example, how the instances of Indianness expressed in the city's outlook were running parallel to the stories of my informants who were all keen to mark out, through their tastes, behaviour and choices, their pride in India. However, it was primarily my way of playfully envisioning the camera as a creator of relations (rather than as an object for 'shooting' or 'capturing' evidence), which gave interesting and at times unexpected results. Addressing it as part of a triad composed also of the photographing subject (me, the anthropologist) and the photographed subject, I experimented with its use as a creator of new ties with my interlocutors. This would also often generate interesting inversions of the roles of subject and object. Figure 3.2 is the most evident result of such process.

In this picture, Neeraj, at the time a 28-year-old journalist, pretends to meditate under a McDonald sign in a shopping mall in South Delhi. This

Figure 3.2 My interlocutor Neeraj posing. Photograph by Paolo Favero.

photograph, although 'taken' by me, was actually 'created' by Neeraj. It was born as a consequence of our shared interest in photography and of the discussions we had had over the years on the meaning of modernity in India. Neeraj instructed me here about how to compose the image, what should be seen in it and what not. He told me when to click, what kind of depth of field to use, and so on. Doing this, he offered me a privileged insight into the refashioning of the meaning of the colonial dichotomies in the context of contemporary Delhi. He reproduced, in fact, a scene displaying a stereotypical posture representing 'India' – a meditation posture, within a 'modern' commercial setting (epitomized by the dominating McDonald's sign). In this way he recreated visually the idea that 'tradition' exists (and is shaped) only within 'modernity', visually translating Mitchell's (2000) and Rofel's (2001) notions of modernity as a stage within which differences are shaped and generated.[13] This episode was fundamental to my understanding of the refashioning of the colonial dichotomies among my interlocutors, and offered me a new and unique insight into their lifeworlds.

A shared or relational photographic 'event' (Caldarola 1985) such as the one described here can hence allow us to gain access to new perspectives on our fields and our interlocutors. Suddenly, in the situation above, the roles of subject and object became inverted. I found myself 'into someone else's story' (MacDougall 1994: 35) – that is, into Neeraj's own ironical display of his own life. What made this possible, I suggest, is the playful and relational use of the camera, a use far removed from the realist notions of documentation, description, illustration and explanation. Approaching the camera as an instrument of 'truth-making' (Taylor 1994: xiii) rather than as a frame through which to gaze at the world from a safe distance, I placed the camera at the very centre of my interaction with Neeraj, using it as a creator of knowledge. In such ways the camera functioned as the trigger for that unique and contextual process of self-narration. Image-work at large offers evident advantages for relating to our interlocutors. As a language closer to the experiences of most of the people we come in touch with, photography (and film too) can be useful to interpellate individuals, allowing (and inviting) them to point out new events, objects and situations for us, and hence to involve themselves in our work. If playfully involved in the process, subjects may also, as in the case of Neeraj, choose to act in front of the camera, displaying new angles of their own identities, which we may explore later on, in an ethnomethodological fashion (Garfinkel 1967), through different – and perhaps more conventional – ethnographic means.

A creative relational use of the camera can therefore help us in actively involving our interlocutors in the process of meaning-making. It can bring

to the fore the nature of knowledge as a 'processual aspect of human social relations' (Banks 2001: 112) rather than as a static thing 'out there'
waiting to be discovered and 'documented'. A strategy that depends very
much on a capacity to rethink the agency and meaning of technology, this
is a technique that I have recurrently shared with my visual anthropology
students. At the beginning of my courses I always 'force' them in fact to go
out, armed with such notions and visualizations, in a public space of their
choice, and describe its character by taking close-ups of the people passing through. Forbidding the use of zooming, I hence force them to enter
into a triangular relation with other human beings through the camera.
Needless to say, such a process inevitably generates unexpected reactions
and insights.

Photo Exhibition and the Constructive Disorientation

During my fieldwork breaks in the late 1990s, I realized that my photographic material about Delhi and Bombay had the potential to communicate something about my experience of conducting research in
metropolitan India to my European friends and colleagues. Such material
also seemed to ignite in them reflections regarding contemporary India.
In 2001, I therefore decided to produce my first photographic exhibition,
called 'India Does Not Exist' (see Figure 3.3).

Hosted for the first time in a restaurant in Italy, and later on, among
other places, at the Etnografiska Museet (ethnographic museum) in Stockholm,[14] this exhibition attempted to address wider audiences and provoke
in them a reflection regarding the conventional representations of India
that dominated the European media scenario of the epoch. The show
'played' principally with the viewers' own associations. Building on strategies of inversion, negation, provocation and confusion, 'India Does Not
Exist' attempted to offer a counter-stereotype of 'India' (i.e. more precisely
of the European phantasm of 'India'). Selecting specific and very narrow
perspectives, the show offered a glimpse into the subcontinent from the
exclusive point of view of its metropolises. Modern architecture and middle-class life presented one view of 'India' that in the 'pre-Slumdog Millionaire era'[15] was quite absent from European media. In a way this show
dealt more with the European phantasm of 'India' and its politics than
with India itself. At the same time, however, it also presented insights into
Indian middle-class life and a view of India as a 'producer of modernity'
(Chatterjee 1993), away from the rhetoric of contrast described earlier.

Besides the specific choices of content that I enacted, the exhibition
created its provocation primarily through the adoption of a visual lan-

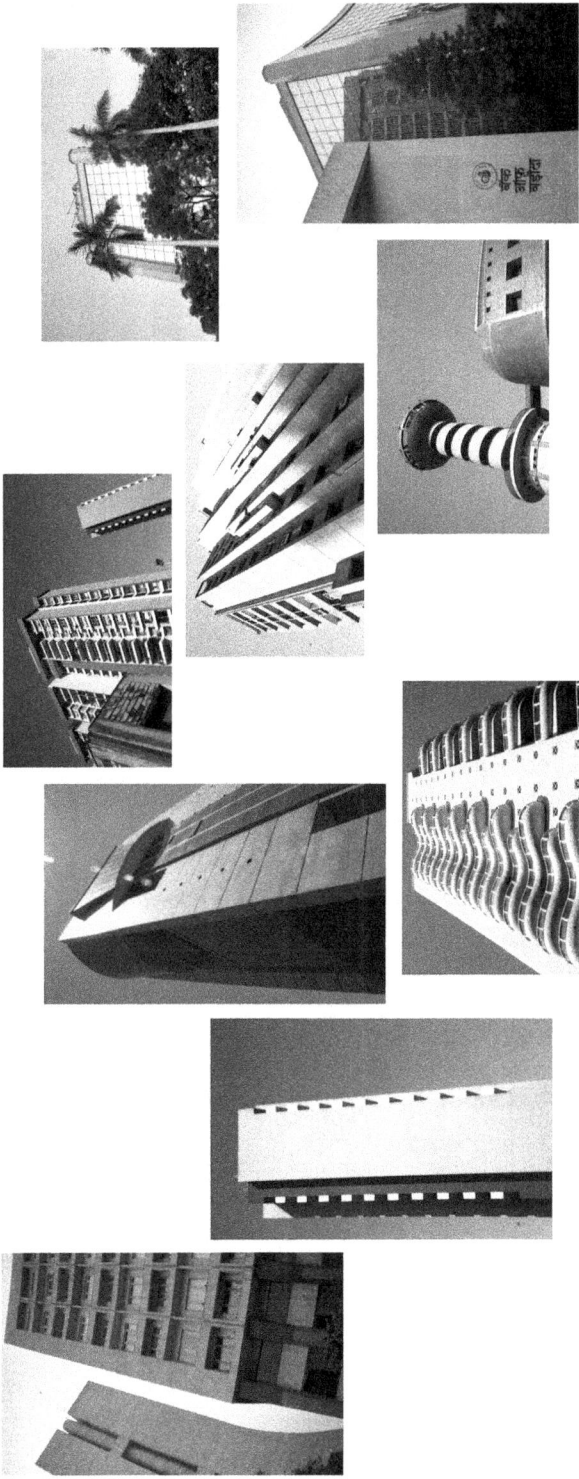

Figure 3.3 Composite of photographs belonging to Paolo Favero's exhibition on Indian modernity.

guage able to create in the viewer an association with abstract notions of
modernity. The skyscrapers of Delhi and Bombay, displayed in the first
part of the exhibition, are for instance portrayed through the same aesthetics that dominated the photographic portrayals of American modernity in the 1960s, the style through which the iconic representations of
the Empire State Building were produced. Hence the images are in black
and white, highly contrasted, offering 'low angles' that produce somewhat claustrophobic perspectives for the viewer, right below the buildings portrayed. Moreover, the streets with their life are cut off from these
first portraits, thus producing a series of decontextualized visions of the
buildings. Through such dialogue between content and form, the viewers
are invited to take part in a 'Manhattan experience'[16] in an Indian context,
and to suspend their expectations on Indian exoticism. Such constructive
disorientation is generated also through the exploitation of the dialectic
between the individual images – what Roland Barthes (1977) called 'syn-
tax' – and between the images and the physical space of display. At Stockholm's ethnographic museum, a narrow corridor introduced the viewers
to this 'India'. They were therefore 'forced' to enter the exhibiting space
through decontextualized representations of modern Indian architecture.
Starting to wonder, as I was able to gather by observing them, whether
this was about India at all, they would, by the seventh picture, be met by a
small sign containing a text in Nagari (see the image to the extreme right
in Figure 3.3). This allowed them to start orientating within India again.
At the end of the tunnel they would then see two walls decorated with a
top–down view of Delhi (Figure 3.4) and with a young girl sitting in a pub.
Behind these walls, a series of portraits of middle-class life in Delhi were
to be found.

'India Does Not Exist' constructed hence its message through the dialogue between 'content' and 'form' – that is, through the simultaneous
choice of subject for the photographs and of the aesthetical choices regarding their presentation. In this dialogue a tension was generated between
what the images in question 'denoted' (i.e. the object itself, the analogon,
Barthes 1977) and what they 'connoted' (the ideological dimension surrounding these images, indicating the cultural/social understanding regarding the object being represented). Through this tension, the (invisible)
assumptions that inform social actors' meeting with images of India were
allowed to be brought to the surface, revealing hence some aspects of the
history and politics of European representations of India. This became
particularly evident on one occasion, when a disappointed visitor commented, 'This is not what I was expecting! This has nothing to do with
India!' By leaving aside the most 'recognizable', 'stereotypical' signs of

Figure 3.4 New Delhi. Photograph by Paolo Favero.

India, and by generating a number of short circuits and instances of disorientation, the exhibition forced the viewers to progressively construct meaning as they explored the space. Meaning, in this context, was hence created through the ongoing negotiation between the images themselves (remanding to the photographer's intentions), the viewers, and the invisible expectations and assumptions about the real 'India' – about the meaning of 'modernity' and 'globalization' that they brought into this exchange. Within such a context, the viewers' own 'knowledge-seeking-strategies' (Färber 2007) became of fundamental importance. This led me therefore to stop envisioning my role as that of a conveyer of knowledge and a provider of explanation and description, and to enter instead the role of the provoker of reactions. Such rhetorical use of disorientation, counterpoint and provocation as means of communication transformed the space of the exhibition 'from a space of representation to a space of encounter' (Basu and MacDonald 2007: 14). Using a strategy of display and sharing, which is perhaps epistemologically closer to the world of art than of science, 'India Does Not Exist' constitutes, therefore, an example of experimentation with a relational and processual production of knowledge.

Video Installation and the Distracted Spectator

The above-mentioned experiment raised in me a growing curiosity for understanding (and exploiting) the different ways in which spectators may produce knowledge as they explore a visual product. With the video installation Indica Mistica Mediatica (from here onwards IMM) we attempted to explore and exploit this issue further. I decided to give more space to the agency of the spectators while inserting elements of cultural critique in conventional public entertainment venues. Born through a collaborative reflection with an electronic music composer[17] on how to implement 'India Does Not Exist' with a soundscape (thus making it more user-oriented), IMM turned into a 34-minute-long video installation, translating the syntactic relation between photographs present in the exhibition into a linear filmic narrative. Consisting of 1,600 frames, it is a cavalcade of digitized analogical photographs re-edited in video form,[18] introducing the viewer, as was the case for 'India Does Not Exist', to a provocative vision of India. Expanding on the material presented in the exhibition, IMM contains black and white photographs of Delhi and Bombay but also colour photographs as well as a number of short texts (slogans and quotes). Images of skyscrapers, of people dancing in discos, etc. are hence brought into a counterpoint dialogue with quotes (coming from various sources) praising the exotic charms of the country. Elements of psychedelia too (in both sound and image) are inserted, evoking another fundamental chapter in the European imagination of India. Scans of visual ethnographic material, gathered from Indian advertisements and news, are also present in the installation in order to offer insights into Indian popular culture from the inside.

IMM was designed for screenings in wide public places. Launched in a popular club in Turin, Italy, the installation was later on projected at conferences, clubs, bars and universities. Always displayed in crucial passage points, it was also selected for the Environment Film Festival in Turin 2002.[19] Trying to insert elements of cultural critique and reflections regarding the politics of representation into a leisure space was indeed an interesting challenge. I had to face here, in fact, a 'distracted spectator', one not only free to take possession of the product displayed on her/his own terms (entering and exiting the space at their own pleasure) but also distracted by the plethora of other stimuli that public places can offer (see Figure 3.5).

Figure 3.5 Video installation Indica Mistica Mediatica. Photograph by Paolo Favero.

To capture the attention of such moving and distracted spectators, the installation needed to develop stratagems able to get a message across in a direct and immediate way. The installation relied in fact on a number of aesthetical stratagems fundamental for capturing the distracted eyes of the viewers and for getting the message across to them. To achieve this, the spectators get, in the first place, immersed in the images, being surrounded by them from two (later on in larger venues even five) sides – an effect obtained also by keeping the club's regular light arrangement to a minimum. Secondly the installation itself contained many lighting effects – changes of tone, colour, etc. – that, dialoguing with the pace of the music, attracted the attention of the distracted eye of the (never guaranteed) viewer. Moreover, key messages in the shape of images, words and quotes were repeatedly delivered to the audience through the use of repetitions and loops. For capturing the eye of a distracted spectator, everything needed to be direct and immediate, and the message had to rely mostly on the very editing, rhythm and visual character of the images. All this work required therefore an in-depth problematization of the role of the spectators and of their movements within the physical space of the display. A question fundamental to all forms of visual (and other) communication (Barthes 1993),[20] this problematization has been extensively neglected in visual anthropology (Banks 1992). Paraphrasing Basu's comment on ethnographic film, we could say that anthropological/ethnographic visual work somehow does appear as a 'genre in search of an audience' (Basu 2008: 103) and lacks in an in-depth problematization of the identity and role of the viewer. The creation of IMM, along with the production of the photographic exhibition mentioned above, made me conscious about the role and meaning of the spectators in the construction of knowledge contributing to the birth of an interest that I would later on develop in theoretical and methodological terms.

Conclusions

In this chapter I have advocated for the need to entangle the practices that characterize anthropological image-making with those belonging to the fields of art and communication. A creative experimentation with new languages, practices and technologies of representation and display is fundamental, I have suggested, for allowing the discipline to find new venues for sharing its knowledge. It is therefore pivotal for allowing the anthropologist to go public and partake in the debates that take place in non-academic arenas. In other words, such creative experimentations can be seen as proper political acts. In this chapter I have, however, also shown how a creative use of audiovisual media can allow us to close the gaps with those individuals who inhabit our multiple lifeworlds and who do not master academic terminology. I have also suggested how such work can offer us a different and more participative understanding of our interlocutors' lifeworlds, allowing us to incorporate them in the process of meaning-making and knowledge creation. These are not, however, the only benefits of audiovisual experimentation. Such practices can in fact give us precious theoretical insights, helping us to rethink the assumptions that inform our work. Such a critical rethinking, I suggest, is particularly important today, given the growing spread of new image-making practices and devices. Participative, interactive and non-linear films (Gallaway, McAlpine and Harris 2007; Birchall 2008), Web 2.0 and mobile-phone-based possibilities for sharing and making images (de Souza e Silva 2006; Chesher 2007; Leadbeater 2008; Shirky 2008) are in fact progressively changing social actors' conventional notions on the meaning and essence of photographs and films (Favero 2013).

The insights we may gain from such a rethinking are indeed many. In the first place, it teaches us to address our spectators as 'emancipated' actors (Rancière 2009). Today's audiences are in fact increasingly skilled in editing and post-production,[21] and hence are no longer prey to objectifying notions of reality and representation. As a consequence, anthropologists must learn to take a distance from the out-of-date notions of 'visualism',[22] realism, and the 'myth of photographic truth' (Sturken and Cartwright 2001) that still dominate the discipline. Instead they must look upon their audiences as co-creators of meaning rather than passive receivers of a preconfigured knowledge. In other words, we must here take the opportunity for enacting a grounded rethinking of the conventional approaches to image-work that characterize our practice. Bringing to the surface knowledge's processual nature (see below), this insight can also respond to the need for more reflexive approaches to both field research and communication.

Secondly, this rethinking forces us to become aware (and exploit further) the entangled nature of 'content' and 'form'. Anthropologists tend to focus primarily on what Sanjek (1991) called 'ethnographic validity' – on principles of theoretical transparency, of methodological rigour and of continuity between the raw material (field notes, raw footage) and the end product (be it a text, a film, etc.). The obsession with 'anthropological relevance' (Wright 1998) makes them neglect the fundamental role played by aesthetics in allowing them to communicate with their audiences. As Ricoeur (1986) suggested with regards to text, knowledge allows itself to be communicated only through a process of 'textualization', and hence through authorial choices (see also Foucault 1977). Style, aesthetics and form are therefore always omnipresent in, and constitutive of, our works.

Ruby, for instance, has suggested that ethnography too is nothing but 'a specific style or group of related styles of scientific presentation', and that 'ethnographers make syntactical, lexical, and other decisions based on a tacit model which they acquired in graduate school, in the field, and at professional meetings' (Ruby 1975: 105). Referring explicitly to images, Banks (1992) has suggested that anthropologists look upon photographs and film primarily as 'research material'. For them, these are 'documents' 'capturing' what is 'out there' – 'proofs' of the 'authentic' contact with the 'lived reality' of the others. This, I suggest, is still visible today in many of the ethnographic films that circulate in the academic market. Very often anthropologists address images as mere 'illustrations' of anthropological knowledge, and it is only seldom that they are capable of allowing them to become, as Lucien Taylor (1996) suggested, constitutive of knowledge. A creative work with audiovisuals should help to remind us that images are not only material but also 'photography' and 'cinema' and 'hypermedia'. We need to bring the question of the dialogue between form and content back to the heart of our agenda. I believe there is something to gain from this, not only for image-making anthropologists but for the anthropological community at large.

Thirdly, I believe that the experimentation with new ways for producing and communicating our work can lead us to rethink the silent assumptions that characterize our approach to knowledge. Through the examples discussed above, knowledge appears as the result of an ongoing performative negotiation between the various actors involved in the image-making event – namely, the image-maker, the interlocutors, the audiences and the technological means at their disposal. The processual nature of knowledge is here allowed to come to the fore. A playful audiovisual experimentation is therefore immediately related to our theoretical understanding of the ways in which we produce knowledge.

As the 'systematic production of novelty' (Pickstone, in Basu and MacDonald 2007: 2), experimentation is a transformative process that allows/forces us to rethink and update the meaning of our practice as image-making anthropologists. After all, as Ruby (1975) suggested, a visual anthropologist needs to be an expert in both anthropology and visual communication. Perhaps it is time for the anthropologist to stop envisioning image-making as an act of communication and start relating to it as a form of relationship creation. Rather than transferring knowledge (from the maker/sender to the receiver), anthropologists can envision their work as an experiment in what Bourriaud (1998) has called 'relational aesthetics' – an activity of production of relations with the world, with the help of signs, forms, actions and objects. Inspired by the notion of the 'interactive artist' (Rokeby 1995: 152), the anthropologist could become a mediator, leaving the construction of meaning open to the dialogic encounter between the product displayed and the emancipated viewers.

Paolo Favero is associate professor in Film Studies and Visual Culture at the Department of Communication Studies, University of Antwerp. With a Ph.D. in Social Anthropology from Stockholm University (focusing on questions of globalization and cultural identity among young people in Delhi, and resulting in a book entitled *India Dreams*), Paolo has devoted the core of his career to the study of visual culture in India and in Italy. Presently he conducts research on image-making practices in contemporary India. Paolo has taught at the University of Lisbon, University College London, University of Foggia (Italy) and Stockholm University, and has published, among others, for *Visual Studies*, the *Journal of Material Culture, Cultural Anthropology, Social Anthropology,* and *Anthropological Quarterly.* Paolo is also an active filmmaker. In 2004 he directed 'Flyoverdelhi', a film on youth in Delhi that was screened by Swedish and Italian national broadcasters.

Notes

1. I use 'image-making' as a single term that can include both moving and still images, and hence make sense of all the hybrid spaces and practices that have emerged as a consequence of the introduction of new digital technologies.
2. With the term 'relational art', Bourriaud refers to 'a set of artistic practices which take as their theoretical and practical point of departure the whole of human relations and their social context, rather than an independent and private space' (Bourriaud 1998: 113).
3. With 'polysemy', Volosinov indicated that signs and representations carry varied layers of meaning (cf. Cubitt 2001).
4. Bonito Oliva used this phrase in a television interview.
5. Fusing 'pleasure in seeing the previously unseen to power in the form of a knowledge with normalizing aspirations' (McQuire 1998: 192), such documents of racial difference were however also quick to abandon the boundaries of academia. Displayed at fairs, in journals, on postcards etc., they became fundamental tools for raising popular awareness about the diversity of the world.
6. Funding for fieldwork was granted by the Bank of Sweden Tercentenary Fund, and smaller scholarships by SSAG (The Swedish Society for Anthropology and Geography), HSFR (Swedish Board for the Humanistic and Social Sciences), the Lars Hierta's Minne Foundation and the Hierta-Retzius Foundation and STINT (the Swedish Foundation for International Cooperation in Research and Higher Education).
7. I highlight here my usage of the word 'sanctioned', given that the Indian economy has been progressively opening up, in particular during the 1980s under the prime ministership of Rajiv Gandhi.

8. This moment has recently been depicted by many authors (e.g. Kamdar 2007; Taroor 2007; Gupta 2009).

9. The 'phantasm' was, in my usage, the 'instrument' through which my interlocutors approached, interpreted, felt and contextualized the images that surrounded them. Following Agamben (1993), who used the phantasm to describe what linked (and at the same time blurred the boundary between) the internal and the external, the real and the imaginary, I approached the phantasm as what mediates not only between agents and their external space but also between the 'here' and 'there', the 'now' and 'then' of our daily experiences, between emotion and intellect, between collective and individual images, hence bringing together discourses and memories (in my case with different geographical and historical roots) that lie unspoken in our everyday lives (see also Ivy 1995).

10. The *kabab* is the generic term used for dry, oven-cooked, meat-based dishes in North India.

11. *Bhangra* is the traditional Punjabi folk music that today has been receiving international fame through the technological revivals carried on mostly by Indian DJs living abroad.

12. For a discussion of this, see, among others, Rushdie (1992); Ramusack (1995); Hutnyk (1996a, 1996b, 2000); Khilnani (1997); Hottola (1999); and Wilhelm and Rawlinson (2000).

13. Rofel suggests that modernity is at best compared with the 'floor of a boxing match' where different 'rhetoric, claims, and commitments to modernity get put into play' (Rofel 2001: 638). In her words, modernity is 'something people struggle over' (ibid.). It is an arena in which different representations of what it means to be modern are involved. Mitchell (2000) promotes a similar idea suggesting that modernity is basically a staging of differences enacted in a realm of representation. According to him, the forms of difference involved here are mainly of two types. One type refers to geo-cultural differences. In its upholding of the divide between the modern and the non-modern, 'modernity' also upholds a distinction between the 'West' and the 'non-West'. Modernity is constructed through the marginalization and exclusion of those elements that question the norm (read 'modernity' and 'West').

14. In Stockholm the show went under the title 'Indien som inte finns', i.e. 'India does not exist'.

15. I believe that Slumdog Millionaire was pivotal in introducing Euro-American audiences to a changing India.

16. This was a description of my work given by Marcus Banks.

17. The music of this work was composed and played by Fabrizio de Piccoli.

18. The process leading to the creation of IMM took a couple of months, and was based on the selection, scanning, 'cleaning' (in Photoshop) and archiving of original negatives, and then the editing of them in Final Cut in the form of a film made up of photographs. Once finished, the first film would be handed to my colleague who would construct a first draft of the soundtrack. Then we would proceed dialoguing with the work until it was finished. The large number of frames depended on the fact that I used no filmic effects but rather composed each effect, such as zooming in and out, and changing contrast and colour, by acting upon the original photograph in Photoshop. All images were also produced so as to contain a different physical dimension, making visible the production of the material and the intrinsic relation between still and moving images. Finally, mention should be made of the fact that the soundtrack contains a series of sound files of sonic impressions that I had collected in Delhi and Bombay in the areas where I was photographing.

19. The installation was placed to run in a loop on monitors placed in one of the corridors leading to the various halls hosting the films.

20. Barthes (1993) has suggested how an image is composed by the encounter between *operator* (photographer or, stretching, also filmmaker), *spectrum* (target object; subject of image) and *spectator* (ourselves, or those who view).
21. Bourriaud (2002) has suggested that post-production can be seen as a metaphor for our age.
22. 'Visualism' is the term that depicts the 'modern' notion that seeing is equal to believing (Fabian 1983 and Dundes 2004).

References

Agamben, G. 1993. *Stanzas: Word and Phantasm in Western Culture*. Minneapolis: University of Minnesota Press.

Asad, T. 1995. *Anthropology and the Colonial Encounter*. New York: Prometheus Books.

Banks, M. 1990. 'Talking Heads and Moving Pictures: David Byrne's "True Stories" and the Anthropology of Film', *Visual Anthropology* 3: 1–9.

———. 1992. 'Which Films are the Ethnographic Films?', in 'Film as Ethnography', ed. P. Crawford and D. Turton. Manchester: Manchester University Press, in association with the Granada Centre for Visual Anthropology, pp. 116–29.

———. 2001. *Visual Methods in Social Research*. London: Sage.

Barthes. R. 1977. *Image Music Text*. London: Fontana Press.

———. 1993. *Camera Lucida*. London: Vintage.

Basu, P. 2008. 'Reframing Ethnographic Film', in T. Austin and W. de Jong (eds), *Rethinking Documentary: New Perspectives, New Practices*. New York: MacGraw Hill.

Basu, P., and S. MacDonald. 2007. 'Introduction: Experiments in Exhibition, Ethnography, Art, and Science', in P. Basu and S. MacDonald (eds), *Exhibition Experiments*. London: Blackwells.

Berger, J. 1972. *Ways of Seeing*. London: Penguin, pp. 7–44.

Birchall, D. 2008. 'Online Documentary', in T. Austin and W. de Jong (eds), *Rethniking Documentary: New Perspectives, New Practices*. New York: MacGraw Hill.

Bourriaud, N. 1998. *Relational Aesthetics*. Dijon: Les Presses du Reel.

———. 2002. *Postproduction: Culture as Screenplay: How Art Reprograms the World*. New York: Has & Sternberg.

Caldarola, V. 1985. 'Visual Contexts: A Photographic Research Method in Anthropology', *Studies in Visual Communication* 11(3): 33–53.

Chatterjee, P. 1993. *The Nation and Its Fragments*. Princeton, NJ: Princeton University Press.

———. 2006. *The Politics of the Governed: Reflections on Popular Politics in Most of the World*. New York: Columbia University Press.

Chesher, C. 2007. 'Becoming the Milky Way: Mobile Phones and Actor Networks at a U2 Concert', *Continuum: Journal of Media & Cultural Studies* 21(2): 217–25.

Cubitt, S. 2001. *Simulation and Social Theory*. London: Sage.

de Souza e Silva, A. 2006. 'From Cyber to Hybrid Mobile Technologies as Interfaces of Hybrid Spaces', *Space and Culture* 9(3): 261–78.

Dundes, A. 1980. 'Seeing is Believing', in C. Delaney (ed.) *Investigating Culture: An Experiential Introduction to Anthropology*. London: Blackwell.

Edwards, E. 2006. 'Photographs and the Sound of History', *Visual Anthropology Review* 1/2: 27–46.

Fabian, J. 1983. *Time and the Other: How Anthropology Makes its Object*. New York: Columbia University Press.

Färber, A. 2007. 'Exposing Expo: Exhibition Entrepreneurship and Experimental Reflexivity in Late Modernity', in P. Basu and S. MacDonald (eds), *Exhibition Experiments*. London: Blackwells.

Favero, P. 2003. 'Phantasms in a "Starry" Place: Space and Identification in a Central New Delhi Market', *Cultural Anthropology* 18(4).

———. 2013. 'Getting our Hands Dirty (again): Interactive Documentaries and the Meaning of Images in the Digital Age', *Journal of Material Culture* 18(3): 259–77.

Foucault, M. 1977. 'What is an Author?', in D. Bouchard (ed.), *Language, Counter-Memory, Practice*. Ithaca, NY: Cornell University Press, pp. 124–27.

Galloway, D., K. McAlpine and P. Harris. 2007. 'From Michael Moore to JFK Reloaded: Towards a Working Model of Interactive Documentary', *Journal of Media Practice* 8(3).

Garfinkel, H. 1967. *Studies in Ethnomethodology*. Englewood Cliffs, NJ: Prentice Hall.

Grimshaw, A. 1997. 'The Eye in the Door: Anthropology, Film and the Exploration of Interior Space', in M. Banks and H. Morphy (eds), *Rethinking Visual Anthropology*. New Haven, CT: Yale University Press, pp. 36–52.

———. 2001. *The Ethnographer's Eye*. Cambridge University Press.

Gupta, A. 1998. *Postcolonial Developments: Agriculture in the Making of Modern India*. Durham, NC: Duke University Press.

Gupta, D. 2009. *The Caged Phoenix: Can India Fly?* Stanford, CA: Stanford University Press.

Hannerz, U. 1998 'Other Transnationals: Perspectives Gained from Studying Sideways', *Paideuma* 44.

Herman, E.S., and N. Chomsky. 1994. *Manufacturing Consent: The Political Economy of the Mass Media*. London: Vintage Books.

Horst, H., and D. Miller (eds). 2012. *Digital Anthropology*. New York: Berg.

Hottola, P. 1999. *The Intercultural Body: Western Woman, Culture Confusion and Control of Space in the South Asian Travel Scene*. Joensuu, Finland: University of Joensuu.

Hutnyk, J. 1996a. *The Rumour of Calcutta: Tourism, Charity and the Poverty of Representation*. London: Zed Books.

———. 1996b. *Dis-Orienting Rhythms: Politics of the New Asian Dance Music*. London: Zed Books.

———. 2000. *Critique of Exotica: Music, Politics and the Culture Industry*. London: Pluto Press.

Ivy, M. 1995. *Discourses of the Vanishing: Modernity, Phantasm, Japan*. Chicago: University of Chicago Press.

Jackson, J. 2011. http://chronicle.com/blogs/brainstorm/films vs articlesbooks/31291

Jay, M. 1989. *The Rise of Hermeneutics and the Crisis of Ocularcentrism: In the Rhetoric of Interpretation and the Interpretation of Rhetoric*. Durham, NC: Duke University Press, pp. 55–74.

Kamdar, M. 2007. *Planet India: The Turbulent Rise of the Largest Democracy and the Future of Our World*. London: Simon & Schuster.

Khilnani, S. 1997. *The Idea of India*. New York: Farrar Straus Giroux.

Leadbeater, C. 2008. *We-Think: The Power of Mass Creativity*. Glasgow: Profile Books.

Loescher, M. 2005. 'Cameras at the Addy: Speaking in Pictures with City Kids', in A. Grimshaw and A. Ravetz (eds), *Visualizing Anthropology*. Bristol: Intellect, pp. 55–68.

MacDougall, D. 1994. 'Whose Story Is It?', in L. Taylor (ed.), *Visualizing Theory*. New York: Routledge, pp. 27–36.

———. 1997. 'The Visual in Anthropology', in M. Banks and H. Morphy (eds), *Rethinking Visual Anthropology*. New Haven, CT: Yale University Press, pp. 276–95.

———. 1998. *Transcultural Cinema*. Princeton, NJ: Princeton University Press.

McQuire, S. 1998. *Visions of Modernity: Representation, Memory, Time and Space in the Age of the Camera.* London: Sage.

Mitchell, T. 2000. *Questions of Modernity.* Minneapolis: University of Minnesota Press.

Pink, S. 2006. *The Future of Visual Anthropology: Engaging the Senses.* London: Routledge.

———. 2007. *Doing Visual Ethnography.* London: Sage.

Pink, S., and L. Hjorth. 2012. 'Emplaced Cartographies: Reconceptualising Camera Phone Practices in an Age of Locative Media', *Media International Australia* 145.

Pinney, C. 2009. 'What Do Pictures Want Now? Rural Consumers of Images in India', in E. Edwards and K. Bhaumik (eds), *Visual Sense: A Cultural Reader.* Oxford: Berg.

Prosser, J. 1998. *Image-Based Research.* London: Routledge.

Ramusack, B.N. 1995. 'The Indian Princes as Fantasy: Palace Hotels, Palace Museums, and Palace on Wheels', in C.A. Breckenridge (ed.), *Consuming Modernity: Public Culture in a South Asian World.* Minneapolis: University of Minnesota Press.

Rancière, J. 2004. *The Politics of Aesthetics: The Distribution of the Sensible.* New York and London: Continuum.

———. 2009. *The Emancipated Spectator.* London: Verso, pp. 1–23.

Ricoeur, P. 1986. *Tempo e Racconto.* Milan: Jaca Book.

Rofel, L. 2001. 'Discrepant Modernities and their Discontents', *Positions* 9(3).

Rokeby, David. 1995. 'Transforming Mirrors: Subjectivity and Control in Interactive Media', in Simon Penny (ed.), *Critical Issues in Electronic Media.* Albany: State University of New York Press, pp. 133–58.

Ruby, J. 1975. 'Is an Ethnographic Film a Filmic Ethnography?', *Studies in the Anthropology of Visual Communication* 2(2).

———. 2000. 'Introduction', in J. Ruby, *Picturing Culture: Explorations of Film and Anthropology.* Chicago: University of Chicago Press, pp. 1–39.

Rushdie, S. 1992. *Imaginary Homelands: Essays and Criticism 1981–1991.* New York: Penguin.

Said, E. 1995. *Orientalism.* Stockholm: Ordfront.

Sanjek, R. 1991. 'The Ethnographic Present', *Man* 26(4).

Schneider, A., and C. Wright. 2010. *Between Anthropology and Art: Contemporary Ethnographic Practice.* Oxford: Berg.

Shirky, C. 2008. *Here Comes Everybody.* London: Penguin Books.

Sturken, M., and L. Cartwright. 2001. *Practices of Looking: An Introduction to Visual Culture.* Oxford: Oxford University Press.

Taroor, S. 2007. *The Elephant, the Tiger, and the Cellphone.* Delhi: Penguin, Viking.

Taussig, M. 2009. *What Colour is the Sacred?* Chicago: University of Chicago Press.

Taylor, L. 1994. *Visualizing Theory.* New York: Routledge.

———. 1996. 'Iconophobia', *Transition* 69: 64–88.

Tobing Rony, F. 2001. *The Third Eye: Race, Cinema, and Ethnographic Spectacle.* Durham, NC: Duke University Press.

Wesch, M. 2009. 'YouTube and You: Experiences of Self-Awareness in the Context Collapse of the Recording Webcam', *Explorations in Media Ecology* 8(2): 19–34.

Wilhelm, F., and H.G. Rawlinson. 2000. 'India and the Modern West', in A.L. Basham (ed.), *A Cultural History of India.* New Delhi: Oxford University Press.

Wright, C. 1998. 'The Third Subject: Perspectives on Visual Anthropology', *Anthropology Today* 14(4): 16–22 [E-journal].

Chapter 4

A LANGUAGE FOR RE-GENERATION
Boundary Crossing and Re-Formation at
the Intersection of Media Ethnography and Theatre

⸺ ❦ ⸺

Debra Spitulnik Vidali

As I write, the story of Re-Generation is not over. In 2009 and 2010, I created and produced a verbatim documentary theatrical work entitled *'RE-GENERATION: A Play about Political Stances, Media Insanity, and Adult Responsibilities'*, based on my ethnographic and interview research into young adults' experiences in the United States.[1] I wanted to get young peoples' voices out – out onto the theatrical stage. I had never done theatre before. And I had never originally thought of doing theatre with the material that I collected during 2006–9. But there I was doing it. I wanted to get voices out, and, perhaps even more, I wanted my material to be useful – useful beyond the proverbial ivory tower.

After wading through over a thousand pages of research transcripts from over sixty hours of recorded material, I developed a 45-page dramatic script that took 80 per cent of its lines directly and verbatim from what people had said in research interviews and conversations. Literality, realism, creative licence, and form-breaking simultaneously drove the project. The words and experiences of over ninety young adults were used to create fifteen dramatic characters, including Shockwave, a hip-hop artist who thinks the main route to political engagement is music and not the ballot box; Crystal, who feels she needs to hide her political views because she's in the minority among her peers; Tina, who has a million better things to do than pay attention to news and politics; Gianna, who starts out apathetic but then decides to get more informed after entering the workforce; and Jin, who works intensely on the Obama 2008 campaign.

Scenes about media use and political engagement reproduced those documented during my participant observation fieldwork. The play's script went through several revisions in 2009, with the assistance of Amreen Ukani, a former undergraduate student, and Ken Hornbeck, a seasoned artistic director specializing in 'theatre for social change'. Hornbeck and I refined and workshopped *Re-Generation* in 2010, and had four public showings that year with a total attendance of 170 people. In 2011, I produced a video of the play, which has since been screened countless times in classroom settings, at special events and at conferences across the globe. The material has been integrated into undergraduate classes on citizenship, as well as courses in media studies and communication for development, and has been used as a springboard for students to write papers on topics such as American politics, social stereotypes, conflict resolution, social media, and the nature of apathy.

Using the double meaning of 're-generation' intended in the original play title, to be about generation and about renewal or new growth, I developed the Re-Generation Initiative as an ongoing public scholarship project in 2011. The initiative, shaped by the input of an advisory collective of artistic directors, social scientists, humanists, parents, teachers, students, actors, videographers, and so on, is a work in progress, evolving as opportunities arise, as people join and partner, and as energies and inspirations expand and contract. In 2012, we produced four very diverse theatrical projects (at UCLA; Kennesaw State and Emory universities in Georgia;

Figure 4.1 Final scene from the play *Re-Generation*, staged in 2010. Angele Masters as David, in foreground. Surrounding, L to R: Jin (Emma Calabrese), Shockwave (Kris Valeriano), Michael (Niyi Oni), Liz (Bianca Copello), and Tina (Moi Li). Photo by Aubrey Graham. All rights reserved, Debra Vidali.

and Malmö University, Sweden), inspired in part by the original theatrical work. There is a public Re-Generation Initiative Facebook page, a website, and a YouTube channel that currently hosts more than a dozen original videos. The core idea is to use these formats and spaces for 're-generating well-being, civic engagement & community dialogues through creative theater projects, storytelling, ethnography & multi-platform events'.[2]

In addition to translating my own research to the theatrical stage, I have become a midwife, developer, spokesperson and co-writer for other projects about young people's relations to contemporary politics, media, community and the world. The Re-Generation journey has developed in both a linear and a rhizomatic mode of production. There is a combination of long-term engagements, short intensively incubated projects, and episodic bursts of production. Many activities in this last category are responsive to current events and public conversations, such as debates about gun control or the education system in the United States. I am the founder, and have been the point person for the initiative – from campus connections to online media development/communication – but at the same time I have been trying to grow Re-Generation as a project with distributed ownership, one that develops depending on who becomes invested, joins the conversation, and moves it forward organically.

At every step, as we engage in conversations and performing arts representations of what it means to live together and be in a democracy together, this work pushes conventional academic boundaries and concepts. The work presents great challenges, if not outright upheaval, to the division between subjectivity and objectivity, the definition of knowledge, and the value of individual ownership. In addition, my own research boundaries are pushed and expanded by the work's collaborative and potentially recursive nature. The performances, screenings, Facebook wall, and other social media comment zones generate new data, as audiences comment on the performance pieces and their own relations to media, society and democracy.

This work has not replaced my ongoing work as a social scientist investigating the phenomenology of civic engagement and the discourses of connection and disconnection. At the same time, it has been difficult, if not impossible, to maintain a strict division between 'applied' research and 'pure' research, between Re-Generation as public scholarship and Re-Generation as one more arena of social science scholarship, without the label 'public' affixed to it. It is unclear which adjective best suits this latter category, or even how the category itself is most productively configured. Is that 'regular' or 'ivory tower' or 'non-public' scholarship? An airtight division between scholarship that is 'public' and scholarship that is 'not public' is not always tenable or desirable (Knauft 2006; Borofsky 2011; Vidali 2011; Willinsky 2011; and Vannini 2012).

This chapter tells the unfinished story of this collaborative, experimental, activist process in (public) hybrid scholarship. I discuss in more detail the genesis of the project, the creative process, and the types of motives that pushed me to 'go public' and to bend the form of ethnographic presentation. I also weave a sociocultural analysis into this account, highlighting specific challenges encountered at the intersection of ethnography, public scholarship, and theatre. I argue that many of the challenges encountered in the production, circulation and reception of public scholarship are shaped by well-known cultural logics and tensions that pervade academic life, particularly those that define the production of what we consider 'work' and 'self' in the academy. These logics and tensions are both spoken and unspoken. Moreover, they are deeply linked through forms of symbolic and economic capital to the political economy of the academic and public scholarship marketplaces (Bourdieu 1988; Lutz 1995; and Pippen 2013). Just as they create the possibility for value, they create the possibility for friction: ideological friction, boundary-crossing friction and status friction.

These cultural logics work through familiar oppositions such as: science vs. art, objectivity vs. subjectivity, fact vs. fiction, general vs. particular, theory vs. method, and author vs. audience. These dualities are fundamental as metaterms in the very genealogy and social organization of modern Western academic life. In addition, very specific, Western, modern assumptions and ideologies about self and intentionality inform these dualities. These are less explicit as metaterms in everyday academic parlance, but they are, nevertheless, important components of the ideologies of communication that surround the production, dissemination and reception of knowledge and public scholarship. They pertain to concepts of the unitary self, predetermined meaning, and authorial authority.

Space limitations prevent a fuller analysis of these socio-cultural-political processes at a general level. In this chapter, I highlight where they impact the Re-Generation work, and allude to them as part of the ongoing field of relations that more broadly impacts work in newer or newish areas of intellectual production. My writing is a blend of storytelling and analysis. Through the narrative, I illustrate the dualities, culturally specific assumptions, communication ideologies and academic frictions that have been both prominent and productive as I have moved forward with Re-Generation projects. I also share some specifics on how the first *Re-Generation* play was crafted, to illustrate how anthropological work can be rendered into a playscript.

The Public Issues, My Issues, and Some Research Findings

For over two decades, my research has been centred on media ethnography, public sphere theory, and the power of language. In 2006, I became very interested in issues of engagement and disengagement among young Americans. I was drawn to this topic as a public sphere theorist and media ethnographer focused on explicating the phenomenology of political subjectivity, and as a concerned American citizen and parent. I designed a research project that involved focus group conversations, interviews, and participant observation fieldwork with young people in Atlanta about their relations to media, the value of news, the meanings of 'being informed', and whether this mattered for democracy. The premise of the work is that the theorization (and documentation) of public spheres from an ethnographic and phenomenological standpoint requires close examination of the social circulation of discourse at the level of powerful institutions and everyday talk (Spitulnik 1996; Vidali 2010, 2014). The analysis centres on the micro-processes of mediation that occur through people's appropriation of public discourses as they articulate stances of connection, disconnection, and normative citizenship, and as they discuss general topics such as the meaning of democracy and the role of media.

A cross-section of over ninety young people aged 18–25 were in the initial phase of the research.[3] The project produced countless pages of participant observation field notes and over sixty hours of recorded material, totalling more than a thousand pages of transcribed talk. The project continues to run, with longitudinal research with some of the original people studied, as well as with new individuals, many of whom are involved in ongoing Re-Generation projects.

Shortly after the inauguration of President Barack Obama in 2009, I decided to share in writing many of the remarkable and also very ordinary stories that I had the privilege to hear. The research results challenge existing conceptions of stereotyped apathy, as well as stereotyped activism, and I wanted to communicate that to a wider audience. I was particularly struck by how the conversations that people had in interview and focus group situations seemed to be very different from the ones that they typically had with peers. They shared uncertainties, struggles and frustrations over our public life and our complicated media landscapes (Snapshot 1). They talked about the conflict avoidance, superficiality and quick judgments that occur between peers when people find themselves on different sides of the political spectrum (Snapshot 2).

TRANSCRIPT SNAPSHOT 1. Tuning out: Media overload and news fatigue

Kelly:[4] I'm so frustrated with what's going on over there [Iraq]. Well, I don't know, actually I don't know how I feel about it. But I don't even pay attention to it anymore. It's every day, it's on every day.

Vanessa: hmmmm

Kelly: And I just can't follow it like that.

Vanessa: And it seems like the more and more we get into it even though we have been over there I think I heard that like within a month, we will have been fighting this war as long as we were involved in World War II, which is crazy to think about to me, but like it seems like as much as we talk about it we say the same thing over and over again.

Kelly: And whenever it comes on, I just, I don't pay attention.

Conversation Group 231 (24 October 2006)

TRANSCRIPT SNAPSHOT 2. Polarization and conflict avoidance

Debra: Are you having some political discussions with some people? Or – is that something you, you do?

Ken: Not usually. I mean, if anything, it's just … in passing. Like: 'Oh who are you voting for?' Like, 'Oh, I'm gonna vote for McCain'. And they're like, 'Why on Earth? like, he's crazy'. Like, 'Get out your pistols and like wave 'em around in the air', and stuff like that. And it's kinda like, 'Oh no, like Obama, like "blah blah blah"'. And then they're like, 'Okay let's not talk about this'. And it's kinda like (*laughing*), 'Yeah let's not talk about this'. And then we just go. So … I haven't had like a more than like a three-, four-minute conversation.

Individual Interview 1112 (8 February 2008)

I was also excited by the possibilities of a non-academic piece of writing to break through familiar generational divisions, accusations and lamentations. Many of the young adults' sentiments about news overload, media hype and political polarization seemed to be no different from those of older adults. Over the past decade, both low media credibility ratings and high distrust of national politics are evidenced at quite similar levels in all generational brackets in the United States (Patterson 2002; Jones 2009). Furthermore, the steady decline in media credibility ratings and the rising distrust of national politics have been trending over time at similar rates among Americans, at all generational levels.[5]

Rather than seeing young people as 'distant others' – naive, apathetic, self-absorbed, or multi-tasking themselves into oblivion – I began to imagine ways that older adults might learn from, identify with, and even be empowered by the voices of younger adults.[6] I began to entertain the idea that generational commonalities may be more important than generational differences. Young adults might speak in more vivid ways about their relations with media, or politics, about their feelings of connection and disconnection, or their desires to feel relevant, make a difference, and figure out where they stand in the world. They may speak more vividly about these things and perhaps feel them more powerfully and poignantly as part of a broader process of coming into young adulthood (Arnett 2014). At the same time, it seemed right to also create public work that would not pigeonhole such issues as exclusively belonging to 'the youth'.

One of the most striking things that emerged in the research is the ambivalence and frustration that many young people feel about the American voting process and the overall political system.[7] Like many older Americans, they are grappling with whether or not their vote counts, and whether or not our current political system is too big and too tightly controlled by powerful interests for there to be significant representation and change in areas that matter to them. Even during the height of young voter registration and 'engagement' during the 2008 presidential election season, many young Atlanta residents in my study had serious doubts about whether their votes mattered. While the *act* of voting, particularly as a first time voter in an exciting presidential election, was highly valued by most, a good number of those who were not casting ballots in swing states expressed frustration that their vote would be irrelevant within a highly polarized two-party, winner-take-all electoral college system.

For others, the issue was not about having one's vote being just one among many in a state whose outcome was already known; it was about not seeing an ideological fit with the candidates. For example, several defined themselves as 'fiscally conservative, but socially liberal' and did not see this self-definition as lining up with either of the two major parties. Many in this category, along with others, explicitly stated that they were choosing one candidate over another simply because he/she was 'the lesser of two evils'. In contrast, a small number stated that they were not voting precisely because they objected to the idea of voting for 'the lesser of two evils'. For them, a non-vote was like a vote: a vote for their conscience, a rejection of the existing voting system. Strikingly, across these wide-ranging stances of frustration and doubt, few seemed to be aware of the existence of other political parties besides Democrat and Republican.

In the end, the public scholarship became driven not just by a desire to share research results, but by an ethical imperative. The weight of young people's reflections highlighted not only a trust deficit and a relevance deficit, but a democracy deficit and a mentoring deficit. More than just relaying these sentiments and analysing their significance in terms of linguistic and social theory, I wanted to create a form of public scholarship that would potentially help young people to get past places of frustration and stuck-ness – something that might empower and transform; something that might in a very small way create some ripples to help to remediate the deficits that I saw.

I thus entered the project – and the interviews themselves – with a hyphenated identity: not as a detached researcher (if such a position is even possible), but as a social scientist, educator, parent and citizen who was concerned about the quality of life and the quality of democracy in America. Although much of my previous research has focused on the very active, unexpected and counter-hegemonic engagements that people have with media, post-Marxist critical theory has deeply informed my perspective on the nature of media power, the perils of consumer society, and the ways that media negatively impact the fibre of society and democratic politics. So both the original research questions and the shape of the first project centred on the degree to which people experienced connections between media and power, and between media and the quality of life. In addition, I attended closely to how interviewees themselves discussed degrees of connection and disconnection, and what kinds of frames they used to describe apathy and activism (Snapshots 3 and 4).

TRANSCRIPT SNAPSHOT 3. On apathy, activism, and being told to 'shut up'

Debra: What do you say to the young person your age who might think the same thing as you … but they don't wanna change things, or … they say, well, there's nothing I can do about it or it's not really relevant to me.

Liz: Um, well I think if it- people who are my age who feel like apathetic and stuff like that, like on one hand a lot of people will be mad at them and I suppose I was like that at one point in my life, like mad at them, like how can you be like this? People are dying, how can you be like this, you know, you're being lied to, how are you not pissed off, you know? But at the same time, you hafta understand like the- where this person comes from within society, like it- is- are they naturally lazy or apathetic or does society like break them down and make it so that they- you know, feel like they can't change anything? Or like are the conditions of the society that you vote every four years and then you don't have a voice- because you have those people out there who are like, if you don't vote, you don't have a voice, you know, or like, you know, if you're against the war, then shut up, you know, like Bill O'Reilly. If you are this, then 'shut up', he says 'shut up' all the time.

Individual Interview 3121 (8 August 2007)

TRANSCRIPT SNAPSHOT 4. On making a difference

When I see these people sittin' on the corner bitchin' about oil and shit like that with signs – pissing people off when they're driving, stuff like that, yellin' at 'em, I mean, that's fine, these people are activists, they have something they believe, but you know, they're all gonna go home and like just waste fossil fuels like the rest of [America]. And that's fine, I'm glad these people have these opinions because it's not that I don't disagree with 'em, but I just-I totally am using all this shit … I mean it's hard to be an American and not do all of that. You know? I mean because our lives are kinda set up that way, too, I mean it's hard not to have a car … Don't get me wrong, I'm glad there are people like you sending emails and standing on corners and stuff like that, I just don't really know if it's gonna make much of a difference.

Individual Interview 3402 with David (9 August 2007)

The Popular Book Idea: Dashed on the Seas of Industry Categories

In February 2009, I pitched a book idea to a prominent New York City agent who regularly works with academics on trade press books. The format was mainly a Studs Terkel type of approach, mixed with a *Bowling Alone* (Robert Putnam) and *The Mommy Myth* (Susan Douglas) type of tone, though with less social history and less authoritative closure. The proposed title was *Re-Generation: Portraits of Apathy and Engagement through the Words of Young American Adults.* My university faculty development office had set up meetings with the book agent during her one-day visit to campus. Pre-meeting, I sent a two-page proposal to the university office, so that this could be sent to the agent beforehand.

The whole meeting was a fascinating disconnect. The agent focused half the conversation on why it would be hard to place my book in a bookstore or on a book list because 'there is no marketing category for "sociology slice of life documentary"'. 'What about Studs Terkel?' I asked, trying to make a connection with the well-known Chicago-based radio interviewer who published several books of extended interview transcripts from his oral history research.[8] 'Studs Terkel is Studs Terkel,' she said, 'not a category'.

The agent focused the other half of the conversation on whether or not I might 'have a more interesting book to write', one which might be more of a page-turner, maybe something about the dangers of social media. 'Do you have any stories about a young girl who made a big mistake by getting involved with an internet stranger?' she asked. 'That would get a lot of interest. Anybody who was physically or psychologically harmed?' Maybe I had something that would fit in the parenting section of the booklist.

'There's always a big market in the self-help genre', she offered. 'Maybe something you have here would be useful for parents to read if they want to understand their kids better'.

'No', I told her. 'That's not what I want to do'. Many things ran through my mind; most I did not say. Yes, there are some fragile people and some sad stories in my research; and yes, parents might be able to learn from the stories that I have to tell – I would hope so. But I do not want to write a moral panic book; I do not want to write a sensationalist, exploitative page-turner; and I do not want to spell it all out. I want the stories to speak for themselves. I want people to go into the voices and stories and see what is there for them. I do not want to be the authority. Well yes, I do, a little bit. But mainly I want to be the medium for the stories to get out. I tried one last time: 'Isn't there a category for "current events" or "contemporary society"? Wouldn't this fit there?' I asked.

'No. People aren't buying books in those areas. Maybe social history, presidents, war, something like that, but not books about young people'. The agent was very generous with her time and expertise. She tried one last time: I was pressed to identify my audience. 'Who do you want to read this?' 'Who is your targeted audience?'

I had a generic answer, again focusing on the fact that I had stories to tell, portraits to paint. As I rambled, I imagined her mind racing to the obvious conclusion that I would bomb on a book tour, and never rise to the level of witty night-time talk show guest.

She delivered the truth yet one more time: young people will not read a non-fiction book about young people – and neither will adults probably, unless it is parenting advice. 'A documentary film made for television – yes, that would be good. Then people can hear and see for themselves what is going on in their lives and what they have to say. But not a book', she concluded.

Without female victims, explicit parenting advice, or the name Studs Terkel, I had no chance. Without a documentary television show approach, I had no genre I could call home. Without a witty, New York City level of panache, I was a bore. I was lucky, probably, to have been rejected so quickly by this agent. Still, as I moved beyond this conversation to develop a theatrical work, the issues of 'industry categories' and 'my targeted audience' followed me. So, too, did the idea of a documentary film.

Genesis: Fusing the Split Brain

'Ever think of turning your research into art?' The sign announcing a Center for Creativity & Arts (CCA) project grant caught my eye as I walked

across my campus one day on a lunch break in spring 2009. Not really; but yes, actually, somewhere in my mind and spirit, I have thought many times about turning my research into art. In fact, I have had dance and poetry and creative writing in my soul since I can remember. My split brain between 'research as analytical, fact-based work' and 'art as creative, expressive work' developed, along very predictable cultural lines, from childhood forward.

In 2001, the fusion of the split brain accelerated. I was pregnant with my first child. I became fundamentally changed by the alchemy of mother-hood – and parenting. My work became more heart-centred. I worried more about what kind of world we were creating for the next generation. I felt a fierce urgency to merge the personal, the political and the professional.

Making a difference, being relevant, working on humanitarian causes, working against social injustice, and contributing to human well-being are not antithetical to anthropology; in fact they are very much part of the core lineage in American anthropology. Still, during a very troubling national political climate in the early 2000s, it seemed to be practically taboo to overtly engage in national politics or to even talk much in the workplace about politics, unless one was firmly positioned through ex-tensive research and publications as an expert. In such modes, one speaks through the research and mutes one's own politics. Objectivity is secured as the dominant professional voice, while unruly and unreliable subjectiv-ity stays home and is made invisible (cf. Lutz 1995).

When I saw the CCA sign in 2009, '*Ever think of turning your research into art?*', I was already at the edge of wanting to break into new types of conversations and communities, beyond the conventional discourses promoted at the centre of the academy, at the centre of anthropology: that science is one thing and art is another; that objectivity and reason need to rise above subjectivity and heart; that attestations of personal politics and family are potentially suspect in the workplace.

The Playscript: Creative Licence, Ethnography and Analysis

Ethnographic work in cultural anthropology fundamentally involves the discovery, documentation, analysis and re-presentation of everyday life as it is lived and experienced, with its implicit cultural logics, webs of mean-ing-making, ways of being-in-the-world, and ways of seeing reality. While there are many styles of ethnographic writing, a pervasive rhetorical aim is to re-present worlds, voices and lives in vivid and compelling ways – alongside, or around, or between the anthropological analysis.

In recent decades there has been an increased experimentation with the ethnographic form itself, and greater discussion of what is at stake in the selection of different forms. One particular facet of this ongoing conversation concerns the degree to which the ethnographer takes an active, explicit voice in stating the analysis versus the degree to which 'the analysis' is embedded in the ethnographic presentation without conventional signposting. Entextualization is an unavoidable part of the process, at either end of this spectrum.[9] As life, actions and conversations are infinitely contextualizable, with no fixed beginning or end as they pertain to the horizons of meaning, the ethnographer necessarily selects, edits and frames pieces of 'ethnographic data' as he or she relays and translates a moment of witnessing, and then presents research insights to a readership. Such entextualization is part of our craft. Entextualization processes are more obvious when ethnographic writers create excerpt-commentary units, or build other kinds of frames around data excerpts, be they field notes of witnessed scenes, extended vignettes that reproduce overhead conversations, or quoted speech.

If 'raw' material is re-presented without an overtly marked surrounding analysis, however, how would one know that there is an analysis? And what would distinguish this from a documentary, non-anthropological re-presentation of something that happened – or from any other category of 'non-fiction', for that matter? These are the questions that loom large around various types of experimental ethnography.

With the popular book idea on hold, I began to imagine: What would it be like to produce an ethnographic work that looks more raw than cooked? With a less explicit analysis? And without so many signposts? I applied for the CCA project grant, to support the drafting of a full-length playscript based on research transcripts. I wrote out a detailed treatment of both the overarching architecture of the play and the specific characters that were to populate the work. The treatment included the key themes and type of stances of engagement/disengagement that had emerged from the research, as well as a map for a sequence of specific scenes that would allow the themes and stances to travel and be juxtaposed throughout the piece, via an alternation of conversational interactions, individual monologues, and break-out spotlights. The treatment also included a close mapping between individual dramatic characters and specific research transcripts (and even targeted excerpts) that were to be the source of characters' lines. The goal was to retain the raw literality of research participants' actual words, media habits and political stances, but to re-embed and fuse them into a smaller set of compelling and representative types, within a form of staged theatre that had action, relationships, movement, and story over time.

Seven characters were modelled after unique individual research participants and the corresponding transcripts from recorded interviews/conversations (Table 4.1). Eight others were created as composite characters, to represent amalgams of individuals who shared common traits, or to vehicle a bundle of traits and issues that were important to represent within the overall piece. For each composite character, several transcripts and disparate transcript excerpts from more than one individual were cued as the sources for monologue and dialogue lines (Table 4.2). Pseudonyms were used for all.

After creating this detailed treatment, I was eager to collaborate with someone who had theatre experience and who could be a sounding board for script development. With the CCA grant, I was able to provide support for Amreen Ukani, a former undergraduate student and aspiring creative writer who had also worked on a few theatrical productions. Using the specific transcripts and transcript extracts that I had cued, and using the character sketches, storylines, and play architecture that I developed, Ukani pulled potential monologue and dialogue lines from the transcripts and began to embed them within the format of a playscript.

Table 4.1 Engagement Types and Sources for Re-Generation Characters Based on Single Research Participants (Vidali, 2009–2012)

DAVID: Full-time worker
cynical + apathetic
transcripts of two conversations

JANINE & MICHAEL: Married, working-class couple
concerned + informed on mainly local issues
transcript of one conversation with a couple

LIZ: Student activist
critical + active
transcripts of two conversations

MAX: Accountant
concerned + semi-engaged
transcripts of two conversations

RYAN: College friend
humorous + engaged
text messages of one individual, sent to research participant who provides a basis for composite character Jin

SHOCKWAVE: Hip-hop artist, entrepreneur
cynical + active
transcripts of two conversations; participant-observation fieldwork

Table 4.2 Engagement Types and Sources for *Re-Generation* Characters Based on Multiple Research Participants (Vidali, 2009–2012)

AJ: Student, avid news consumer
serious + involved in international issues
transcript of one conversation with one person; invented dialogue; participant-observation fieldwork

ALICIA: Single mother
worried + disengaged
transcripts of two separate conversations with two different people

CRYSTAL: Student, political minority
frustrated + engaged
transcripts of three conversations with one person; transcripts of two conversations with a second person (this second person is also one source for Gianna); participant-observation fieldwork

GIANNA: Job seeker (post-college)
(un)informed + sharp
developed from multiple individuals in transcripts of two focus group conversations; transcripts of two individual conversations with same person (this person is also one source for Crystal); participant-observation fieldwork; invented dialogue

JIN: Student, campaign volunteer
idealistic + engaged in mainly national issues
transcripts of two conversations with one person; transcript of one conversation with a second person; participant-observation fieldwork with both people; text messages between second person and a friend (friend used as source for Ryan's texts)

PAUL: Student, follower
confused + idealistic
developed from multiple individuals in transcripts of two focus group conversations; transcripts of two individual conversations with same person (this person is also one source for Jin); participant-observation fieldwork; invented dialogue

TINA: Career-driven student
practical + apathetic
developed from multiple individuals in transcripts of two focus group conversations; transcripts of two individual conversations with same person; participant-observation fieldwork; invented dialogue

ZACK: Entrepreneur, social media addict
serious + engaged
transcripts of two conversations with same person; additional short lines from multiple individuals in transcripts of two focus group conversations; participant-observation fieldwork

While it was essential to see how far the experiment could go using only the words that were on the transcripts, it was also essential to create a web of meanings, juxtapositions and convergences on the stage that recreated the myriad stances of engagement and disengagement, as well as the complex entanglements of these within individual life trajectories, that were discovered in the research. This is precisely where re-presentation blurs with analysis, and vice-versa. In my case, the anthropological analysis resided in the processes of construction, extraction, editing and juxtaposition that both preceded and informed the development of the initial treatment and my decisions about where to cue the transcripts. It also happened during the extensive conversations that Ukani and I had as we worked together on scene reorganization, character development, rewrites, and experiments with invented sections designed to function as bridges.

My work as a linguistic anthropologist also informed the script development, as I attended to processes of intertextuality in the data, particularly the back and forth echoing of commonly used words and phrases that circulate in media and in conversation. To a great degree, the entire work was conceptualized as a Bakhtinian project: a vehicle for staging the dialogicality and social life of voice and language. This shaped the way I worked with media sound bites and other poetic echoes in the playscript itself. For example, I wrote the first scene, 'Generational Babel', as an improvised scene with repeated lines and actions that build into a cacophony: a generational tower of Babel. The entire cast is on stage, and each character has one or two tag lines that they repeat multiple times, and that are echoed throughout the play: 'Sometimes, the real world is just too much'; 'You have an effect on the world'; 'I want my vote to count'; 'It's my responsibility', and so on. Both the overt and covert intertextuality within the ethnographic theatre project produce what could be called an anthropological analysis.

During the summer of 2009, the project evolved through eleven versions of a document. As Ukani crafted monologues and dialogues with the cued-up transcripts, I wrote scenes based on the participant observation fieldwork and overheard dialogue. Field notes were translated into scenes of voter registration campaigns, friends watching televised presidential debates, bar patrons playing a debate-watch buzzword drinking game, and other scenarios. In addition, I developed several segments of text message exchanges, to be projected behind the actors on a large flat-screen monitor.[10]

By August 2009, we had a 45-page playscript for a two-act play. In this first full draft, approximately 90 per cent of the playscript lines were verbatim from the transcripts, overheard dialogue and text messages. Support for Ukani's involvement was limited to the summer, timed to match her impending departure to Portland for graduate studies in creative writing. Through later revisions in autumn 2009 and throughout workshops in 2010, using the input of numerous people, most prominently artistic director Ken Hornbeck, the playscript was refined further and became approximately 80 per cent verbatim.

Too Many Characters? An Unknown Genre? 'A Talking Back'

The play has fifteen characters. What? Unthinkable for a small production house. A nightmare for casting. A nightmare for scheduling rehearsals. A monster for budgeting. How can the audience follow so many individual characters? Poor artistic director. How could he or she coach so many actors simultaneously? *Oy*, the personalities! The dramas!

This predictable litany of concerns did not cross my mind, as I started to write the *Re-Generation* play. My goal was to create a representation of the range of young people's experiences and the complexity of political subjectivity, as evidenced in the research. The sheer number of characters needed to create this kind of tableau was a challenge for dramaturgy and for some audience members. One theatre professional who attended the April 2010 workshop production said that the piece had 'too many characters', suggested that it 'be reduced to just 5 characters', and went on to offer rich feedback along the lines of conventional dramatic story arc development:

> The triangle of AJ–Paul–Jin works well. There are great tensions when Paul is vying for the attention of Jin, but not really being as politically astute as Jin would like him to be. And then also when Paul is trying to go along with his activist friend AJ, but then learns some things that put a rift into the friendship. These would be the things to concentrate on developing.

A similar reaction had occurred a few months earlier, from a theatre professional after reading the first draft in autumn 2009. This person remarked:

> What is this? Is this a debate? Where is the action? What happens? Who are these people? I just don't see any character development or dramatic development that sticks as identification points for an engaged experience of theatre.

Still another theatre professional provided a supportive reading on a later draft in summer 2010, but urged streamlining the piece:

There are so many voices. You gotta figure out what is your voice, Debra. What message do you want people to get? That could come down to a moral message, a political message, or a message about what action you want people to take.

These interpretations highlighted how the project was coming up against industry categories. The feedback pushed me to strengthen the work; it also made me wonder about its value. The comments also created an allergic reaction. I recoiled from the idea of distilling and highlighting 'my message', or the idea of privileging a conventional narrative structure. I was steadfast that the goal of crafting a script directly from research transcripts with a mosaic of stances of engagement and disengagement was worth pursuing as an experiment in ethnographic re-presentation. Some theatre professionals supported this and kept providing encouragement. With an additional CCA grant and other sources of funding, it was possible to create four performances at Emory University's Schwartz Center for Performing Arts in 2010.

Responses on the feedback forms at the November 2010 performances indicated that the conscious complexity of character types worked. Here is a sample of responses to the question: 'What do you think about the play?':

'Excellent. Really got to the messiness of these discussions'. *Whitney, 29, graduate student*

'It was really interesting to see the different viewpoints. I thought that the way it was presented was very effective'. *Curtis, 22, undergraduate student*

'Very well developed characters. Innovative use of technology on stage with text messages'. *Brett, 22, undergraduate student*

'It was very realistic and eye-opening!' *Laura, 21, undergraduate student*

In contrast to one of the first theatre specialists, who read the work and literally said, 'What is this? Is this a debate?', the project's genre was nailed by one audience member as a 'talking back' and a 'counter story'. Sheri Davis-Faulkner, a crunk feminist theorist and then graduate student, who had also contributed to the initial research, posted on the Re-Generation Facebook wall:

Re-Generation: A Play is a first person 'talking back' (bell hooks) against the dominant narrative of apathetic and uninformed U.S. youth. It is a counter-story that lifts up legitimate reasons for the diversity of responses that youth have to the political marketing promoted through media.

Listening to the Street

So how was the weaving done, using raw material from disconnected conversations, interview events, and participant observation fieldwork? Let me describe some of the conscious complexity in more detail, along with more information on how individuals were woven into relationships with each other. Additional audience reactions are also explored.

There is a group of seven characters who all know each other, and whose paths cross many times during the course of the play. Some are friends with each other, some are in romantic relationships with each other, and most are in college together. They watch the 2008 televised presidential debates and election night returns together, they text each other, and they talk to each other about relationships, about political and social causes, about troubles finding employment, about figuring out who to vote for, and so on. Some are in college during Act I and have graduated by Act II, so we see how the pressures of being in the job market and having to earn a living can change young people's orientations towards politics and media. These characters are: Tina, Paul, Jin, AJ, Gianna, Crystal and Ryan.

In addition, there are eight characters who do not all know each other, and who have loose or zero connections to the aforementioned group of seven interrelated people. Two have finished college, one is in college, and the other five never went to college. Of these, there is a single mother who is a writer, a young married couple who manage a hardware store, an independent hip-hop artist who sells his CDs on the street and who has two children, and a sharp but apathetic shop worker who goes from paycheck to paycheck. These characters are: Zack, Max, Liz, Alicia, Janine and Michael, Shockwave, and David.[11]

Characters were developed to show a spectrum of socioeconomic backgrounds, life circumstances, and orientations to media and politics. A few are avid news consumers, others are wilfully ignorant of current events; some are naive, others are misinformed. There is one social media addict and early adopter who is working on his own social media start-up company. Many of the characters are shown texting, multitasking, and talking about Facebook. Their emotional and political stances could be described as apathetic, uncertain, idealistic, cynical, activist, depressed, anxious, confused and optimistic.

The overarching architecture of the play is a hybrid of chronological narrative and non-chronological spotlights. This serves the main compositional/analytical goals of juxtaposing different voices and stances, and showing some degree of change and consistency in stances and struggles over time. Short scenes of dialogue and interaction between characters alternate with break-out monologues and spotlighted moments. The staging is raw and the action minimalistic.

This first *Re-Generation* play starts in late 2007, during the build up to the U.S. presidential primaries, and it ends in late 2008, just after the election of President Obama. Many scenes and conversational moments centre on current events and hot button issues that engaged research participants during the original fieldwork period, such as the war in Iraq, the crisis in Darfur, health care reform, and concerns over immigrant workers. There are a few story arcs (the election cycle, Jin and Paul's relationship, Paul and AJ's relationship, Gianna's job search) and many character throughlines. There are some potential cliffhanger questions, but due to the play's length and cast size, they are not maximized for dramatic tension.

The fact that this was a relatively unknown genre for many performance attendees produced interesting reactions. The piece's documentary 'rawness' was seen as both a strength and a weakness. Many who were non-U.S. citizens readily related to the genre, because they had seen similar 'voices of the people'-type productions in their own countries (e.g. the Netherlands, Poland, Czech Republic, France, Venezuela and Italy). Many newcomers to the genre commented on the 'fresh' approach, and appreciated the 'minimalistic' staging and the wide range of voices. Others felt it was hard to follow. And some cringed. Some found the voicing of stances and the heavy reliance on monologue to be too strident. I was charged with promulgating too much of my own ideology. There were concerns that I was not adhering to social scientist's standards of representativeness and objectivity. I found myself searching for language for this during the talk-backs, at times placing the characters and case studies in relation to national statistics, and at other times backing off from the social scientist's frame and focusing on the work as a form of humanistic anthropology, interested in storytelling, voices, and experimental forms of re-presentation.

A few audience members were uncomfortable during any extended monologues that represented political stances greatly different from their own. It was as if they had unknowingly stepped into a political-dramatic zone that was not their usual echo chamber. By contrast, others were appreciative of the windows opened by hearing diverse voices and vivid dilemmas. Some were touched by seeing versions of their former selves. Many were moved when they saw themselves in characters such as Tina, the busy college student, and began to think about perhaps being different: less apathetic, and more passionate about causes like the characters Liz and Jin. Others saw themselves in Tina, and felt validated as Tina, without any need to change.

Responses on the post-show feedback forms and discussions during talk-backs highlighted these connections. The decision to proliferate in the name of accurate ethnography (which was actually a reduction from the data), rather than reduce in the spirit of conventional dramaturgy, was validated. In the written responses to the question *Which characters do you identify most with? Why?*, many claimed to have connected with some of the characters. For example:

'Each and every character had characteristics that I really resonated with'. *Sophia, 19, college undergraduate*

'I feel/have felt like many…'. *Tim, 43, community member*

Others wrote about resonances with individual characters:

'Max. I care, I think about things, I'm fairly aware, but I don't feel powerful or meaningful in the political sphere, or completely satisfied with any of the options available to me'. *Katharine, 19, college undergraduate*

'AJ. I'm not completely informed, but I often find myself more informed than those around me. It's frustrating'. *Sarah, 19, college undergraduate*

While the work as a text was finalized in the first instance as a written playscript, and in the second instance as an embodied performance by live actors, it was in many respects not final at all. The lack of closure and open-endedness for different types of engagements and possible finalizations became apparent during the audience talk-backs and on the feedback sheets. Audience engagements were as much a mosaic of reactions and stances as those that were vehiced by the play's characters. A sample of some of the written responses to the question *What do you think the biggest message of the* play *is?* conveys this diversity of interpretation:

'Think! Then Act'. *Will, 45, community member*

'There is always noise and no single correct way to narrow down the noise to the important things. There are many ways to be an individual and caring person outside of just politics'. *Nathan, 22, recent college graduate*

'Youth *are* civically engaged – in different ways, at different levels. The 24/7 news media and economic pressures make people disengaged'. *Lilly, 28, graduate student*

Significantly, Will, Nathan and Lilly, all in their own ways, answered the question that the theatre professional quoted earlier had wanted me to answer while the work was being drafted: 'You gotta figure out what is your voice, Debra. What message do you want people to get?' If I had wanted to convey a neat, discrete message in a traditional sense then I might have decided to drive a more singular message. Equivocation and open-endedness were preferred, however, not only because they relayed my take on the research, but because they granted space for audience members to come to conclusions too.

In a post-show interview, one colleague Sam Cherribi, a professor of sociology and former member of the Dutch Parliament, described this as a kind of Brechtian project, 'bringing people to listen to the street, to listen to what's going on in the streets like a doctor listening to my heartbeat'. He went on to comment that the performance itself is a way of 'building community with the audience', a means of immunizing ourselves 'against the forces of fragmentation that are really haunting our societies now'.[12] For Brecht, the renowned twentieth-century German playwright, director, and theatre critic who pioneered a new form of politically and socially engaged theatre, this kind of realism is 'the basis of art's enormous and proper social significance' (Brecht 1964: 223). Scenes are played as pieces of history and this allows spectators to 'criticize human behavior from a social point of view' (ibid.: 85). Consonant with a range of approaches from across the social sciences and the humanities, the point in Brechtian theatre is to see ourselves, and be moved to action, as we better understand the various influences on the ways that human beings behave.

As I moved forward with the project, I began to see alignment and resonances with such long-standing traditions of theatre for social change, theatre of the oppressed, and applied theatre (Boal 1979; Prendergast and Saxton 2010). It was as if I had backed into Brazilian theatre revolutionary Augusto Boal and bumped into Brecht, with an experiment that I was calling ethnographic theatre based on verbatim talk. Not knowing much about these traditions beforehand facilitated the leap into an unknown interdisciplinary, experimental ethnography space. I first went on intuition. I did not overthink it or try in advance to line it all up with disciplinary canons and greats.

Compartmentalization and Incommensurability

Ever think of turning your research into art? The sign played with a division. The division is useful and also troubling. It figures in the production of scholarly knowledge, the creation of disciplinary pursuits, and the stories that we tell ourselves. Lurking behind the 'research that can be turned into art' formulation is an implicit division between culturally specific categories of 'knowledge' understood as a type of 'content', on the one hand, and 'expression' understood as a kind of 'form', on the other. On this model, the conversion of research into art happens when research is the factual content and art is the new, non-traditional form through which the research is expressed. Research is the stuff. And art is the new way that it can be packaged or shared.

The untold story is that the pre-conversion version of 'the research' is expressed in whatever happens to be understood as the most disciplinarily appropriate form of expression for the home field of the researcher. In the home discipline, there are the normal, unmarked and expected forms of expression for delivery of research content – a chart, a graph, a data set, a symbol, a formula, the absence of formulas, a narrative style, a publication length and format, a publication venue, a typeface and font size, a mode of argumentation, and so on. There is a standard relation to methodology, a recognizable researcher voice, and an accepted relation to credentialing. There is the argot: the key words, phrases and sentence structures that signal inclusion in the disciplinary home. There is the ancestor worship: the figures to be honoured and invoked. There is the warfare: the positions to attack and defend; the tactics that are approved and even expected. There are the discipline-sanctioned forms of adventure: where it is important to travel, and what it is important to explore and discover.

Analogous to the research/art dichotomy, some forms of public or applied scholarship are also described as a clear-cut two-step process: first the research, then the application. But not all are. Within the narrative of two discrete steps, the first step – 'pure research' – can be construed as 'neutral' and independent from potential application and public relevance – a reinforcement of the ivory tower. The second step – 'application' or 'public version' – is typically the phase when 'non-neutrality' is potentially more acceptable, be it through direct advocacy, explicit statement of opinion, or some other form of 'personalizing' or 'politicizing'. The complication with the narrative of two discrete steps, however, is that a strict compartmentalization of value-laden investment, with no ideological values in the 'pure' phase, or unconnected values in the two phases, is a fiction. Ethical, political and ideological decisions and stances inform human labour at every step, including research design and selection of research topic. In my case, both academic interests and personal, political and public issues motivated the research, and the public scholarship based on and inspired by the research. The process has been simultaneously two-step, split, hybrid, hyphenated and recursive.

The first theatrical project – through conception, development, execution, and post-performance reporting – was structured by a set of *applied questions* informed by ethics, critical media literacy, and civics: How do different people relate to democracy in America? Does voting matter? What does it mean to be a good citizen? How do media contribute to or detract from democratic engagement in society? How do friendships affect relations to politics and news media? And so on. I did not intend the playscript to answer these questions definitively, but imagined that the staging of young people's stories and actual words – those of Alicia, Vanessa, Kelly, Jackie, Ken, Liz, David and many others – around such issues would contribute to others being able to develop insights for themselves. But as stated earlier, the initial research, even before the first theatrical project was even imagined, was also structured by such questions, more generally aiming to develop an anthropological analysis of the experiences of young adults regarding their connections and disconnections with media, politics and the public sphere. The very fact that many young people themselves struggle with these types of question is part of the findings (Vidali 2014).

In addition, it is important to highlight that regardless of whether or not there is a fictional compartmentalization of value-laden interest, all two-step processes – the 'research', which is then translated for 'the public' – have the challenge of translation. Translation processes on a two-step model might work smoothly when there is linearity and literality. As with translations from one language to another, the process works well when there are good translation equivalents and when there is enough grammatical commensurability to also support 'the same' flow of ideas within a message delivery structure in the second language. Such issues also impact translation – or simply having conversation – across different disciplines and subdisciplines. For the case of theatre and anthropology, the languages of conventional scholarly anthropological production and theatrical production are only partly commensurable. The semiotic systems are not fully alignable.

The communication modalities of ethnographic theatre (like those of film/video) are more varied and far reaching than those of conventional scholarly publications. They include spoken language, other sounds, lighting, signage, text and image projection/overlay, and potentially greater variation and manipulation of the temporal flow of a viewer's encounter with the material than that afforded by conventional print publication. In addition, the pacing and layering of different elements is more dynamic within moving image products and theatrical products than it is within conventional print products. Such multimodality activates multiple sensory channels to different degrees at different moments, creates complex affective experiences, and even disrupts linearity.

Furthermore, with theatre and performance, the viscerality of human bodies and voices is heard and seen in co-present three-dimensional space. What happens to communication possibilities – at the levels of production, reception and textuality – when a primary dimension of the communication involves real, living human bodies? Physical and expressive immediacy of 'the other' creates identification or disidentification in a more urgent way than the printed word. Possibilities for empathy, inter-subjectivity and understanding change and proliferate.

Product vs. Process; Ownership vs. Collaboration

Partial incommensurability between mainstream forms of academic anthropology and theatrical work exists because the two disciplines involve different orders of knowledge production as well as different kinds of possibilities for audience positions. On the conventional model of scholarly knowledge production, results are *products*: scholarly findings and publications. What we developed with the *Re-Generation* theatrical work was both *product and process*: a text, a performance, and an interactive process with open-endeness and multiple stances. While all anthropological work, and work in any discipline for that matter, develops a product that invites a process of interaction, such a process is usually unmarked and secondary. When the process is highlighted, for example in what Bishop (2012) describes as 'participatory art', the scholar-knowledge producer-cultural producer-artist is less a producer of objects and more a co-producer of situations, dialogical practices and ephemeral products.

As an ethnographic interviewer turned playwright and collaborator, I opened up 'my' material to others to inhabit and activate. During revisions, workshops and rehearsals, some verbatim dimensions of the script were challenged by seasoned actors and directors (Figure 4.2). Long monologues and dialogic exchanges, some of which were already highly edited down from extended stretches of speech, were cut further in the interest of pacing, delivery, message and impact. Significantly, for the *Re-Generation* actors, many transcription choices for verbatim representation of pauses, disfluencies and fillers ('um', 'like') were found to be too confining, too artificial, too redundant, or a hindrance to the memorization process. These elements were cut and then often added back in by actors themselves. They inserted disfluencies and rhythms in both similar and different locations than those in the original transcripts. This worked more powerfully for the theatrical production than my faithful transcription efforts, since they were more organically developed by the actors, in tune with their own sensibilities for character portrayal.

Similarly, creative infusion occurred as actors breathed life into the characters: people who had become disembodied and even merged through the transcription of live utterances into written chunks of texts within the pages of a playscript. The implication of this is nothing new to people who do theatre, but it is fundamentally radical for the way anthropologists typically view ownership and control of ethnographic representations. One

Figure 4.2 Actor Angele Masters (L) providing script feedback and edits to author during *Re-Generation* rehearsal, 2010. Photo by Moi Li.

extreme case of this was with the character Paul, the confused follower, who was so enriched and expanded by what actor Anish Shah brought into the portrayal, that my own understanding of Paul – and the actual individuals who were the sources of this composite character – expanded accordingly. Through the workshop, rehearsal, and rewriting process, the character Paul developed in alignment with Anish's reading and inhabitance of Paul. Anish was thus analogous to being a co-author, an analyst, *and* an additional research participant, as well as being an actor cast to perform a scripted role. Through similar types of creative infusions from artistic director Hornbeck and others in the cast, ethnographic ownership and authority became shared across the project's development.

We Are All Social Scientists? We Are All Artists?

Is there an impasse when there is great incommensurability across different forms of knowledge production? Or is constructive dialogue and understanding possible? It depends on who seeks commensurability and connection. It also depends on who is doing the work of translation. I shift from translating one discipline into the other (code-switching in both directions with a multilingual identity) and from holding the two as incommensurable (doing parallel work with a split identity). I also work simultaneously in both arenas in a hybrid non-two-step fashion, where 'translation' – better understood as intellectual work in a third space – happens more intuitively and less explicitly.

Frictions are inevitable with any inter-/multi-disciplinary intellectual product and process. Some use the word 'transdisciplinary' to signal an attempt to avoid frictions by bypassing or rejecting the imposition of disciplinary-based evaluations. 'Trans' used in this fashion is an attempt at a re-frame towards something that is 'beyond' or 'post' discipline. But even if 'discipline' is *heralded* as averted, placed in the past, or taken off the table, reactions and evaluations that echo disciplinary standards and conversations still occur (Pippen 2013).

Even *within* 'a' discipline such as anthropology, there are discourses and subfields that are only partly commensurable, as they are informed by different orders of knowledge. In some cases, for example, the divisions between social anthropology, humanistic anthropology, linguistic anthropology, cultural anthropology and biological anthropology are just as great as the divisions between disciplines *outside* of anthropology. Behar, for example, writes about the construal of 'artsy ethnographers' (Behar 2007:145) as a threat to the 'commitment to maintaining the sobriety and respectability of anthropology within the university system' (ibid.:

154). While some might see this tension as greatly exaggerated in Behar's writings, and as something that the discipline has largely moved passed by now, others see a real impasse. With the Re-Generation projects, reactions in my field have ranged from enthusiasm and strong support to disparagement, bafflement and avoidance.

In one extreme case, a colleague stated: 'You might be happier in another department'. Strikingly, this was a context where I was not expressing unhappiness, but rather excitement about the new direction in ethnographic theatre that I had recently embarked on. The exchange is worth relaying in detail as it exemplifies the complexities of translation, impasse, cultural logics, and friction highlighted above. I started the conversation in an attempt to describe some of my recent work. This was met by the colleague's sharp interruption: 'We are all social scientists here, Debra'. The phrasing, tone, and surrounding context implied a collective 'we' that I was not considered part of. I rejected the exclusion. I again started to explain how the work builds on ethnography and anthropological theory, and takes them in a new direction, one with continuities to previous work in anthropology, performance studies and ethnographic writing. Again, I was interrupted as the colleague almost scornfully proclaimed that my approach was either naive or hubristic, seemingly unaware that there was a disciplinarily time-tested way of doing ethnography and being an ethnographer. The colleague went on to challenge the value of staging verbatim material by saying, 'I can get students to read my research transcripts'. I endeavoured to be civil and constructive in the conversation amidst the overtones of hostility and condescension. I tried to continue the conversation about how the person might experiment with a project that stages excerpts from their own research transcripts – but that was a non-starter. Fortunately, this was the only instance of such extreme negativity. And as with all interlocutors – positive, excited, curious, baffled, silent, negative – it presents a rich opportunity to clarify the methods, values and goals inherent and emergent in this kind of work.

The Re-Generation journey has been hard work. I have employed professional actors and seasoned artistic directors, engaged professional videographers and lighting technicians. I have invited others to work with my research data. We have placed material on YouTube, Vimeo, Facebook and a website. The work has activated the joys and dangers of boundary crossing, creativity, re-formation and merging. It invites a process that aligns with Bourdieu's call 'exorcise the domestic'; to unpack and purge those elements of academic culture that impede the human spirit (Bourdieu 1988: xi). It is a process through which mainstream disciplinary expectations of ethnographic closure, individual ownership, muted politics, and downplaying of the artistic are released and challenged. It is my hope that we find language to frame such pursuits, not as a question of *either* social science *or* art, but as fundamentally both, and also beyond. It would be a language of inclusion and addition, rather than exclusion and subtraction. And it would still be a language of anthropology.

Debra Spitulnik Vidali is associate professor in the Department of Anthropology, Emory University, and the founding director of the Re-Generation Initiative. Vidali's work centres on critical epistemology, ethnographic theatre, experimental ethnography, political subjectivity, democracy & citizenship, public sphere theory, discourse circulation, and media ethnography. Recent publications and projects include: '*Kabusha* Radio Remix, Your Questions Answered by Pioneering Zambian Talk Show Host, David Yumba (1923–1990)', a multi-sensorial ethnographic installation co-created with Kwame Philips; 'Civic Mediations', a Special Issue of *Ethnography* 15(1) (2014), guest edited with Thomas Tufte; *Slices of Time*, a collaborative ethnographic theatre project; and *Re-Generation: Portraits of (Dis)Engagement*, theatrical productions (2009–2012).

Acknowledgements

Parts of this research were presented at: the Consortium for Communication and Glocal Change (Ørecomm) seminar on 'Performing, Writing and Doing Ethnography' (Roskilde University, Denmark); the International Association for Media and Communication Research (IAMCR) conference in Istanbul; the University of Georgia, Athens; LUISS University's Centre for Media and Communication Studies, Rome; and Indiana University, Bloomington. I am deeply indebted to the convenors and interlocutors at these events for the opportunity to shape this work. Special thanks go to Aiden Downey, Ioulia Fenton, David Gere, Ilana Gershon, Bobby Gordon, Oscar Hemer, Ken Hornbeck, Henry Scott, Thomas Tufte, Amreen Ukani and Nicola Vidali for their support and feedback. I also wish to express my deepest gratitude for the research and production support received from the Fox Center for Humanistic Inquiry, Emory Center for Creativity & Arts, Theater at Emory, Emory University Research Committee, Scholarly Research and Inquiry at Emory, Halle Institute for Global Learning, Center for Ethics, Campus Progress, and the many people who have contributed on Re-Generation projects as actors, co-writers, artistic directors, research assistants, and interlocutors.

Notes

1. The playscript, now titled, *Re-Generation: A Verbatim Documentary Play about Media and Civic (Dis)Engagement*, has an excerpt hosted on the author's Academia.edu page.
2. From the 'About' line on the Re-Generation Initiative Facebook page: www.facebook .com/ReGenerationINITIATIVE
3. See Vidali (2010) for discussion of research methods.
4. Names of research participants and audience members are pseudonyms unless otherwise noted.
5. '4th Annual TV News Trust Poll', by Public Policy Polling, 6 February 2013 (http:// www.publicpolicypolling.com/main/2013/02/4th-annual-tv-news-trust-poll.html); 'U.S. Distrust in Media Hits New High', by Lyman Morales for Gallup, 21 September 2012 (http://www.gallup.com/poll/157589/distrust-media-hits-new-high.aspx); 'Further Decline in Credibility Ratings for Most News Organizations', by Pew Research Center, 16 August 2012 (http://www.people-press.org/2012/08/16/further-decline-in-credibility-ratings-for-most-news-organizations/1/).
6. The publicly circulating imagery of youth and young adults as naive, disaffected and self-absorbed is pervasive, and even crops up in young people's documentations of themselves (e.g. Wesch et al. 2007).
7. See Vidali (2014) for more discussion and examples.
8. Studs Terkel (1912–2008) was a Pulitzer Prize-winning author and radio personality, well known for his contributions to U.S. oral history on the topics of race, work, Second World War and the Great Depression.
9. See Silverstein and Urban (1996) for detailed discussions of entextualization in relation to discourse analysis.
10. Multiple sources were used for the text messages: verbatim text messages that research participants had shared with me, verbatim utterances from research recordings and participant observation, and invention.
11. A number of extras also appear in the first *Re-Generation* production: there are three bar patrons and four passers-by. In the 2009 playscript, a few street scenes also contained parts for protesters against the war in Iraq. They carried signs, but did not have direct speaking roles. This ambient feature was removed in the 2010 production to streamline the street scenes and to alleviate casting challenges.
12. Interview excerpt can be viewed on the Re-Generation Initiative YouTube channel.

References

Arnett, J.J. 2014. *Emerging Adulthood: The Winding Road from the Late Teens through the Twenties.* Second edition. Oxford: Oxford University Press.
Behar, R. 2007. 'Ethnography in a Time of Blurred Genres', *Anthropology and Humanism* 32(2): 145–55.
Bishop, C. 2012. *Artificial Hells: Participatory Art and the Politics of Spectatorship.* London: Verso.
Boal, A. (1974) 1979. *Theatre of the Oppressed.* New York: Theatre Communications Group.
Borofsky, R. 2011. *Why a Public Anthropology?* Honolulu: Center for a Public Anthropology.
Bourdieu, P. 1988. *Homo Academicus*, trans P. Collier. Stanford, CA: Stanford University Press.

Brecht, B. 1964. *Brecht on Theatre: The Development of an Aesthetic*, ed. and trans. J. Willett. New York: Hill and Wang.

Jones, A.S. 2009. *Losing the News: The Future of the News that Feeds Democracy*. Oxford: Oxford University Press.

Knauft, B. 2006. 'Anthropology in the Middle', *Anthropological Theory* 6(4): 407–30.

Lutz, C. 1995. 'The Gender of Theory', in R. Behar and D.A. Gordon (eds), *Women Writing Culture*. Berkeley: University of California Press, pp. 249–66.

Patterson, T.E. 2002. *The Vanishing Voter: Public Involvement in an Age of Uncertainty*. New York: Vintage Books.

Pippen, R. 2013. 'Transdisciplinarity, Interdisciplinarity, Reductive Disciplinarity, and Deep Disciplinarity'. Keynote address presented at Interdisciplinary Futures Symposium, Emory University. http://www.youtube.com/watch?v=X31J9gm1KXM

Prendergast, M., and J. Saxton. 2010. *Applied Theatre: International Case Studies and Challenges for Practice*. Bristol, UK: Intellect.

Silverstein, M., and G. Urban (eds). 1996. *Natural Histories of Discourse*. Chicago: University of Chicago Press.

Spitulnik, D. 1996. 'The Social Circulation of Media Discourse and the Mediation of Communities', *Journal of Linguistic Anthropology* 6(2): 161–87.

Vannini, P. 2012. 'Introduction: Popularizing Research', in P. Vannini (ed.), *Popularizing Research: Engaging New Genres, Media, and Audiences*. New York: Peter Lang, pp. 1–10.

Vidali, D.S. 2009–2012. Re-Generation: A Verbatim Documentary Play about Media and Civic (Dis)Engagement.

———. 2010. 'Millennial Encounters with Mainstream Television News: Excess, Void, and Points of Engagement', *Journal of Linguistic Anthropology* 20(2): 372–88.

———. 2011. 'The University and the Public Sphere', *The Academic Exchange* 13(2): 1–3. http://www.emory.edu/ACAD_EXCHANGE/2011/spring/lead.html

———. 2014. 'The Ethnography of Process: Excavating and Re-generating Civic Engagement and Political Subjectivity', *Ethnography* 15(1): 12–31.

Wesch, M., and Kansas State University students. 2007. 'A Vision of Students Today'. http://www.youtube.com/watch?v=dGCJ46vyR9o&feature=relmfu

Willinsky, J. 2011. 'Rethinking What is Made *Public* in the University's Public Mission', in R. Rhoten and C. Calhoun (eds), *Knowledge Matters: The Public Mission of the Research University*. New York: Columbia University Press, pp. 290–314.

Chapter 5

SOCIAL MOVEMENTS AND *VIDEO INDÍGENA* IN LATIN AMERICA
Key Challenges for 'Anthropologies Otherwise'

⸺⸺⸺∞∞∞⸺⸺⸺

Juan Francisco Salazar

Indigenous social movements in Latin America have been at the forefront of renewed struggles around cultural difference, the right to self-representation and self-determination, as well as calls for a plurality of ways of belonging and being. This chapter provides a brief critical account of the ongoing engagement by media anthropologists in indigenous media practices, arguing that media anthropology has been at the forefront of the study of social movements and their communication and media practices. I offer a brief description of how communication and media have taken a central role in rearticulating identity politics within indigenous social movements in Latin America by tracing the development since the 1980s of CLACPI, the Latin American Council of Indigenous Peoples' Film and Communication.

This chapter is also a reflection of my experience engaging in multisited ethnographic research on Indigenous media practices for over a decade, and working alongside a range of organizations in Chile and elsewhere in Latin America through my participation in the CLACPI festivals in Chile 2004, Mexico 2006, Bolivia 2008, Colombia 2012 and Chile 2015. Over these years, my work has embraced engagements with a range of subjectivities and 'institutionalities', including indigenous media and cultural activists; translocal, non-indigenous activist 'collaborators'; and media practitioners from a range of local and international institutions. I often found myself productively caught up in the projects I was involved with, often taking an active role in enabling the very activities I was examining – a process that Faye Ginsburg and Rayna Rapp have recently called 'ethnographic entanglement'. Ginsburg and Rapp locate entangled ethnography as a term emerging within the vocabulary of engaged anthropology, which they differentiate 'from legacies of applied, action, and advocacy projects to capture a sense of the recent expansion of research that encompasses everything from collaboration to activism' and where the researcher 'has stakes in the process being documented, and may even play a role in determining the outcome of circumstances that emerge serendipitously' (Ginsburg and Rapp 2013: 188).

The story of Indigenous video in Latin America is recounted here as a tale of (dis)encounters between indigenous cultural/media activists and producers, anthropologists and communication/media researchers and practitioners, with its own moments and spaces of convergence and divergence. I have been particularly interested in the productive friction that emerges as the perspectives of engaged anthropologists, indigenous cultural activists and media producers rub up against each other in relation to the complex processes of what Erica Wortham has termed 'making culture visible' (Wortham 2002, 2013).

One enduring tension, whose pull and push can be traced back to the very beginnings of anthropology, has to do with the politics of representation of Indigenous cultures and knowledge, in which anthropological knowledge in general – and visual anthropology and ethnographic film in particular – have developed a particular mode of imagining and representing Indigenous peoples and cultures. More than a decade ago, at the advent of today's ubiquitous digital media landscape, Faye Ginsburg cautioned that without an expanded intellectual and empirical base, visual anthropology and the practice of ethnographic film 'were in danger of becoming atavistic and myopic' (Ginsburg 1994), something that today, with the expansion of reality television, has become almost commonplace in the global mediasphere. Writing as early as 1994, Ginsburg referred to a cultural 'parallax effect' by which Indigenous media ought to be understood as arising from 'a historically new positioning of the observed behind the camera so that the object – the cinematic representation of culture – appears to look different than it does from the observational perspective of ethnographic film'. The possibilities of this parallax effect, as Ginsburg argued, were in the prospect for repositioning ethnographic film alongside indigenous media in order to offer 'a fuller comprehension of the complexity of the social phenomena we call culture' (1994, 158).

Twenty years on, Ginsburg's admonitory observation remains up-to-date and a challenge that rests seriously unattended. Despite noteworthy exceptions, the anthropology of Indigenous media in Latin America remains locked in the internal vicissitudes of critical anthropology and visual anthropology. On the other hand, by creating, imagining and re-inventing traditional social relationships through the moving image, In-digenous organizations, communities and individual producers have established new forms of cultural resistance and revitalization that go well beyond the public impact that anthropologists and communication researchers have been able to make. Consequently, I argue that Indige-nous media has been effective in decolonizing methodologies by shifting relations of power away from anthropological knowledge practices. This process may ultimately lead to productive ways of rethinking and redo-ing part a long tradition of engaged research in anthropology (Hale 2006, 2008), thus envisioning the potential for politically engaged public anthro-pologies, or 'anthropologies otherwise' (Restrepo and Escobar 2005).

Indigenous Social Movements
in an Age of Public Anthropologies

In *The Indigenous Emergence in Latin America*, Chilean anthropologist José Bengoa (2000) drew a series of observations around what he termed the emergence of 'the indigenous question' in times of globalization. The phe-nomena he was referring to was the emergence in Latin America during the 1980s of vigorous Indigenous social movements sweeping across the region, surfacing around 1992 at the Earth Summit in Rio de Janeiro, and coinciding with commemorations of the 500th anniversary of Columbus's voyage to the Americas. These were the first massive mobilizations in a new wave of social unrest in an age of globalized capital, that rejected and mobilized against official celebrations that spoke of the 'fifth centenary of the "discovery" of America' and of the '"meeting" of two cultures'. Ben-goa, as only one of many other Latin American and U.S. cultural critics writing at the time, presented an epitome of ethnic resurgence processes that crystallized in virtually the whole of Latin America in what was then described as a new pan American movement of Indigenous peoples of the continent. The most significant event, of course, was the Zapatista insur-gency in Mexico, begun on 1 January 1994.

The unprecedented features of this new political and cultural strug-gle for identity politics had to do with a set of complex processes taking place simultaneously across the region, including an emergent diversity of oppositional movements that marked a transition away from previous processes of 'national-popular' projects (Hale 1997). Yet this oppositional moment at the beginning of the 1990s was concurrent with broader polit-ical and economic change, such as democratization processes in several countries in the southern cone of Latin America, the penetration of global capital and the impact of structural neoliberal reforms bringing about a swarm of privatization and deregulation policies.

Indigenous organizations springing up in the early 1990s became key emergent actors (Stavenhagen 1997) in bringing about a new set of demands for rights, namely: rights to traditional knowledge; rights to indigenous languages; rights to sustainable development; rights of nature; rights to indigenous medicine; and communication rights. For Bengoa, this struggle for new rights was a sort of 'reverse conquest', where indigenous peoples, in their demand for new modes of cultural and political recognition, became vociferous and active against being cast as silent witnesses to 'the wedding of free markets and representative democracy' (Bengoa 2000: 59).

Increasingly, efforts towards self-determination of indigenous peoples became framed in the language of 'recognition': recognition of cultural difference, recognition of an inherent right to self-government, recognizing the obligations of the State to international standards, binding or not, and so on. Shifting the issue of recognition to the forefront of identity politics eventually led to many Latin American countries reforming their national constitutions and supposed a reorganisation of the rights' debate from the realm of the symbolic into the performative. Recognition, as Nancy Fraser and Axel Honneth (2003) argue, has become a keyword of our time, rearticulated by contemporary critical theory as a fundamental category in efforts to conceptualize the current struggles over identity and difference, and to decompress the normative basis of political claims.

Today there are over 650 Indigenous nations in Latin America, all with different legal statuses and demographic and socio-political features, comprising close to fifty million people, or roughly 10 per cent of the total population of Latin America. Bengoa has more recently sustained that this 'Indigenous Emergence' has been the most important socio-political phenomenon in Latin America during the last two decades, and argues that a first cycle of this process of ethnical identity reconstruction has begun to exhaust, but is giving way to a second cycle (Bengoa 2009). For Bengoa this new phase is strongly marked by a new wave of indigenous leaderships of local public institutions and municipalities, epitomized on a major scale by the rise of Evo Morales to power in Bolivia since 2006 and the 're-foundation' of Bolivia as a plurinational state in 2010. What this new situation entails is the challenge of a new form of indigenous or ethnic citizenship (De la Peña 1999; Salazar 2004; Bengoa 2009), in which to be a national citizen and a member of an indigenous nation is not a contradiction.

Besides the question of citizenship, another key dispute in terms of recognition has been fought over communication rights related to the rise – sometimes coordinated, sometimes spontaneous, and most times self-organized – of new practices and processes of indigenous communication, which since the mid-1980s have emerged, developed and consolidated to different degrees in several countries in the region. These certainly point to broader (and concurrent) forms of political action, social action and civil disobedience. In many cases these disputes for new rights and new political spaces are characterized by precarity. By this I do not mean deprived conditions of production (which in many cases is the norm), but the condition of precarity as a political concept emerging as a platform (Neilson and Rossiter 2008) from where the struggle of indigenous political and cultural rights is organized and from where an 'insurrection of subjugated knowledges' (Foucault 1980) becomes possible.

At the time that new social movements were emerging across the continent in the early 1990s, Arturo Escobar was expressing concern that as a novel body of literature had appeared, mostly in Western Europe and Latin America, 'dealing with the nature and role of social movements in relation to the crisis of modernity and the possibility of new social orders', anthropology was 'largely absent' from this emergent debate on questions of political practice (Escobar 1992: 396). This has also been noted by Gibb (2001) who lamented too the 'invisibility' of social movements in anthropology during the 1990s, arguing that anthropologists have generally not played a prominent role in theoretical and conceptual debates within this field of research, attributing it largely to how 'political anthropology constructs its object, and particularly to the weakness of its concepts of politics and practice' (ibid.: 233). Escobar's early plea for an anthropological research informed by social movements theory and research was an invitation to focus on the political practice of collective social actors (Escobar 1992: 396), as anthropology remained to a large extent on the periphery of social scientific theorizing about collective action (Edelman 2001: 286).

To me this call remains as urgent as ever for those interested in the public impact of contemporary and future anthropologies. Because despite the reimaginings of public and critical anthropologies since the late 1980s, the dilemmas of ghosts past remain unresolved and manifold: in many contexts, the politics of commentary and critique embedded in anthropological knowledge continue to cast a veil of mistrust that shapes the ethics of anthropological intervention and the association of anthropologists to dubious, and often dominant, forms of political, economic, religious or military power. To a large extent, critical anthropology continues to pay scant attention to Indigenous social movements – in Latin America and elsewhere – while engaged anthropology (Low and Merry 2010) still scuffles to find a foot as a form of public sharing or a collaborative practice in support of cultural activism and social justice. In my opinion this remains the case despite recent notable anthropological engagements with networked social movements for global justice and against corporate globalization (Juris 2004, 2008) and the materialization of militant anthropologies (Scherper-Hughes 1995; Juris 2007), protest anthropologies and direct action (Graeber 2009; Maskovsky 2013), activist anthropology (Hale 2006) and 'other anthropologies/anthropology otherwise' (Restrepo and Escobar 2005: 99).

Moreover, anthropology has not only been late in arriving at an engagement with social movements theory and practice; as John Postill (2008) has noted, its late arrival at the study of media and communication is yet again indicative of the discipline's lack of public impact in this field, especially in Latin America where there has been a fertile and established field of research in communication and media for social change since the 1970s (Gumucio-Dagron and Tufte 2006). Events since 2008 in Tunisia, Egypt, Iran, Chile and many other countries, in addition to the Occupy and the *indignados* movements, have compelled anthropologists and communication/media scholars alike 'with the protean phenomena variously termed alternative media, community media, citizens media, tactical media, social movement media, or still other sobriquets' (Downing 2014: 1545). However, unlike their anthropology counterparts, and despite noteworthy exceptions, media studies researchers have been far more active over the past decade and a half in generating a slew of work on social movement media, community media, citizens' media, and alternative media (Downing et al. 2001; Rodríguez 2001, 2011; Downing 2014).

Nonetheless, an important body of anthropological work has developed with a particular interest in studying the centrality of media in Indigenous peoples' cultural processes of self-representation and social movements more broadly, paying closer attention to media practices and circuits, rather than media content and audiences, whether globally (Ginsburg 2002; Wilson and Stewart 2008), or with a particular focus on Latin America (Wortham 2002, 2013; Salazar 2002, 2003, 2004, 2005, 2009, 2014; Schiwy 2003, 2009; Smith 2006; Himpele 2008; Salazar and Córdova 2008; Zamorano 2009; Córdova 2011, 2014; Zamorano and León 2012; Gleghorn 2013). In many ways this body of work situates media anthropology at the forefront of the discipline. However, media anthropology and communication research have yet to be able to capture the full intellectual and political impact of Indigenous video practices and social processes. In this way, Indigenous media has come to fill in a gap, growing as a novel knowledge practice from the fissures of the Latin American cultural and mediascapes to emerge as a force and a space of cultural production in its own right.

Decolonization of Anthropological Knowledge through Indigenous Media Practices

After almost thirty years of development, growing within the fissures of commercial and state mediaspheres, Indigenous video in Latin America – *video indígena* – continues to be framed today through a multiplicity of interrelated perspectives and voices: as a survival and fighting strategy in the creation and recreation of indigenous imaginaries (Sanjinés 2013; Córdova 2014); as a metaphor of Indigenous resistance (Rodríguez 2013); as a means by which indigenous organizations and mobilizations articulate new claims on national politics (Zamorano 2009); as a life project, an ideology, a political attitude (García 2013); as an appropriated and self-consciously resignified *postura* or political position, vital to indigenous struggles for self-determination (Wortham 2004: 366); as a political practice for articulating an activist imaginary (Salazar 2004 in reference to Marcus 1996; Ginsburg 2002); as a proposal for cultural seduction (Carelli 2013); or as an integral practice of 'cosmoexperience' (Champutiz 2013).

In this particular way, indigenous media is a defiant form of political activism. But the term itself also invokes a series of social relations that lie beyond a videotape, a television programme, a YouTube video or any other product of information and communication. It demands the consideration of a formal socio-technical assemblage of technologies, resources, social organizations, legal frameworks and bureaucracies, cultural principles, and imagery, into a representational and performative form embodied in processes that extend beyond the completed product. This is what Faye Ginsburg (1994) has called 'the embedded aesthetics' of indigenous media and what Amalia Córdova (2011) has recently translated as '*estéticas enraizadas*', where cultural products must be understood within the social and cultural systems in which they are produced, circulated and used.

Indigenous video production in Latin America continues to position itself as a distinct field of cultural production – a signifying practice separate from national cinemas, popular and community video, and tactical media practices. It inhabits its own representational space and it has started to create parallel circuits of production, dissemination and reception of cultural materials, which point towards what Ticona and Sanjinés call the 'end of the hegemony of the literate and the beginning of a decolonization of the intellect' (Ticona and Sanjinés 2004 in Salazar and Córdova 2008). This issue of decolonization is central. Maori educator Linda Tuhiwai Smith states the issue clearly when claiming that 'the struggle for the validity of indigenous knowledges may no longer be over the recognition that indigenous people have ways of knowing the world which are unique, but over proving the authenticity of, and control over, our own forms of knowledge' (Smith 1999: 104). Smith's model of an indigenous research agenda, imitating the waves of the Pacific Ocean, is a shift away from Western models of conducting research to include a social justice agenda, towards research subjects where the ultimate goal of research is positive transformation and development. In Smith's model, healing, mobilization, decolonization and transformation are necessary steps towards self-determination. Finding the strength to overcome injustice in order to mobilize the community for action might lead to decolonizing processes. Smith emphasizes in her explanation of this model that these steps are not to be seen as goals, but as processes 'which can be incorporated into practices and methodologies' (Smith 1999: 116).

As I have discussed elsewhere (Salazar 2004, 2007, 2009; Salazar and Córdova 2008), one way of tracing the genealogy of the contemporary Indigenous media landscape in the region, and the processes of decolonization they imply, is by looking at the development of the Coordinadora Latinoamericana de Cine y Comunicación de los Pueblos Indígenas (Latin American Council of Indigenous Film and Communication, or CLACPI). CLACPI has been critical in creating a discursive space for indigenous media in Latin America. Along the way, it has created new spaces of participation within national media discourses (production, circulation and reception). To date, CLACPI has organized eleven Indigenous film festivals and communication encounters, and the 30th anniversary with the XII International Festival held in Wallmapu (Chile) in late 2015.

Engaged Anthropologists and the Origins of CLACPI

A first phase of CLACPI took place between 1985 and 1992, when the initiative to establish a platform for thinking and making Indigenous media was primarily driven by engaged anthropologists and non-indigenous cultural and media activists advocating ways to strengthen the training, development, production and exposure of Indigenous film and video by, about and for Indigenous peoples.

The idea for a first festival emerged from Alejandro Camino, a Peruvian anthropologist who was then well known as an environmentalist and political activist (Bermúdez 2013: 22). During this first festival in Mexico, Claudia Menezes, a Brazilian anthropologist, then director of the Museo do Índio (Museum of the Indian) in Rio de Janeiro, proposed the formation of a platform to give continuity to the experience of the first festival, and this is how CLACPI emerged (ibid.: 23) as a response to gather the scattered but emerging audio-visual efforts (mainly film and video) in Latin America, with the aim of channelling the growing demands for more valid, vetted means of communication among – and emanating from, by and for – Indigenous communities.

The first CLACPI festival was swiftly organized in 1985 in Mexico City, primarily around a showcase of mostly non-Indigenous 16 mm films shot in the late 1970s and early 1980s by documentary and ethnographic film-makers and by engaged anthropologists and communication scholars interested in Indigenous politics. In this first festival, awards for excellence in cinematographic production went to films made by non-indigenous filmmakers about the plight of indigenous peoples.

It is important at this point to contextualize the setting at the time of CLACPI's creation. Latin America was scarred by severe economic crises sweeping a region already disturbed by political nationalism, right-wing military dictatorships, social inequality, and decades of cultural paternalism and misleading public policies towards Indigenous communities. Until the first years of the 1990s, Indigenous peoples were not constitutionally recognized in any Latin American country, and it has only been in the past two decades or less that some countries, including Argentina, Bolivia, Colombia, Mexico, Ecuador, Peru and Venezuela, have reformed their national constitutions to recognize the pluri-cultural nature of their societies. Other countries, such as Chile and Brazil, have legally recognized the existence of ethnic minorities, but not of Indigenous nations.

In this context, the second festival was held in Rio de Janeiro in 1987, coinciding with the public presentation of two groundbreaking processes of Indigenous video production founded some years earlier. One was a project with Kayapó people in the Brazilian Amazon, 'Mekaron Opoi D'joi' (The One Who Creates Images), initiated by Brazilian photographer/filmmaker Monica Frota with the assistance and vast documentation of U.S. anthropologist Terence Turner (Tuner 1992). The other is the ongoing project 'Video Nas Aldeias' (VNA, or Video in the Villages), headed by photographer Vincent Carelli and originating at the Centro de Trabalho Indigenista (CTI), a Sao Paulo-based non-Indigenous NGO that Carelli had helped to create after he had left the state-affiliated Fundação Nacional do Indio (FUNAI). As Carelli once recalled: 'It was not going to be the State that would change the situation of Indians, but they themselves who must take their destiny in their own hands ... We took part in the general movement of Brazilian civil society in search of alternatives' (Carelli 2004 in Córdova 2014). Although VNA began at the CTI, it is now an independent media centre where Indigenous organizations have today a more prominent involvement, though still under Carelli's direction (Salazar and Córdova 2008).

In 1989, in parallel to the organization of the third CLACPI festival in Venezuela, another exemplary occurrence took place when the Mexican

Instituto Nacional Indigenista (INI) implemented a historic Indigenous media training programme called the Transferencia de Medios Audio-visuales a Organizaciones y Comunidades Indígenas (Transference of Audiovisual Media to Indigenous Communities and Organizations). As part of this project, state-sponsored video centres called Centros de Video Indígena (CVIs) were established in four states of the country. These video centres were still coordinating much of Indigenous video production in Mexico twenty years later, but their influence and omnipresence has de-creased in recent years, giving way to Indigenous-owned or -coordinated video centres like Ojo de Agua Comunicación in Oaxaca. The CVIs are a good example nevertheless of the complex entanglement of Indigenous video and national politics across the region (Salazar and Córdova 2008; Córdova 2014). In relation to this, anthropologist Erica Wortham has demonstrated how the CVIs originated 'at the height of official plural-ism in Mexico' after 1987, whereby a 'government video program created in a transitional institutional setting colludes with the indigenous auton-omy movement – through the work and visions of individual video mak-ers and cultural activists – to produce a social form and process that has gained international recognition while confronting particular challenges in indigenous communities' (Wortham 2004: 363–64).

Despite the good intentions in place during the first three CLACPI fes-tivals, Indigenous organizations and media makers were still outsiders in the process of appropriating moving images with their own voices and perspectives. This tendency continued well into the early 1990s, with fes-tivals held rotationally in Brazil (1987), Venezuela (1989) and Peru (1992), following the inaugural format established in Mexico.

Ruptures within CLACPI

By 1992 a rupture between engaged anthropologists and indigenous me-dia activists was inevitable. I argue that a second stage could be loosely identified between 1992 and 2004 when, responding to generations of in-vading ethnographic, documentary and commercial film crews, Indige-nous communities began to take up the means of audio-visual production and to generate their own narratives and images of themselves. This is also a period of heightened debating and wrangling between Indigenous organizations across the continent about the processes for appropriating communication and media infrastructures and developing an indigenous approach to media making.

At the time, several Indigenous video makers in Mexico began forming the independently run Organización Mexicana de Videastas Indígenas

(OMVIAC) in an effort to create a national organization of Indigenous communicators. It eventually dispersed, leaving video makers to work with independent Indigenous media production centres or with the CVIs channelled through the Mexican state. In June of the same year, during the fourth CLACPI festival held in Cusco and Lima, the organization was restructured to encompass the demands of Indigenous producers for better access to audio-visual technology and for a voice in the processes of decision making, coordination and programming. This event marked an end to the first phase of CLACPI and inaugurated a second phase in which Indigenous organizations took the leadership of the network and the associated events. However the changes would crystallize in two different ways as Indigenous communities in Ecuador took a different route from CLACPI, founding the Abya Yala Network and organizing the Indigenous Abya Yala video festivals. Ecuador's federation of Indigenous nations, Confederación de Nacionalidades Indígenas del Ecuador (CONAIE), played a fundamental role in this process, organizing four Abya Yala video festivals and launching the Quito Declaration of 1994, a foundational document which asserted the right of Indigenous peoples to the creation and recreation of their own image.

Between CLACPI's fourth festival in Lima and Cusco in 1992 and the following event held in Santa Cruz, Bolivia in 1996, Indigenous groups in Bolivia began forging a national strategy for Indigenous video production. In his account of the emergence of Indigenous video in Bolivia in the late 1980s and early 1990s, Iván Sanjinés (2013) notes:

> *Queríamos romper con las miradas que se habían estado dando desde la antropología donde hay investigadores que llegan y ven una realidad, en el caso del cine se entregan cámaras, y se pone atención a cómo mira tal individuo o pueblo, cómo graba con la cámara, etc. pero al final tratado como un objeto, no como un sujeto y mucha veces no se piensa en como responder a requerimientos concretos desde una visión de procesos.*

Translation: We wanted to break with the anthropological gaze where researchers come and see reality, in some cases film cameras are delivered, and attention is paid to how such an individual or group sees the world, or how people use the camera, etc. but ultimately they always treated us as an object, not a subject, and many times did not think how to respond to specific requirements from a processual perspective.

The fifth festival in Bolivia was launched along with a consulted, long-term strategy of building a national plan for Indigenous media training and production, including international and regional workshops. This model marked the beginning of what we consider to be the paradigmatic experience: the Plan Nacional Indígena de Comunicación Audiovisual (PNICA or National Indigenous Audiovisual Communication Plan) in Bolivia and the formation of the Coordinadora Audiovisual Indígena-Originaria de Bolivia (CAIB or the Bolivian Indigenous-Aboriginal Audiovisual Council). The PNICA was implemented following a nationwide consultation, becoming an extensive nationwide media training and production initiative to support Indigenous self-representation, training Indigenous people from diverse nations and communities in video production. The PNICA is jointly coordinated by the media training centre, Centro de Formación y Realización Cinematográfica (CEFREC) and CAIB, which includes three of Bolivia's primary Indigenous organizations. Productions address community needs and overtly seek to counteract the effects of mass media on the communities. Themes range from journalistic reportage to traditional stories, told through short fictions, documentaries, news programmes for television, music videos, and video letters. The resulting work – though widely acknowledged and circulated at Indigenous film and video festivals both within Bolivia and elsewhere in Latin America – is not in distribution. Paradoxically, in La Paz, CEFREC houses the most extensive Indigenous video archive in Latin America, making it the main centralized media collection site of CLACPI (Salazar and Córdova 2008).

CLACPI as an International Network

The current structure of CLACPI was consolidated in the seventh festival held in Chile in 2004, a structure that has remained in place in subsequent festivals in Mexico 2006, Bolivia 2008, Ecuador 2010, Colombia 2012 and Chile 2015 under the leadership of Mapuche cultural activist and filmmaker Jeannette Paillan. This signposts a third phase that starts after 2004 when CLACPI has been consolidating itself as an international network whose impact has been fundamental in opening up a new 'associative political space' (Yashar 1998) – both discursive and performative – through which to represent and enact new imaginaries of ethnic citizenship, nation, a sense of identity, and a manifestation of dissent.

The last four CLACPI festivals have taken place amid great political turmoil in the countries where it has been held: in Chile in 2004 during the peak of the conflict between the State and the Mapuche; in Mexico in 2006 during a violent crackdown of the military police against teachers in Oaxaca; in Bolivia in 2008 and Ecuador in 2010 in the middle of periods of massive popular unrest; and in Colombia in 2012 against the backdrop of the ongoing killings and massacres of Indigenous leaders and farmers in diverse regions of the country.

As Bolivian communicator Iván Sanjinés contends, since Colombia 2012, CLACPI has become a space of intercultural encounter between indigenous and non-indigenous realities but with the view that it is possible to go about building a better world by dismantling the structures of injustice – both economic and social, on which they are based – and making visible the urgent glances clamouring that another world is possible. Most important, the forthcoming CLACPI festival in November 2015 in Chile will celebrate thirty years of CLACPI, in recognition that the Indigenous social movements emerging across Latin America have also been pivotal in forging a new front of public intervention allowing Indigenous cultural activists to 'shoot back' (Ginsburg 1999: 295) to dominant structures by way of 'reversing the colonial gaze' and by 'constructing their own visual media, telling their own stories on their own terms' (Prins 2004: 518).

Given the critical times we live in, anthropology – and any form of engaged knowledge production for that matter – has an ethical challenge to revise and rethink the terrain of the political and the social within which to make a meaningful contribution to public culture and transformative politics (Osterweil 2013). Consequently, the key challenge for an 'anthropology of social movements' cannot be to just 'document indigenous activism more fully than other observers can' (Warren and Jackson 2005: 3). This is what I find most interesting about Restrepo and Escobar's formulations of 'other anthropologies/anthropology otherwise', or the political potential of 'situated anthropologies' linked to new visions and forms of political action emerging from contemporary social movements. That is, the authors' suggestion that 'the space in which anthropology is practised is fractured where multiple and contradictory historical, social, cultural and political locatedness of the different communities of anthropologists and their anthropologies coexist' (Restrepo and Escobar 2005: 100).

From Land to Screen: A Collaboration towards 'Anthropologies Otherwise'

As this book attempts to show, a growing number of anthropologists are both expected to and inspired to ensure that their work engages with public issues and questions, and has some kind of 'impact' or influence beyond academia. In this last section of the chapter I reflect back on my own work carried out primarily between 2000 and 2010 but which is in many ways a continuing and enduring project of commitment to an ongoing process.

The seventh CLACPI festival was held in Santiago de Chile in June 2004 and coincided with the completion of my research project and Ph.D. dissertation titled *Imperfect Media: The Poetics of Indigenous Communication in Chile,* which included a 52-minute collaborative documentary film titled *De la Tierra a la Pantalla* (From Land To Screen), shot in Santiago, Temuco and the Alto Bio-Bio region in southern Chile. This premiered at the festival.

I had moved to Australia in 1998 at the beginning of a period of heightened tension between the Chilean state and the Mapuche organizations. The research project I conducted between 2000 and 2004 was in direct response to what had mistakenly been framed by the media and Chilean public sphere as 'the Mapuche Conflict'. The implications of framing a 'Mapuche' conflict is that only the actions by indigenous actors are to blame for the violence and social unrest in the south of the country and in Santiago, exculpating the other main actors with direct responsibility: the state and its policies, the corporate interests in the area, and the indifference and contempt from Chilean society in general.

In June 2001, I held the first meeting with Mapuche video maker Jeannette Paillan with the intention of co-producing a documentary film project on the Mapuche struggle for communication rights. Our first encounter, in a warm small flat on a cold downtown Santiago night, was brief and clear cut. Jeannette agreed in principle to be part of the project, and was very specific in terms of what was expected of it, as she had been involved in several projects by filmmakers and anthropologists – not all of them with positive outcomes.

The film is divided into three broad parts. In the first, the characters introduce how they see the Mapuche conflict, how it may be understood from a Mapuche perspective and how it has been criminalized in the media. The narrative is structured around a series of interviews with several Mapuche activists. The second part looks at the role of communication and information technologies in the Mapuche political agenda. The characters define what indigenous media is in the context of Mapuche cultural activism. The final part takes a closer and more intimate look at the work of Jeannette Paillan,[1] and the way she conceives and puts indigenous media into practice. In this sense, the film brings together different techniques and narratives, blurring the genres of conventional documentary, experimental video art and ethnographic film, all of which raise a possible fourth dimension to be considered – the issue of appropriation.

I never regarded the film as an ethnographic one in the strict sense of the genre. There was no scientific (anthropological) description of the Mapuche culture conducted within a pre-established theoretical framework. This is not to say that the video programme does not have anthropological value, as there was indeed prior involvement with the subjects involved. In this regard, the film is not merely a one-off involvement in another culture, so it is not a conventional documentary either, where a crew of outsiders working under the industrial constraints and conventions of documentary filmmaking come to a community, take the pictures and leave. The narrative style and audio-visual treatment is neither strictly ethnographic nor exactly a conventional documentary as it also takes some elements from video art aesthetics (Salazar 2004). At the end, I was more interested in 'doing visual ethnography' (Pink 2001) whereby I could stress the importance of using video for ethnographic research. Interviews are a key element in the telling of the story as a way of giving confronting testimonies and controversial opinions on the addressed topics. The main characters interviewed narrate the story and evoke their subjectivity as a window to their realities. I do want to stress though that the film required certain cultural knowledge, and the process of making it fell closer to what Pink (2001, 2004) calls 'applied visual ethnography'.

The film became a device for collaborative research. In the winter of 2002 we spent four weeks together in the Bio-Bio Region in southern Chile, a historical iconic place of Mapuche resistance where Jeannette Paillan was documenting the forced removal of Pehuenche families from their ancestral lands and their re-localization in government-sponsored farmlands. This area had seen highly controversial disputes between the government, Mapuche and pro-Mapuche groups, environmental NGOs and corporate interests, around the building of the Ralco Hydroelectric Plant, Chile's largest hydroelectric power plant, with the flooding of sacred land. The conflict subdued after compensations were paid, several Indigenous leaders endured periods of imprisonment, and the completion of the hydro-dam in 2004.

My ethnographic field site – and situated story about Jennette's work – was also her video documentary field site. In a very peculiar way, the two films became an interface of dialogue and collaboration, allowing a deeper form of engagement where, as knowledge devices, they made possible specific forms of intervention into and action on these practices for making culture visible – practices that are in themselves a process of strategic reversal, from where indigenous media makers are able to challenge long-standing cultural stereotypes, and create novel forms of healing historical disruptions in traditional knowledge, social memory and cultural identity.

The video was produced over a period of two years. During this period, a particular form of collaboration developed, which may also be considered as a distinctive form of authorship, associated in this case with the specific principles of authorship involved in new media works. Collaboration over a network, either in real time or not, has become a common pattern of social communication in the realm of new digital ICTs. In this particular case, collaboration was designed in two ways. We were working in 2003 before the advent of social networked media and cloud computing, so Jeannette and I were able to share and discuss aspects of the film by exchanging compressed low-resolution QuickTime files between Australia and Chile, whereby the production and post-production process rather became a question of 'negotiation'. The video design also incorporated the sampling of some of Jeannette's already produced work. In technical terms, sampling refers to the first step of the digitization process, whereby measurements are taken at a particular time and at regular intervals to create a digital (numerical data) version. Her visuals were not only used as archival footage to visualize the current process of indigenous mobilization in the south of Chile, but were sampled to illustrate the political situation of upheaval. After sampling different shots into discrete files, these become modular and variable, so I was able to remix and re-version them into new movies. By remixing clips from her previous works, and combining this with my own footage of activities and interviews, the process was pointing towards a different form of collaborative authorship and a way to look critically at issues of cultural appropriation involved in research.

To my knowledge this remains an innovative and exceptional case of collaborative engaged research in media anthropology and applied visual anthropology in Chile, which was designed as engaged research in the way it approached questions of methodology, principles and ethics as a broad platform for research practice (Kanngieser, Neilson and Rossiter 2014). As previously argued, the film-based research became a privileged site for frontally addressing contingent politics and creating a mutually defined project among research 'subjects'. This project was challenging precisely because it was an exploration in activist anthropological scholarship, where the research process was always open to contradiction, serendipity and reflexive critique. When the film was premiered at the seventh CLACPI festival, it was received with acclaim, and for many years indigenous activists used it as evidence of the Mapuche struggle for communication rights.

In hindsight – and from afar after sixteen years of not living in Chile – I think little has changed there since 2004 in regards to the *'cuestión* Mapuche' (Mapuche problem) and Indigenous rights in general. Chile was the last country in the Americas to sign Convention 169 of the International Labour Organization (ILO), but despite the strengthening of a structure of indigenous rights through the ratification of this convention, the efficacy of its application remains debatable at best. There has certainly been a fruition of the modern Indigenous discourse, which has had high public support in civil society but not in government. At the time of writing this chapter in late 2014, the Chilean Antiterrorist Law continues to be applied to deal with direct action, including numerous incidents like violent land occupations, the burning of private property and huge demonstrations across Santiago and the Araucanía region. Successive governments have failed to contemplate the expropriation of land in the southern region of Araucanía to restore lost ancestral territory to the Mapuche.

In Chile, where 1.5 million people identify as Mapuche (9 per cent of the total population of the country), there is no such thing as an indigenous cinema, and indigenous peoples remain utterly absent and invisible on mainstream media. Most relevant, while other Latin American countries have passed legislation to reform their communication and media sectors to include indigenous and community media, in Chile nothing has been achieved in this area. Anthropological research continues to be concerned with the Mapuche as objects of study. Anthropologists have a responsibility for this failure and a role to play in developing different modes of public engagement.

Conclusion

In a context of cultural and political effervescence surging across Latin America since the early 1990s, the fervent development of indigenous media has had an arrested development. It is a strong, yet often dispersed movement towards opening counter public spheres from where to contest the indifference and coercion of states, and the inefficacy of current legal and cultural policy frameworks to promote indigenous participation and autonomy.

Indigenous media in Latin America has not followed conventional production processes. Today it inhabits a wide range of platforms, including film festivals, international meetings on indigenous rights, academic conferences, local community meetings, and television broadcasts. Indigenous media constitutes a system of social relations and networking aimed at reaffirming communal social solidarities, where local conjunctures are increasingly strengthened and linked through transnational strategies and cross-cultural collaborations across national borders. In most cases, the endeavour for making culture visible becomes a process of strategic reversal, from where indigenous media makers are able to challenge long-standing cultural stereotypes, and create novel forms of healing historical disruptions in traditional knowledge, social memory and cultural identity.

What I have tried to show in this chapter is that the Indigenous media movement in Latin America is an example of how making videos or radio or television programmes is a critical form of 'doing' politics and enacting one's political subjectivities on a daily basis. There is little doubt that the Indigenous movements today are much more complex than in the past. Indigenous scholars worldwide have developed critical frameworks that not only condemn the historical and philosophical bases of Western research and forms of representation but have also contributed to the urgent need to decolonize research methodologies in setting agendas for planning, evaluating, criticizing and implementing public policies, including the media.

Indigenous media practices and circuits have also turned into a field of research and practice that has received coveted attention by anthropologists as an important cultural resource, a critical area of political activism, and a fertile field of theorization in studies of media and culture. In many cases though, indigenous media has also been critical in highlighting the inefficacy of public and engaged anthropologies to have a real impact in social change.

The key lesson to be learnt from the study of Indigenous media in Latin America is the understanding that the relationship between how we know and how we act is inseparable, and that both activist and academic practices are elements required for a transformative political practice. Anthropology has a momentous role to play in commentary and critique about the human and the more-than human processes of worlding emerging at the beginning of the twenty-first century. But the retrenchment in the realm of the theoretical and the textual that allowed cultural critique to stand alone as anthropology's contribution is not enough. I have borrowed Restrepo and Escobar's rubric of 'other anthropologies and anthropology otherwise': first, as a way of complicating, as they argue, 'the picture of a single tradition emanating from the West that defines anthropology as a modern form of expert knowledge'; and secondly, because I strongly disagree with often-prevalent views that privilege cultural critique over direct engagement as the form of activism that public anthropologists should undertake. Direct political engagement and critical analysis ought not necessarily to be separate undertakings (Speed 2008), and I would advocate anthropologists having a distinctive role to play in putting activist scholarship to work, as the efforts of many contemporary engaged anthropologists demonstrates. Latin American anthropologies have endeavoured, with different degrees of success, to address the politics of anthropological knowledge production and to decolonize the relationship between researcher and research subject through the research process itself. However the vast majority of anthropological work concerned with the centrality of communication and media in Indigenous social movements today remains locked in emphasizing the epistemology of textual critique over the ontology of performing engaged research as the fundamental form of ethnographic work.

Juan Francisco Salazar is a Chilean/Australian media anthropologist and video maker. He is an Associate Professor in communication and media studies at the University of Western Sydney, Australia, and is co-author (with H. Cohen and I. Barkat) of the book *Screen Media Arts: Introduction to Concepts and Practices,* 2009. His research and media work on Indigenous media in Chile and Latin America was pioneering in the field of engaged cultural research and is widely cited as an important work in understanding the cultural politics of Indigenous media practices in Latin America. He has produced several documentary and experimental short films that have been exhibited internationally. More recently he has developed an interest in environmental humanities and futures research and has conducted several years of ethnographic work in the Antarctic Peninsula which have lead to several publications and a feature length experimental documentary film titled *Nightfall on Gaia* (2015). He is an ongoing international coordinator of the OURMedia Network since 2004 and since 2012 is co-convenor of the Humanities and Social Sciences Expert Group (HASSEG) of the Scientific Committee for Antarctic Research (SCAR).

Notes

1. Jeannette Paillan's work has always revolved around the conflict between the Chilean state, the Mapuche nation and the corporate interests in the area. Her first film, the 27-minute documentary *Punalka: The Spirit of the Bio-Bio,* was shot in 1994 after two years working with Pehuenche communities in the Bio-Bio region, south of Santiago. It is however in her latest documentary, *Wallmapu,* that Paillan attempts to rethink Mapuche identity as a self-conscious contestation to official history. The film also works as a call to the visualization of a historically rooted national consciousness and attempts to simultaneously uncover both a Mapuche a counter-history and a counter-memory. *Wallmapu* is to date the strongest Mapuche televisual text to tangle video media as a space of negotiation within broader domains of difference within Chilean society. The notion of the Wallmapu becomes in Paillan's work a clear metaphor for locating a Mapuche identity, where the Mapuche struggle is consistently tied to the social solidarities in which it is grounded. The video not only documents and visualizes a history according to the Mapuche – or a certain sector within the Mapuche intelligentsia – but, more importantly, works as a (media/tion) practice of imagining a Mapuche nation, not just within the Chilean nation but also adjacent to it. *Wallmapu* is a text that therefore acts as a kind of 'televisual practice of location' (Wortham 2002), providing a sense of place rooted in a different imaginary; an 'activist imaginary' (Marcus 1996).

References

Bengoa, J. 2000. *La Emergencia Indígena en América Latina*. Santiago: Fondo de Cultura Económica.

———. 2009. '¿Una segunda etapa de la emergencia indígena en América Latina?', *Cuadernos De Antropología Social* 29: 7–22.

Bermúdez, B. 2013. 'CLACPI: Una historia que está pronta a cumplir 30 años de vida', *Revista Chilena De Antropologia Visual* 21: 20–31.

Carelli, V. 2013. 'Video nas Aldeias: una propuesta de seducción cultural', *Revista Chilena de Antropología Visual* 21: 51–63.

Champutiz, E. 2013. 'Productores audiovisuales indígenas de Ecuador: Una práctica integral de cosmovivencia', *Revista Chilena de Antropología Visual* 21: 118–36.

Córdova, A. 2011. 'Estéticas enraizadas: aproximaciones al video indígena en América Latina', *Comunicación y Medios* 24: 81–107.

———. 2014. 'Reenact, Reimagine: Performative Indigenous Documentaries of Bolivia and Brazil', in V. Navarro and J.C. Rodriguez (eds), *New Documentaries in Latin America*. New York: Palgrave Macmillan, pp. 123–44.

De la Peña, G. 1999. 'Territorio y ciudadanía étnica en la nación globalizada', *Desacatos: Revista De Antropología Social* 1 (Spring): 13–27.

Downing, J.D.H. 2014. 'Social Movements Media: Evaluating Fresh Perspectives', *International Journal of Communication* 8: 1544–51.

Downing, J.D.H, T. Villarreal Ford, G. Gil and L. Stein (eds). 2001. *Radical Media: Rebellious Communication and Social Movements*. London: Sage.

Edelman, M. 2001. 'Social Movements: Changing Paradigms and Forms of Politics', *Annual Review of Anthropology* 30: 285–317.

Escobar, A. 1992. 'Culture, Practice and Politics: Anthropology and the Study of Social Movements', *Critique of Anthropology* 12(4): 395–432.

Foucault, M. 1980. *Power/Knowledge*. Brighton: Harvester.

Fraser, N., and A. Honneth. 2003. *Redistribution or Recognition? A Political-Philosophical Exchange*. London: Verso.

García, J.J. 2013. 'El video indígena, un proyecto de vida, una ideología, una actitud política', *Revista Chilena de Antropología Visual* 21: 104–17.

Gibb, R. 'Toward an Anthropology of Social Movements', *Journal des anthropologues*, 85–86: 233–253.

Ginsburg, F. 1994. 'Embedded Aesthetics: Creating a Discursive Space for Indigenous Media', *Cultural Anthropology* 9(3): 365–82.

———. 1999. 'Shooting Back: From Ethnographic Film to Indigenous Production/Ethnography of Media', in T. Miller and R. Stam (eds), *A Companion to Film Theory*. Malden, MA: Blackwell, pp. 295–322.

———. 2002. 'Screen Memories: Resignifying the Traditional in Indigenous Media', in F. Ginsburg, L. Abu-Lughod and B. Larkin (eds), *Media Worlds: Anthropology on New Terrain*. Berkeley: University of California Press, pp. 39–57.

Ginsburg, F., and R. Rapp. 2013. 'Entangled Ethnography: Imagining a Future for Young Adults with Learning Disabilities', *Social Science & Medicine* 99: 187–93.

Gleghorn, C. 2013. 'Reconciliation en Minga: Indigenous Video and Social Justice in Colombia', *Journal of Latin American Cultural Studies* 22(2): 169–94.

Graeber, D. 2009. *Direct Action: An Ethnography*. Oakland, California: AK Press.

Gumucio-Dagron, A., and T. Tufte (eds). 2006. *Communication for Social Change Anthology: Historical and Contemporary Readings*. South Orange, NJ: Communication for Social Change Consortium.

Hale, C.R. 1997. 'Cultural Politics of Identity in Latin America', *Annual Review of Anthropology* 26: 567–90.

———. 2006. 'Activist Research v. Cultural Critique: Indigenous Land Rights and the Contradictions of Politically Engaged Anthropology', *Cultural Anthropology* 21(1): 96–120.

——— (ed.). 2008. *Engaging Contradictions: Theory, Politics, and Methods of Activist Scholarship*. Berkeley: University of California Press.

Himpele, J. 2008. *Circuits of Culture: Media, Politics, and Indigenous Identity in the Andes*. Minneapolis: University of Minnesota Press.

Juris, J. 2004. 'Networked Social Movements: Global Movements for Global Justice', in M. Castells (ed.), *The Network Society: A Cross-Cultural Perspective*. Cheltenham, UK: Edward Elgar, pp. 341–62.

———. 2007. 'Practicing Militant Ethnography with the Movement for Global Resistance in Barcelona', in S. Shukaitis and D. Graeber (eds), *Constituent Imagination: Militant Investigations, Collective Theorization*. Edinburgh: AK Press, pp. 164–78.

———. 2008. *Networking Futures: The Movements against Corporate Globalization*. Durham, NC: Duke University Press.

Kanngieser, A., B. Neilson and N. Rossiter. 2014. 'What is a Research Platform? Mapping Methods, Mobilities and Subjectivities', *Media, Culture & Society* 36(3): 302–18.

Low, S., and S. Merry. 2010. 'Engaged Anthropology: Diversity and Dilemmas', *Current Anthropology* 51: 201–26.

Marcus, G. 1996. 'Introduction', in G. Marcus (ed.), *Connected: Engagements with Media*. Late Editions, no. 3. Chicago: University of Chicago Press, pp. 1–18.

Maskovsky, J. 2013. 'Protest Anthropology in a Moment of Global Unrest', *American Anthropologist* 115: 126–29.

Neilson, B., and N. Rossiter. 2008. 'Precarity as a Political Concept, or, Fordism as Exception', *Theory, Culture & Society* 25(7/8): 51–72.

Osterweil, M. 2013. 'Rethinking Public Anthropology through Epistemic Politics and Theoretical Practice', *Cultural Anthropology* 28(4): 598–620.

Pink, S. 2001. *Doing Visual Ethnography: Images, Media and Representation in Research*. London: Sage.

———. 2004. 'Applied Visual Anthropology: Defining the Field', *Visual Anthropology Review* 20(1): 3–16.

Postill, J. 2009. 'What is the Point of Media Anthropology?', *Social Anthropology* 17(3): 334–37.

Prins, H. 2004. 'Visual Anthropology', in T. Biolsi (ed.), *A Companion to the Anthropology of American Indians*. Malden, MA: Blackwell

Restrepo, E., and A. Escobar. 2005. 'Other Anthropologies and Anthropology Otherwise', *Critique of Anthropology* 25(2): 99–129.

Rodríguez, C. 2001. *Fissures in the Mediascape*. Cresskill, NJ: Hampton Press.

———. 2011. *Citizens' Media against Armed Conflict: Disrupting Violence in Colombia*. Minneapolis: University of Minnesota Press.

Rodriguez, M. 2013. Hacia un cine indígena como metáfora de la memoria de un pueblo y de su resistencia, *Revista Chilena de Antropología Visual* 21: 64–79.

Salazar, J.F. 2002. 'Activismo indígena en América Latina: Estrategias para una construcción cultural de tecnologías de información y comunicación', *Journal of Iberian and Latin American Studies* 8(2): 61–79.

———. 2003. 'Articulating an Activist Imaginary: Internet as Counter Public Sphere in the Mapuche Movement in Chile', *Media Information Australia* 107: 19–29.

———. 2004. 'Imperfect Media: The Poetics of Indigenous Media in Chile'. Unpublished Ph.D. dissertation. University of Western Sydney, Australia.

———. 2005. 'Digitising Knowledge: Anthropology and New Practices of Digitextuality', *Media International Australia* 116: 64–74.

———. 2007. 'Indigenous Peoples and the Cultural Constructions of Information and Communication Technology in Latin America', in L.E. Dyson, M. Hendriks and S. Grant (eds), *Indigenous People and Information Technology*. Hershey, PA: Idea Book Publishing, pp. 14–26.

———. 2009. 'Self-determination in Practice: The Critical Making of Indigenous Media', *Development in Practice* 19(4/5): 504–13.

———. 2014. 'Prácticas de auto-representación y los dilemas de la auto-determinación: el cara y sello de los derechos a la comunicación Mapuche', in *Aproximaciones a la cuestión mapuche en Chile, una mirada desde la historia y las ciencias sociales*, ed. C. Barrientos. Santiago, Chile: RIL Editores, pp. 143–60.

Salazar, J.F., and A. Córdova. 2008. 'Imperfect Media: The Poetics of Indigenous Video in Latin America', in P. Wilson and M. Stewart (eds), *Global Indigenous Media: Cultures, Poetics, and Politics*. Raleigh, NC: Duke University Press, pp. 39–57.

Sanjinés, I. 2013. 'Usando el audiovisual como una estrategia de sobrevivencia y de lucha, de creación y recreación de un imaginario propio', *Revista Chilena de Antropología Visual* 21: 32–50.

Scheper-Hughes, N. 1995. 'The Primacy of the Ethical', *Current Anthropology* 36(3): 409–20.

Schiwy, F. 2003. 'Decolonizing the Frame: Indigenous Video in the Andes', *Framework* 44(1): 116–32.

———. 2009. *Indianizing Film: Decolonization, The Andes, and the Question of Technology*. New Brunswick, NJ: Rutgers.

Smith, L.C. 2006. 'Mobilizing Indigenous Video: The Mexican Case', *Journal of Latin American Geography* 5(1): 113–28.

Smith, L.T. 1999. *Decolonizing Methodologies: Research and Indigenous Peoples*. Dunedin, NZ: University of Otago Press.

Speed, S. 2008. 'Forged in Dialogue: Toward a Critically Engaged Activist Research', in C.R. Hale (ed.), *Engaging Contradictions: Theory, Politics, and Methods of Activist Scholarship*. Berkeley: University of California Press, pp. 213–36.

Stavenhagen, R. 1997. 'Las organizaciones indígenas: actores emergentes en América Latina', *Revista de la CEPAL* 62: 61–73.

Turner, T. 1992. 'Defiant Images: The Kayapo Appropriation of Video', *Anthropology Today* 8(6): 5–16.

Warren, K.B., and J.E. Jackson (eds). 2005. *Indigenous Movements, Self-Representation, and the State in Latin America*. Austin: University of Texas Press.

Wilson, P. and M. Stewart. 2008. *Global Indigenous Media: Culture, Poetics, and Politics*. Durham, NC: Duke University Press.

Wortham, E.C. 2002. *Narratives of Location: Televisual Media and the Production of Indigenous Identities in Mexico*. Unpublished doctoral thesis. New York University.

———. 2004. 'Between the State and Indigenous Autonomy: Unpacking Video Indígena in Mexico', *American Anthropologist* 106(2): 363–69.

———. 2013. *Indigenous Media in Mexico: Culture, Community, and the State*. Raleigh, NC: Duke University Press.

Yashar, D.J. 1998. 'Contesting Citizenship: Indigenous Movements and Democracy in Latin America', *Comparative Politics* 31(1): 23–42.

Zamorano, G. 2009. 'Reimagining Politics: Video and Indigenous Struggles in Contemporary Bolivia'. Ph.D. dissertation. City University of New York.

Zamorano, G., and C. León. 2012. 'Video indígena, un diálogo sobre temáticas y lenguajes diverso', *Chasqui: Revista Latinoamericana de Comunicación* 120: 19–22.

PART II

PUBLIC ANTHROPOLOGY AND SOCIAL MEDIA

Chapter 6

ANTHROPOLOGY BY THE WIRE

———— ✠ ————

Matthew Durington and Samuel Gerald Collins

The city is never a stable place. Spatially, the city shifts with development projects and new construction. Socially and politically, it shifts with the demographics of its population, and with the ways in which the city is represented. Media technologies constantly shift and expand as well. The seedy images of some cities in the United States, like Baltimore in Maryland, that proliferate on television programmes like *The Wire* (Simon 2002) are entirely different from the more positive representations that people hold of their neighbourhoods and communities. But these are more than differing opinions: 'representations' of the city have very real consequences – for funding, for politics, for development and, ultimately, for the survival of neighbourhoods. This chapter discusses a research project that has been conducted in Baltimore since 2011, which intersects media and public anthropology, reframing representations of Baltimore and its citizens from the television series *The Wire* through media technologies transmitted via a wire itself by a group of anthropologists and community members in the city.

'Anthropology by the Wire' is a multi-media research project on urban and visual anthropology in Baltimore; it is part of a National Science Foundation Research Experience for Undergraduates grant at Towson University. In this project, students conduct research on neighbourhoods in Baltimore, utilizing anthropological methods through the lens of a public anthropology with a variety of digital media. A sampling of chronological data in the form of videos, photos, audio, links and text are posted to a website (www.anthropologybythewire.com) in an attempt to reflexively detail the process of collaborative research with a variety of community groups and individuals in Baltimore City. There are pedagogical, research and theoretical goals in the project. We are attempting to retool pedagogy towards an applied ethos and to develop novel media-based research methods while expanding the theoretical boundaries of a public anthropology. To do this we train students in cutting-edge research and technologies, while simultaneously working in an applied fashion to create media of use to our collaborators. Parallel to these goals is the collection of data on various networks that create and utilize this media through social media analytics. In this chapter we detail the theoretical premise of the project and the research process for others who may be thinking of employing various technologies in their efforts to engage a public anthropology practice. Our premise and inspiration are creative commons and open source movements, so we hope that others will utilize our project and replicate it.

But we go further in detailing how anthropologists and others can think of these applied strategies to forward a body of scholarship and research from the outcomes of these endeavours, and perhaps retool or reconsider what we mean by a 'public anthropology'. Nearly twenty years old, public anthropology is a well-known part of anthropological practice and the subject of numerous articles and monographs (Checker 2009). Although widely discussed as a practice, the actual 'public' in public anthropology is rarely addressed, especially the fast-changing nature of that public due to new media technologies and the way research is disseminated and shared. Through a discussion of our ongoing participatory research in Baltimore, this chapter also forwards the establishment of a public as central to public anthropology and, conceptually, how that moves towards what we call a 'networked anthropology' (Collins and Durington 2014).

The utilization of media in anthropological research has often taken the form of supplementary visual teaching materials and the creation of ethnographic films to illustrate various cultural groups under the rubric of visual anthropology (Ruby 2000). In recent years, many anthropologists dissatisfied with this stasis have formulated two strains of direct research with media responding to the changing accessibility of visual technologies. One strain seeks to employ various media, including traditional audio and visual formats, in the process of ethnographic research while simultaneously studying media through an anthropological lens. The other strain is an applied visual anthropology centred on the engaged nature of anthropological work with media technologies (Pink 2007). Both are rapidly adopting and negotiating a slew of Web 2.0 technologies as well. While there is a precedent of applied ethnographic work within traditional anthropology (Erwin 2000), the notion of an applied visual anthropology continues to be explored and defined. It is hard to deny the impact that new media technologies such as the internet, consumer access video production and social media have in terms of fostering participation and the ability of anthropological research to be disseminated to the general public and create new iterations of a public anthropology. This chapter is part of a 'networked anthropology', which combines collaborative and engaged approaches with networked multimedia (Collins and Durington 2012).

Through 'Anthropology by the Wire', anthropologists, alongside students and in partnership with community residents, engage in collaborative, empirical research on people's representations of Baltimore City using a common set of qualitative research methodologies related to media anthropology (Collins and Durington 2011). The research experience produces two interrelated bodies of results: empirical observations on the multiple representations and practices of place in the city; and collaborative media projects designed to help residents of various neighbourhoods to disseminate their own versions of place both to each other and to other social actors in positions to help them, such as non-profit organizations, community organizers, city and state government. The project utilizes anthropological theory based on urban and visual approaches and organized through technology-enabled networks in order to produce data that are of use to participants as well as to the communities in which research is undertaken, thus producing a more contemporary and timely public anthropology.

Participants utilize a variety of technologies to facilitate a networked study of Baltimore, while at the same time forming alternative networks that link them to each other and to communities in potentially meaningful and long-lasting ways. Through collaboration, researchers and community members circumvent the often-commented on digital divide that exists among economically challenged communities who do not have access to certain technological platforms, and, hence, create alternative information channels beyond primary media (D'Costa 2012). Alternatively, our premise is that the digital divide, as once conceived, no longer exists in a world of accessible smartphones and other open technologies. Simultaneously, the information produced about the community and delivered through different media platforms provides a window into the lives of urban residents that is rarely seen in traditional media outlets that tend to exacerbate stereotypes about urban residents. Urban residents and those that live outside of these spaces are often trapped in a cycle of stereotypic and reifying representations of one another – a media-based engaged public anthropology has the potential to change this trend.

A Networked Anthropology

Google 'Baltimore' and a slew of representations will emerge. A scopic regime (Metz 1982) appears on YouTube with the keyword 'Baltimore' producing bonds and fissures between a myriad of media pieces interlinked through suggestion, hashtag or a number of other metadata. Continue to drill down into the search phrase and through music, sports highlights, protests and parody, and one will inevitably come to clips from shows like *The Corner* (Blown Deadline Productions 2000), *Homicide* (Attanasio 1993) and *The Wire* (Simon 2002). One clicks through suggested links to a vignette from *The Wire* to a scene that represents a somewhat problematic but common representation of Baltimore depicting violence and addiction, predominantly affecting a Black urban populous. The line between documentary, fiction and depiction blurs by the volume of media accessed by the user. Mash-ups with popular music and other imagery parallel these and are interspersed with more rearrangements further fracturing an attachment to the initial referent. Much of this digested media skirts fair use and probably violates copyright and redefines representation simultaneously (Aufderheide and Jaszi 2011) to create a media milieu of Baltimore never intended or envisioned by a community of individuals who are now unknowing collaborators. Following the same search word trajectory one can continue to link through multilayered informational cartography and drill down to research videos created between anthropology students and members of a South Baltimore community as part of an urban ethnographic research project called 'Anthropology by the Wire' (Collins and Durington 2011). A video of neighbourhood youth and student researchers dancing at an outdoor festival becomes part of a new representational regime heretofore unimagined and unintended.

All of these media, digested and linked by one Google or YouTube search, are now connected by an individual simply through the act of liking, sharing or commenting while browsing the internet, but not necessarily linked by authorship or participation to anything viewed. The individual is forever tied to the media accessed. If the individual browser is going through a username it makes them an instantly recognized collaborator, which extends and potentially problematizes conceptions of methods and ethics that are changing as rapidly as new mediascapes and technologies. Through social media analytics, the user can become part of a networked anthropology created through the viewing practice and the translation of that experience into connecting nodes. The anthropology students involved in the urban ethnographic research project intended to make a video with community members and post it on YouTube for the community to access and for others to watch. Their anthropology professors are prepared for the intended and unintended consequences of doing fieldwork with their students and community collaborators towards larger research goals. Yet, is anyone involved prepared for the tagging anthropology that has now been created (Collins and Durington 2013)?

This is part of a general shift from place-based relationships grounded in neighbourhoods to 'networks' – those complex media ecologies and information technologies that make up our world (Urry 2007). They also have the power to reshape the notion of a 'public' in 'public anthropology' for the twenty-first century. Networks are 'real' in that we can characterize them qualitatively and quantitatively, but they are also shifting, protean, temporary and chiasmic. Networks are the preferred form of social life and social interaction in an information technology-mediated world; and in a world still dominated by verticality, networked socialites represent possibilities for other kinds of realities – at once more participatory and more democratic (Collins 2008). At the same time, networks are not created equal, with neighbourhoods and residents (considered as nodes) effectively cut off from other, more powerful, networks joining the city to the world system – networks that produce dominant representations of people that they are powerless to contest (Castells 1997). For example, this fundamental inequality was tragically apparent in the Hurricane Katrina disaster in New Orleans, when middle-class residents were able to take advantage of far-flung networks in order to find places to stay and jobs outside of the city, while the city's poorer residents, with their more multiplex, localized networks grounded in neighbourhoods were unable to leave – or, leaving, were unable to mobilize social capital in their new surroundings (Procopio and Procopio 2007). Unravelling these issues means both following the networks of power from local neighbourhoods to institutions, governments, regions and transnational geographies, as well as making new connections.

In a networked anthropology, anthropologists are cognizant of all the perils of social media, while still recognizing the potentials for making anthropological work more relevant to communities and institutions invested in social media. In this methodology, ethnographers, interlocutors, community and audience are all networked together; the course of the research is really the elaboration of that social network. Ultimately, the goal is to transform relationships and to form new ones through this networked content and through community partnerships that might then be generative of new collaborative possibilities. These are the data that networked anthropology utilizes, but they are also the media that communities utilize to network their own future. What marks networked anthropology as a distinct (and yet still emergent) methodology is this multiplying decoupage of interested agents, connections, appropriations and re-appropriations.

For a younger generation engaged with social media, the world exists to be recorded, shared and distributed: Facebook, YouTube, Flickr, Twitter, Instagram and other social media are testament to this documentary zeitgeist. But we would argue that social media is, at least in part, suggestive of an anthropological instinct to collect data, and to engage in analysis and self-reflection vis-à-vis multiple collaborators and audiences. There has never been more interest in exploring the vicissitudes of everyday life than today – social media has meant an explosion of media exploring ultimately anthropological questions. How do we live? How do we interact? How do we utilize space? How do we perform identity? What we are developing as a 'networked anthropology' suggests just that: the utilization of various technologies and social media to record and reflect on contemporary society and culture. These questions and tensions inform our media-based public anthropology research.

Anthropology by the Wire

'Anthropology by the Wire' has at least three meanings. Our internet presence through our website – www.anthropologybythewire.com – presents all of these through an archival progression of text and image (Greenspan 2012). First, we are creating representations of Baltimore that run alongside the predominant lens through which the city of Baltimore is primarily viewed, arguably one of the best shows ever created in *The Wire*. This landmark television show has become a touchstone for social science explorations in a variety of texts and curriculum over the last several years (Beilenson and McGuire 2012). We seek to present another way for Baltimore City and its residents to be understood through the production of collaborative ethnographic media with community residents. Second, we are conducting this public anthropology literally through 'the wire' via digital media in a number of different forms, including video, photography and social media. Third, the 'wire' connotes the skein of networked connections between people in the city – connections that re-order the physical geography of the city while still confirming the salience of place. Accordingly, the proposed project is organized along the lines of participatory action research through a networked multimedia. Participatory action research goes by many names (e.g. public anthropology), but what they all have in common is the desire to work with communities towards research with 'real-world' implications for people's lives (Greenwood and Levin 1998). For our project, 'action research', however defined, builds a bridge between the places where anthropologists live and the research they do; action research can be a powerful argument for the relevance of empirical research to everyday life, as anthropologists, students and community members begin an intensive research programme. The ethos of action research undergirds the research programme that results in a set of collaborative media and a new networked anthropology.

The research programme we have developed creates research teams of three to five students who begin with introductions to ethnographic research methods, ethics (when they will prepare applications for human subjects review) and the City of Baltimore. Site research begins with walks through Baltimore's neighbourhoods, mapping and photography, followed by photo and map elicitation-aided interviews with each other, both as an introduction to research methodologies as well as to develop an idea of representations of the city held by students who most likely live outside of the neighbourhood (Harper 2002; Kedia and van Willigan 2005). Students compare their own images and impressions of the city to the often negative portrayals of urban Baltimore in mass media, including local news coverage and television programmes lauded for their so-called realistic portrayals of urban Baltimore, like *The Wire*.

Next, students begin to explore parts of the city based on specific field sites structured in advance by the authors and co-principal investigators. During the pilot of this programme in the summer of 2011, students were placed at three sites in South and West Baltimore: the neighbourhood of Sharp-Leadenhall, historically significant urban squares in Southwest Baltimore, and a new Farmers' Market in West Baltimore. In the second iteration of the project in 2012, students continued work in the neighbourhood of Sharp-Leadenhall and expanded collaborative projects with interlocutors in a variety of other settings. This work has continued in 2013 and 2014. Students engage in archival work in the sociohistorical backgrounds of Baltimore neighbourhoods. Then, with the help of members of the community acting as consultants, students survey the neighbourhood using structured, timed observations of population and behaviours combined with photographed resource surveys of businesses, schools and public areas (Low 2000; Taplin, Scheld and Low 2002). In addition, students engage in participant observation of public events in the neighbourhood, including public meetings and festivals.

The next stage involves 'transect walks' of the neighbourhood with members of the community, who explain the relevance of place, and lead students on a 'tour' of their daily round in the neighbourhood (Taplin, Scheld and Low 2002). In combination with these, students engage community members in unstructured interviews guided by photo elicitation and critical reflection from the community on media representations. Through preliminary analysis of ethnographic data, students then contrast these visions of urban Baltimore as a 'place' to both their initial impressions and to mass media portrayals. Finally, students garner consent and engage in structured interviews and focus groups with people in the community in order to assess community needs with regards to self-representation of their neighbourhood, and begin to edit together media projects documenting the neighbourhood from the perspective of residents using audio recordings, maps, photographs and video obtained from previous stages of research. These project outcomes are then posted to the collective research website alongside reflexive contextual materials posted throughout the entire research process.

Media projects combine text, audio and visual data to present the neighbourhood as a dynamic, multifaceted 'place' intimately linked to the lives and aspirations of its denizens. The media are then released to communities to be utilized in a variety of ways. But these are also data for anthropological research. Accordingly, students engage in transcription and preliminary content analysis of interview data and narratives, utilizing open-source qualitative analysis software like Weft QDA or commercial packages like Transana, to do coding and analysis using a 'grounded theory' approach (Woods and Dempster 2011). Finally, students present their preliminary data and accompanying media projects to each other and to community consultants for critical feedback, leading recursively back upon networks to form new media in the space of this critical reflection. Further networks are established through the research website by those who view it and share it on other social networks. NodelXL analytics allow us to map these networks as they are formed. Particular emphasis is placed on integrating data gathered from different media; indeed, this is the hallmark of the networked anthropology we have been developing.

Products from this work serve a number of purposes. Media produced between students and local community collaborators is disseminated to surrounding residents, stakeholders, developers, tourists, and political entities that are assisted by further context on various communities. And through this research, participants ultimately gain a stronger grasp of the global networks that transect local communities. In the case of Sharp-Leadenhall, our main fieldwork site, a primary thrust is to contradict a slew of imagery that has shaped an aberrant perception of this community and its residents over time.

Sharp-Leadenhall

Since its first settlement, the people and institutions of Sharp-Leadenhall have played a pivotal role in the history of African Americans in Baltimore. As many free Blacks settled in the community, it became a centre for the anti-slavery movement with the founding of the Baltimore Abolitionist Society. This later became the African Academy of Baltimore, one of the first schools for free Blacks in the United States. Despite this rich history, the last several decades have seen Sharp-Leadenhall under siege from socioeconomic and political forces, which have diminished its size, population and sense of cohesion and purpose. Since the Second World War, this historic community has borne the brunt of urban renewal, highway planning, real estate expansion and sport stadium construction. Ethnographic research initiated in 2006, which foregrounds the Anthropology by the Wire project, examines the cultural context of community residents, surrounding stakeholders and institutions concerning these phenomena (Durington et al. 2009). The research is participatory and collaborators in the community are continually 'talking back' (Hooks 1989) through a variety of mediums. This collaborative ethos informs academic outputs, including articles and videos, that are continually produced as the project continues to grow and diversify through Anthropology by the Wire.

In the summer of 2006, at the genesis of the collaboration that would inform Anthropology by the Wire five years later, researchers met with several community leaders who make up the board of the Sharp-Leadenhall Planning Committee in Baltimore. This committee is a non-profit organization that is involved in issues of equitable housing and other neighbourhood concerns. In 2006 property values had been increasing exponentially over the previous five years. Sharp-Leadenhall had become a 'hot neighbourhood' on developer and real estate agent speculative maps. The committee's efforts focused on retaining the actual make-up and citizenry of a community undergoing rapid gentrification in the latent era of gentrification prior to the 2008 housing collapse in the United States. They agreed that one of the ways to embolden the neighbourhood and inform social policy was to highlight the area's unique history. The committee worked strategically to include the neighbourhood on a proposed Heritage Walk being developed by the City of Baltimore. Historical narratives collected during research by both traditional ethnographic field notes and videography would also inform the narratives for an entrepreneurial endeavour by the committee to create a walking tour for this new recognition of the community.

Primary fieldwork has focused on documenting the history of the neighbourhood through the collection of life histories of remaining and recently displaced residents as well. Archival research produced a number of sources, photos and other materials documenting the historical and current conditions of the community. A strong emphasis has also been placed on the capacity of research and academic outputs to provide resources to the community being studied. During the initial research and since, we have collected statistical data, engaged participant observation in a variety of settings in the community, and conducted interviews with new residents, developers, politicians and a variety of other actors. On the recommendation of our collaborators, a major impetus for research has been placed on the creation of a historical archive of press clippings, planning documents, photographs and other materials alongside the collection of videotaped life-history interviews with current and former residents. While many interviews may be compiled and edited into various media-based research outcomes, the longer unedited interviews are turned over to the Sharp-Leadenhall Planning Committee for archival purposes.

In subsequent iterations of research design between 2008 and 2010, students working with professors in Sharp-Leadenhall were encouraged to volunteer for events in the community, including the creation of a concession operation for Sunday home games for the Baltimore Ravens, a National Football League franchise. The intent here is to push out illegal vending operations attached to tailgating for the games from Sharp-Leadenhall. Students combine service learning experiences with traditional research for the completion of assignments in a variety of courses taught by the authors. As part of the fieldwork methodology, it has been a paramount concern to enlist constant feedback from the community. A continuous dialogue occurs at monthly strategy meetings and through frequent informal discussions as ethnographic documentary videos are created.

Short ethnographic documentary videos with community collaborators provide historical social mapping of the community as well. These videos utilize students in sound, shooting and other production capacities. Each video includes interviews at historical landmarks in the community, including a Baptist church, a park named after a former resident of the neighbourhood, and two abandoned storefronts that serve as evidence of a past local entrepreneurial economy, to name a few. Community collaborators choose additional sites that have symbolic meaning and that thus define Sharp-Leadenhall as a place. This has led to a number of research epiphanies and the documentation of deep historical ties to the community for displaced residents particularly. One collaborator has been able to trace back his paternal and maternal history within the community for over a hundred years, including the house he was born in, through the research process.

Active members of the Sharp-Leadenhall Planning Committee have assisted with interview contacts and helped to create volunteer opportunities such as tutoring neighbourhood youth by university students. Local business owners give interviews and assist in volunteer efforts. The local Baptist and AME churches assist in the historical archive process by fostering communication with elderly residents who have moved out of the community, and with younger families who return for church services on Sundays but are currently living in outlying counties of Baltimore. Lastly, the idea to create a web presence for the Sharp-Leadenhall committee was agreed on to assist in communicating with community members who have left, and to counter negative representations of the community. Web domains have been purchased and there are ongoing efforts towards helping the community organization to develop these. As research progresses, photo elicitation projects and the collection of oral histories has continued to gauge sentiments concerning encroaching development. Much of this fieldwork has demonstrated that new development often equates with displacement, and emboldens a belief that racial and class divisions in the city are being reinforced rather than dissipated in the twenty-first century. Much of this has to do with the perception of urban areas as lacking green space and not being clean, with all the concomitant stereotypes. A central project in Anthropology by the Wire confronts this representation and perception directly.

The residents of Sharp-Leadenhall are negotiating a cultural identity that relies on historical residency while confronting forces of displacement driven by both economic and symbolic forces through processes like gentrification. These housing pressures compound employment issues as a spiking unemployment rate among residents is exacerbated by a scarcity of resources in the neoliberal economy. One of the primary needs articulated by research collaborators in the community has been to document the historical and contemporary contributions of its citizens towards urban sustainability within the community, and throughout Baltimore. This need is articulated alongside a desire to confront stereotypic images of urban residents through popular culture representations. Establishing local history through research while simultaneously creating positive media about the community is the primary thrust of collaborative work, with a particular focus on creating representations of family life and housing to confront the recent effects of gentrification on the community, and to show other ways the community is sustainable.

The local organizations that we continue to work with – the Sharp-Leadenhall Planning Committee, a new non-profit organization called the South Baltimore Partnership, and the Ebenezer AME church – have all suffered through and are attempting to confront forces of urban renewal and displacement. Historical processes that have decreased the standing of the community are present in the socioeconomic and housing conditions that plague the community to this day. They are caught in a wake of deindustrialization and revitalization that may benefit commercial components of the City of Baltimore, but do not necessarily impact local communities such as Sharp-Leadenhall, particularly those in the shadow of the Inner Harbor.

As Harvey further describes, 'The "armpit of the east" had been the out-of-town image of Baltimore in the 1960s. But by transforming the entertainment spectacle into a permanent image, it became possible to use it to lure in developer capital, financial services, and entertainment industries, all big growth sectors in the US economy during the 1970s and 1980s' (Harvey 2001 139). These new growth sectors, such as the Inner Harbor, did not benefit the original urban residents who lived in the shadows of these new developments and who served as a constant reminder of Baltimore's recent disenfranchised past. The efforts of developers and city leaders did not include these residents. In fact, these developments could be described as something much more nefarious than simple free-market practices.

In 2015 Baltimore finds a considerable amount of its housing stock over leveraged and underwater through deleterious financing on the edge of a slow national economic recovery. As is the case with many other cities in the United States such as Philadelphia (Maskovsky 2006), Baltimore has systematically denied African-American neighbourhoods of capital, and removed much of the authority that residents may have once had to define their own communities. These are only exacerbated in a global economic recession. In response to these processes, grass-roots community organizations and activists have worked to keep their communities intact. The intention of Anthropology by the Wire is to assist these efforts through collaborative media projects that create more realistic and positive representations of Baltimore, and of Sharp-Leadenhall specifically.

The Clean and Green Team, and the New Nature of Networked Collaboration

One of the other tangential collaborative efforts that has occurred between researchers and members of the community is to locate and assist with the acquisition of grants to assist a variety of efforts. In the spring of 2011 it was announced that Baltimore would hold its first Grand Prix Racing event in close proximity to Sharp-Leadenhall. A grant was procured by the president of the Sharp-Leadenhall Planning Committee, who serves as the 'centrewoman' of the community, to help to 'spruce up the place' for tourists. Alongside this grant was a YouthWorks project that sought to provide summer funding to employ youth in different communities throughout the city to assist in 'clean and green' efforts such as gardening and other agriculture-related schemes. This was to compensate for an increasing closure rate of youth recreational centres throughout the city and a general lack of resources and employment opportunities for urban youth.

Around this same time, funding was given to support Anthropology by the Wire through the National Science Foundation, and the decision was made to work collaboratively with the Sharp-Leadenhall Planning Committee to create a documentary of the youth who would be hired as the 'Clean and Green Team' of Sharp-Leadenhall in the summer of 2011. Student researchers went through a series of seminars, walking tours and dialogue with community members for an ethnographic orientation. Local teenagers were introduced to student researchers and a theme for the video was agreed; videotaping then took place over a series of weeks, edits were discussed and a short ethnographic documentary was eventually produced. Each of these stages of production was guided by an ethos of participatory research and shared anthropology to create a mutually beneficial outcome. The final product has production value, presents urban Baltimore and its youth in a positive way, and becomes an alternative representation of the city; the community now has a new video to promote their identity and to assist with fundraising. For us, the media gives us insights into the way Baltimore youth experience questions of social class, race and gentrification in their lives – how they make sense of the city as a growth machine. For our student ethnographers, they have had the experience of both undertaking fieldwork and media production. For the community, they have been able to leverage the video for subsequent funding of the project in 2012 - 2015, offering a tangible result of our collaborative efforts.

Now that the video is posted on the Anthropology by the Wire website, all parties who have viewed the video analytically or who show it off to grandparents form a networked anthropology. This networked anthropology is created by both viewing practices and through the metadata attached to the videopost. A YouTube network shows the central connections the video has with high density and high centrality vis-à-vis other videos with 'Sharp-Leadenhall' as a keyword or tag. The network and collaborative process expands as the audience grows from actual participants to random individuals online searching for 'Baltimore' on YouTube – the same process as described at the beginning of this chapter in an ever-expanding networked anthropology. The question becomes how this is negotiated in terms of a reframing of the nature of collaboration, and the ethical consequences of these connections made in digital mediums.

Conclusion

Through Anthropology by the Wire we seek to provide an alternative format, content and delivery mechanism for the history and current issues facing Baltimore residents by collaborating with local residents in the production of research and media about their community and the surrounding Baltimore region. The ultimate goal of the project is to utilize digital technologies to discuss urban life, identity and representation in such a way that both interrogates the racial politics of place and that outlines new possibilities for cooperation between academic institutions and urban neighbourhoods involving civic education and resource sharing.

In anthropology, we are able to imagine metaphorical connections between different entities and then ground them in ethnographic detail. We are used to critiquing the interpretive violence levelled against the city and then seeking grounded explanations by those individuals affected by it, both in a material and a symbolic fashion. On the one hand, there are the powerful stereotypes of the urban inscribed by popular culture that are utilized to pathologize the poor: the city as dangerous, as sexualized, as non-White. On the other, there are discourses and representations that allow for expeditious capital expropriation: the city as the site of redevelopment, investment, and phantasmagorias of capital (Sassen 1996; Harvey 2001). Both of these 'top–down' representations have together wreaked havoc on the texture of neighbourhoods in Baltimore over the last sixty years through the guise of urban renewal and other social engineering, transforming some working-class neighbourhoods into pathologized ghettos, and others into gentrified 'rejuvenated' zones for a capital investment premised on the absence of that neighbourhood's residents.

But these are not the only representations being proffered by Baltimore residents. People variously seek to exert control over the way they are seen by the outside world as well as each other. They may work to record their histories, to build solidarity with each other, to sponsor festivals and cultural events, to make their voices heard in city council meetings, to challenge zoning, to demand more city services, to protest, and to form affinities with like-minded groups across the city, the nation, the world. Whatever the case, the stakes here are high, with the very existence of neighbourhoods, communities and the city itself hinging on the ability of its inhabitants to demonstrate its worth to the world of power and capital outside it. These different interpretative frames bring together individual agency and institutions in powerful ways, denying some the ability to interpret their own lives, while others are able to author the city to their liking. Further complicating our understanding, the different discourses on the city are not neatly divisible into 'top–down' and 'bottom–up'; they overlap in significant ways, with different groups appropriating the language of other groups for their own purposes in a kind of heteroglossia inflected by the realities of political economy. One person's community activism can become a way of commodifying the city in new ways; conversely, people try to develop coherent senses of self using images derived from media spectacle.

The goal of Anthropology by the Wire is to introduce students to a series of overlapping methodologies commonly used in qualitative research in order to gain an understanding of Baltimore as a contested space. The project takes participants into this swirling vortex of conflicting and contradictory interpretations with the intent of stimulating critical thought about the processes of representation and self-representation in order to suggest new directions for research as well as new ways of incorporating the city into academic speculation, and to expand a notion of public anthropology towards a networked anthropology. In fact, the research project itself – in particular, its focus on self-produced, new media – is a template for the development of a new type of applied visual anthropology, as interrelated techniques lead simultaneously to both data and collaborative projects. Perhaps this can contribute to a continued engaged notion of media-based anthropology practice. The methods are designed to build upon each other, to repeat and to be utilized by other social scientists through a creative common ethos. Collaborative research, with all the pitfalls therein, develops and represents the city as a site of contested representation and identification, with the production of knowledge to help denizens of Baltimore's neighbourhoods to support their own self-representations. Check the website after you read this and see where we are today, and perhaps the reader will become a part of this networked anthropology.

Matthew Durington is an associate professor of anthropology at Towson University in Baltimore, MD. A visual and urban anthropologist, his research includes work on suburban teenage heroin phenomena in the United States, and housing and racial identity in South Africa. Recent work through the project Anthropology by the Wire focuses on socioeconomic issues in Baltimore. Together with collaborator Sam Collins, he has recently published the book *Networked Anthropology* (2014), and is designing mobile apps and games for curricula.

Samuel Gerald Collins is an anthropologist at Towson University in Baltimore, MD. His present work examines the urban as the confluence of people and social media. He is the author of various books, book chapters and articles, among them *All Tomorrow's Cultures: Anthropological Engage-*

ments with the Future (2008), *Library of Walls: The Library of Congress and the Contradictions of Information Society* (2009) and, with co-author Matthew Durington, *Networked Anthropology* (2014).

Acknowledgments

This material is based on work supported by the National Science Foundation under Grant No. 1062843. Any opinions, findings, conclusions or recommendations expressed are those of the author(s) and do not necessarily reflect the views of the National Science Foundation.

References

'Anthropology by the Wire', *Tagging Anthropology*. Retrieved 10 October 2012 from http://anthropologybythewire.com/post/27337664018/tagging-anthropology

Attanasio, P. (creator). 1993. *Homicide: Life on the Streets*. New York: National Broadcasting Corporation.

Aufderheide, P., and P. Jaszi. 2011. *Reclaiming Fair Use: How to Put Balance Back in Copyright*. Chicago: University of Chicago Press.

Beilenson, P., and P. McGuire. 2012. *Tapping Into The Wire: The Real Urban Crisis*. Baltimore, MD: Johns Hopkins University Press.

Blown Deadline Productions. 2000. *The Corner*. New York: Home Box Office.

Brodkin, K. 1998. *How Jews Became White Folks: And What That Says About Race in America*. New Brunswick, NJ: Rutgers University Press.

Castells, M. 1997. *The Power of Identity*. New York: Oxford University Press.

Checker, Melissa. 2009. 'Anthropology in the Public Sphere, 2008', *American Anthropologist* 111(2): 162–69.

Collins, S.C. 2006. 'If I'm Not in Control, Then Who Is?: The Politics of Emergence in Multi-agent Systems', in *An Imitation-Based Approach to Modeling Homogenous Agents Societies*, ed. G. Trahkovski. Hershey, PA: IDEA Publishing, pp. 93–114.

———. 2008. *All Tomorrow's Cultures*. New York: Berghahn Books.

Collins, S., and M. Durington. 2011. *Anthropology by the Wire*. National Science Foundation Research Experience for Undergraduates Grant Project 1156767, www.anthropologybythewire.com

———. 2012. 'Coming to Terms with Networked Anthropology', *Anthropology News*. Retrieved 6 April 2012 from www.anthropology-news.org/index.php/2012/05/01/coming-to-terms-with-networked-anthropology/

———. 2013 'Tagging Culture: Building a Public Anthropology Through Social Media', *Human Organization* 72(4): 358–368.

———. 2014 *Networked Anthropology: A Primer for Ethnographers*. Londong: Routledge.

D'Costa, K. 2012. 'The Diminishing Digital Divide', *Scientific American*. Retrieved 7 May 2012 from http://blogs.scientificamerican.com/anthropology-in-practice/2012/04/30/the-diminishing-digital-divide/.

Durington, M., S. Gass, C. Maddox, A. Ruhf and J. Schwermer. 2009. 'Civic Engagement and Gentrification Issues in Metropolitan Baltimore', *Metropolitan Universities Journal* (20)1: 101–14.

Erwin, A. 2000. *Applied Anthropology: Tools and Perspectives for Contemporary Practice*. Needham Heights, MA: Allyn and Bacon.

Greenspan, E. 2012. 'A Review of Towson University's Anthropology by the Wire Course and anthropologybythewire.com', *American Anthropologist* (114)2: 357–58.

Greenwood, D., and M. Levin. 1998. *Introduction to Action Research*. Thousand Oaks, CA: Sage.

Harper, D. 2002. 'Talking About Pictures: A Case for Photo Elicitation', *Visual Studies* (17)1: 13–26.

Harvey, D. 2001. *Spaces of Capital: Toward a Critical Geography*. New York: Routledge.

Hooks, B. 1989. *Talking Back: Thinking Feminist, Thinking Black*. Cambridge, MA: South End Press.

Kedia, S., and J. van Willigen. 2005. *Applied Anthropology: Domains of Application*. Westport, CT: Praeger.

Levine, S. 2003. 'Documentary Film and HIV/AIDS: New Directions for Applied Visual Anthropology in Southern Africa', *Visual Anthropology Review* 19(1/2): 57–72.

Low, S. 2000. *On the Plaza*. Austin: University of Texas Press.

Maskovsky, J. 2006. 'Governing the "New Hometowns": Race, Power, and Neighborhood Participation in the New Inner City', *Identities: Global Studies in Culture and Power* (13): 73–99.

Metz, C. 1982. *The Imaginary Signifier: Psychoanalysis and the Cinema*. Bloomington: Indiana University Press.

Pink, S. 2007. *Visual Interventions*. New York: Berghahn Books.

Procopio, C., and S.T. Procopio. 2007. 'Do You Know What It Means to Miss New Orleans? Internet Communication, Geographic Community, and Social Capital in Crisis', *Journal of Applied Communication Research* 35(1): 67–87.

Ruby, J. 2000. *Picturing Culture: Explorations of Film and Anthropology*. Chicago: University of Chicago Press.

Sassen, S. 1996. 'Whose City Is It? Globalization and the Formation of New Claims', *Public Culture* (8): 205–23.

Simon, D. (executive producer). 2002–2008. *The Wire* (television series). New York: Home Box Office.

Taplin, D.H., S. Scheld and S. Low. 2002. 'Rapid Ethnographic Assessment in Urban Parks', *Human Organization* 61(1): 80–93.

Urry, J. 2007. *Mobilities*. Malden, MA: Polity Press.

Williams, B. 1988. *Upscaling Downtown: Stalled Gentrification in Washington, D.C.* Ithaca, NY: Cornell University Press.

Willigen, J. van. 1986. *Applied Anthropology: An Introduction*. South Hadley, MA: Bergin & Garvey Publications.

Chapter 7

PUBLIC ANTHROPOLOGY IN TIMES OF MEDIA HYBRIDITY AND GLOBAL UPHEAVAL

───────── ❦ ─────────

John Postill

Like other professionals, anthropologists work in a public environment that has undergone profound technological changes over the past ten years. New forms of publicness have arisen out of three converging global trends, namely the rise of 'viral media' such as Facebook, YouTube and Twitter, the mainstreaming of 'nerd politics' epitomized by Wikileaks and Anonymous, and the digitization of public spaces. I will now consider each of these trends in turn.

First, with the proliferation of new social and mobile media around the world, millions of citizens now have in their hands the ability to decide how and with whom to 'share' digital information and commentary (Postill, 2014). There is nothing new, of course, about forwarding messages through electronic means. What is novel is the sheer scale, routinization and sophistication of the new culture of 'sharism' (Mao 2008), with the ubiquitous 'Likes' and 'tweets' of social media indexing the shift. If ten or twenty years ago internet users could readily forward emails with hyperlinks to their contacts, today the very architectures and business models of social media and smartphones are built on 'sharing' digital contents. While early cyberspace scholars announced the coming of an age of 'virtual reality' (Turkle 1984), what we have seen over the past five years is rather the rise of what I call 'viral reality', or the accelerated co-production of news and opinion by media professionals and amateurs through social and mobile (or 'viral') media (Postill, 2014). This is a flattened informational terrain that the mainstream media must now share with alternative media outlets and millions of digitally savvy citizens. While the mainstream media have retained the ability to set the day-to-day current affairs agenda (Chadwick 2011), they must also contend with the ability of ordinary citizens not only to reach the scene of a media event before reporters, but also with their new power to 'Like' a potentially viral item of news or opinion (Shirky 2008). The study of virality is still in its infancy, but given the participatory nature of their research, anthropologists can play an important part in its development (Postill 2012).

A second shift currently underway is the mainstreaming of 'nerd politics' (*pace* Doctorow 2012), epitomized by formations such as Wikileaks, Anonymous, Spain's Indignados and the global Occupy movement. This is a novel phenomenon whereby geeks, hackers, bloggers, copyleft lawyers and other 'information activists' (Brooke 2011) have learned to take their once niche internet struggles to the heart of the political process by linking them to broader popular demands. A spectacular instance of this trend was the release in November 2010 by Wikileaks via mainstream news media organizations (including the *New York Times,* the *Guardian,* and *El Pais*) of over 200,000 U.S. State Department cables. Less well known are the earlier activities of Julian Assange and fellow information activists that eventually led to significant changes to Icelandic legislation protecting the country's freedom of information, and the strong ties forged between information activists and grass-roots protesters during the Arab uprisings and among the Indignados and Occupy movements. But the crucial point is that it is not only 'tech nerds' who co-produce and share digital contents in support of greater internet freedoms, political and financial transparency, 'distributed' forms of democratic participation, and so on. Thanks to the new viral media environment, even anthropologists who not long ago boasted of being technophobes have now begun to actively participate in these new forms of public engagement (see Chapter 8 on the blog 'Savage Minds', and Chapter 9 on the Open Anthropology Cooperative, this volume).

Third, in many urban centres the explosive uptake of smartphones combined with new forms of civic engagement in the wake of the Arab uprisings are reconfiguring citizens' public ideas and practices (Corsin and Estalella 2011). One defining moment was the mass occupation of Tahrir Square in January 2011 to demand the end of the Mubarak regime in Egypt, followed in real time around the world via a plethora of mainstream, alternative and social media. This successful occupation was an inspiration for citizens worldwide who were demanding political reform and social justice. The Tahrir model was adapted by a small group of hacktivists and other citizens who occupied Madrid's Puerta del Sol square later that year. In turn, the Madrid template was exported to New York by an activist network in Vancouver, giving rise to Occupy Wall Street

(Juris 2012), from where it spread to hundreds of cities around the globe in October 2011. The occupied squares were not only utopian exercises in direct democracy (della Porta 2011). They were also highly experimental 'hackerspaces' (Brooke 2011) in which the mainstreaming of nerd politics acquired a public (inter)face, a manifestation of viral reality, and a context where the disenchantment and fear of the educated middle classes was articulated with that of the general population.

As we face new national and global crises in the coming years (witness, for instance, the June 2013 protests in Brazil and Turkey), it is likely that new and old forms of public engagement will continue to interact and co-evolve. In this chapter I draw from my own recent experience as a public anthropologist to explore some of the ways in which anthropologists can not only 'reach out' to non-academic constituencies via different media, but also help to constitute new forms of public engagement and democratic reform. I argue that an updated understanding of public anthropology is required if we are to transcend the mass media channels of a previous era. The new digital media environment is a 'hybrid' system made up of old and new technologies, actors and practices interacting in contingent ways (Chadwick 2011) as well as a domain of cultural production mired in a deep political and economic crisis. This situation demands open-ended, idiosyncratic and collaborative approaches to public engagement that exploit both the unique affordances of today's digital technologies and the after-effects of the 2011 and 2013 waves of social protest around the globe. I exemplify this argument through my experience with four distinct platforms, namely a mailing list, a research blog, Twitter and Facebook, in a range of public contexts.

Sustaining a Mailing List

Although there is little doubt that today's media environment differs markedly from that of the early 2000s, and even more so from earlier environments, it is unwise to adopt a 'replacement model' of media change in which 'new' media replace 'old' media (Apprich 2013). Thus in a recent ethnographic study set in Italy, Barassi and Treré (2012) found that an 'old' internet technology, the humble listserv, took pride of place among student activists who valued its interactivity and discretion (see also Treré 2012). These authors caution against the current rhetoric around 'Web 2.0' as the age of interactivity and user-driven content, as if email and other earlier technologies had not possessed such affordances. Moreover, they found that young Italian activists were often using social network sites and other 'Web 2.0' technologies in strategically non-interactive ways.

Similarly, Kelty's (2008) ethnohistory of the free software movement reveals the long-standing centrality of mailing lists to the making and remaking of 'recursive publics' around the practices of open-source coding (which in turn, we could add, eventually led to the mainstreaming of nerd politics). These listservs were in fact a key resource in Kelty's archival research (Postill 2010).

Mailing lists have been a mainstay of academic life for decades, and show no signs of decline despite the parallel rise in social media usage amongst academics. The number of European Association of Social Anthropologists' (EASA) networks continues to grow every year, and they all rely on listservs as their main communication tool. For instance, the EASA Media Anthropology Network – which I co-founded and convene – relies on its thriving listserv. Set up by a small group of enthusiasts during the 2004 EASA conference in Vienna, the listserv has continued to spread by word of mouse, and today (2015) boasts some 1,500 subscribers from a wide range of national and professional backgrounds. As stated on the Network's website: '[M]embership of EASA is not a prerequisite for subscribing to the Media Anthropology Network mailing list. The mailing list is open to scholars, research students and others anywhere in the world who have a legitimate interest in the anthropology of media'.

The decision to open the list to non-EASA members, and indeed to anyone with an interest in the subfield, lent it a public dimension, although in practice most active participation comes from scholars and advanced students working within academic institutions. Another formative influence was the informal agreement to focus on the anthropological (and related) study of media rather than on anthropology's presence in the public domain. Nevertheless, we have occasionally engaged with journalists, activists, documentary filmmakers and others working at the intersection of anthropology and public life; but the thrust of the list – and the network as a whole – has always been media-related academic research.

This research-driven agenda is clearly at work in the mailing list's widely praised innovation, its e-seminar series. E-seminars are chaired sessions that unfold around a working paper over a period of two weeks. The sessions were originally designed to 'remediate' (Bolter and Gursin 1999) a familiar offline social script, the co-present academic seminar, so as to serve a dual purpose: to present cutting-edge research in the subfield whilst fostering a sense of collegiality amongst list subscribers.

Now it could be argued that this mailing list – and others across the academic field – is merely a small inward-looking group that does not make a substantial contribution to the public projection of its discipline. However, this criticism would assume that the only meaningful ways of 'doing' public anthropology are either through the mediation of mainstream media outlets or by means of traditional outreach events such as public lectures. On the contrary, mailing lists can be an important means of building and sustaining new publics, and can reach out beyond the walls of academe. In the case of the media anthropology list, we do so in mostly indirect ways, by sharing and co-producing specialist knowledge not only with fellow 'experts' but also with researchers and practitioners from many walks of life, including journalism, activism, technology and film production, many of whom may be 'lurking' on the list.

Too narrow a conception of the notion of 'engagement' can be misleading here, for experience suggests that far from being idle onlookers, lurkers can in fact be active but silent members of a vibrant public. An anecdote will illustrate this point. In December 2012 I presented a working paper to the media anthropology e-seminar. Towards the end of the session I joked about the inclusive nature of these events by suggesting that even lurkers had been busy theorizing during the seminar. To my surprise, soon after making this remark, a colleague recommended the seminars to her Facebook friends and described herself as a lurker who had indeed been theorizing all along, but too busy to post. Although this colleague is also an anthropologist, many of her Facebook friends are not. This is an example of a modest but cumulatively significant type of indirect or unintended outreach. Another instance of unintended publicity would be those occasions when network participants are approached for an interview by journalists or bloggers who have found or been referred to the mailing list.

In sum, even the most seemingly academic of exchanges can find its way into wider public domains through the mediation of inter-field practitioners and technologies (e.g. search engines, 'Like' buttons, tweets).

A Public Research Blog

While mailing lists are taken-for-granted features of most scholars' email routines, blogs occupy a more ambivalent position in academia. Despite the strenuous efforts of leading anthropology bloggers to promote this practice amongst colleagues, blogging remains very much a minority pursuit in the discipline. It is common to find anthropology blogs that were started with great enthusiasm only to be abandoned or neglected within weeks or months. Experience suggests that those rare anthropology blogs that have achieved longevity tend to be collective rather than personal endeavours – for example, Savage Minds (see this volume) and Neuroanthropology.

The reasons for the low uptake and lack of sustainability of personal blogs among anthropologists are complex and would require a separate discussion. I would nevertheless hazard the following two factors. First, blogging requires considerable time and effort, both of which are in short supply amongst anthropologists and other academics facing heavy teaching and administrative workloads in an increasingly competitive marketplace. Second, blogging is a low-status practice regarded as having far less career value than publishing in respected journals or securing research grants. Like other scholars, anthropologists blog against the grain, as a meaningful activity in its own right but with low external rewards (see Warde 2005).

My own research blog is named 'media/anthropology'. Although launched in July 2006, it was only in April 2008 that I started blogging in earnest. I use this site primarily for research, self-promotion and archiving. As stated on the homepage,

> the aim of the blog is to put out in the public domain materials that I am already working with as part of my research activity under the broad theme of media anthropology. The idea is to keep colleagues, students and others informed of my work as well as to keep an online notebook for my own personal use, e.g. as an easy way of tracking down materials that may otherwise have remained hidden in my personal records.

Notice the double disclaimer contained in this passage. First, I imply that this is not the place to find time-consuming 'passionate blogging' (Estalella 2011). Rather this is a site of modest ambitions run by a busy academic. Second, the site has a personal archival purpose riding alongside its public mission. In other words, I am both the sole owner of the blog and a key member of its target audience, not in a 'Dear Diary' confessional mode but as a future seeker of specific contents via Google or the blog's own search engine. Indeed, I sometimes find that a Google search for online materials on a given topic will direct me to my own blog (e.g. 'practice theory')!

Another example of the blog's labour constraints is that, while comments are allowed on the site, I seldom solicit them from readers, as a high volume of comments would add to the burden of running the blog on a very time-limited budget. This reinforces Barassi and Treré's (2012) earlier point about the gap between the potential and actual interactivity of 'Web 2.0' technologies such as blogs and social network sites.

That said, there have been a number of interactive episodes throughout the blog's short history. Thus on preparing for fieldwork in Catalonia in 2010 I wrote a small number of blog posts on the topic of regional nationalism in Spain. Although my aim was to position myself as an impartial observer with a scholarly interest in the subject, some of the comments made by blog visitors challenged this neutrality. After some reflection on the issue – a privilege conferred on the blogger by the asynchronicity of this medium – I decided to steer clear of the topic in future posts so as to maintain access to prospective research participants when working in nationalist circles.

One obvious attraction of owning a personal research blog is the almost complete editorial freedom it allows its proprietor. This is not to say that owners operate in a moral and political vacuum, but in contrast to a collective blog such as Savage Minds, a personal blog requires no communal negotiation on the theme, register or style of its contents. The onus is entirely on the solo blogger. This makes personal blogs idiosyncratic media stamped with an individual's unique traits and preoccupations, the quintessential home of 'me-centric' or 'networked' individualism (Castells 2001; Wellman 2001). Coupled with the time constraints just mentioned and the incessant demand of the medium for new content, the results are often uneven. Thus, in my blogging career I have made virtue out of necessity by turning all manner of materials to hand into unlikely blog posts, including presentation notes, summaries of readings, tweet collections, working papers, reblogged posts, musings on topical issues, and so on. Because of the archival nature of blogs (Estalella 2011), items that were originally neglected by blog readers may reach new audiences when they are 'rediscovered' weeks or months later through a search engine, and shared via social media or other means. Some blog posts have remained perpetually popular, such as the post 'What is practice theory?', an extract from the introduction to *Theorising Media and Practice* (Bräuchler and Postill 2010). Since I posted it in October 2008, this entry has been viewed over thirty-five thousand times and received twenty-two comments, and it continues to draw traffic to the site. This is an example of a high publicity return on a low investment in time and effort.

Twitter's Transient Publics

There are few web platforms as misunderstood as the microblogging site Twitter. One common misconception about this site is that it is an outlet for narcissistic trivia and celebrity self-promotion. While there is some truth to this portrayal, there is far more to Twitter than mindless entertainment. In fact, Twitter is surprisingly conducive to the practice of public scholarship.

The media theorist Nick Couldry (2010) argues that certain powerful (media) practices 'anchor' other practices. For example, televised state ceremonies such as a royal wedding can anchor offline gatherings in pubs and homes (Couldry 2003). This is an intriguing metaphor, but it does not travel well to public microblogging. The term anchor suggests, of course, immobility. Instead, we need dynamic metaphors that can capture how microblogging may be 'spearheading' both socio-political change and the creation of new publics in which anthropologists can play an important part. Looking back at the trajectory of Spain's leading internet activists over the past two years, I regard activist microblogging as a cutting-edge, disruptive practice that has helped to 'unsettle' powerful fields such as politics, journalism and finance whilst creating new transient publics ripe for anthropological intervention.

Launched in 2006, Twitter is today a hugely popular platform where information can be shared and discussed via brief messages known as tweets. Unlike Facebook, Twitter is based on asymmetrical relationships. That is, to establish a visible relation on the site there is no need to be 'friended' by another user; one need only 'follow' them. The result is a huge disparity in users' follower-to-followed ratio – a key index of prestige on Twitter. Thus, while A-list celebrities will typically boast millions of followers, they are likely to follow in return far fewer people. In stark contrast, ordinary users may find it difficult to recruit more than one or two hundred followers, with public scholars generally lying somewhere in between.

Like many other social media platforms, Twitter is free of charge and poses no significant technical challenge to prospective users. However, most novices must embark on a steep learning curve if they wish to be noticed amidst Twitter's relentless torrent of information. Many newbies must also overcome the initial 'culture shock' of a giant platform teeming with half a billion users who generate over 340 million tweets and make more than 1.6 billion search queries every day.[1]

Twitter's 2011 tagline 'Follow your interests' encapsulates one of the chief attractions of the site, namely the ability it confers on users to keep track of those people and issues that matter to them. Interestingly, this tagline mirrors the old ethnographic maxim 'Follow their interests', making Twitter a milieu that is highly conducive to ethnographic research. Most topics are freely created and shared (or 'retweeted') by users themselves, not by the site owners, and arranged into topical threads through 'hashtags' (e.g. #anthropology, #worldcup). Topics that are rapidly gaining in popularity at any given time are publicly listed by Twitter as 'trending' nationally and/or globally. As can be expected, there is fierce competition among certain kinds of Twitter users and groups (including political activists) to create and maintain trending topics.

In recent years Twitter has become integral to the work of activists and protesters around the world, not least in Spain. As one veteran Catalan activist told me in the summer of 2011, when broaching the subject of the

15M protest movement: 'I had no choice but to join Twitter to find out what was going on'. Thus during the mass occupation of Spain's central squares in May 2011, two 15M activists highlighted the role played by Twitter in these terms:

> The assemblies in each of the encampments are essential not only for logistical reasons but also because everyday and mid-term tasks are outlined in their committees. Above all, they are massive, transparent exercises in direct democracy … However, the [movement's] direction is mostly set on Twitter. The hashtags serve not only to organize the debate. They also set the collective tone: #wearenotgoing #wearenotafraid #fearlessbcn … (@galapita and @hibai [2011], my translation)

The importance of Twitter to my own research became clear in December 2010. Having spent four months 'chasing' activists across Barcelona while slowly building a directory of campaigns and groups on my research blog, it was on Twitter that I 'found' them all gathered in one place. More importantly, Twitter became a central rallying space and 'meme factory' for activists and protesters themselves (Postill, 2014). Although Twitter came to be one of my key field sites, I resisted the temptation to turn the inquiry into an 'online community' study (see Postill 2008), and instead continued to 'follow the conflict' (Marcus 1995) across a range of online and offline sites (Postill and Pink 2012). My Twitter persona (@JohnPostill) was that of a UK anthropologist researching new media and activism, with special reference to Barcelona, Catalonia and Spain. In order to keep the flow of information manageable, I limited the number of people I followed to 130–140 users, while steadily building up a following that reached around 1,400 on leaving Barcelona (over 3,000 at present). Twitter was my default aggregator, a 'human-mediated RSS feed' (Naughton 2011) where knowledgeable informants operating in different domains filtered news and commentary on a large set of actors and issues related to my research question.

Over time, I learned to craft my tweets to increase the likelihood that they would be retweeted – for example, by tweeting in English on topics generally discussed in Spanish, or posting messages during peak hours of Twitter traffic in Spain so that they would reach a larger audience. I also made ample use of my interstitial position as a bicultural scholar with access to academic, journalistic and blogging resources in both English and Spanish (and occasionally other languages as well) to feed relevant contents into the appropriate discursive streams. One important part of the process was learning how to play social games on Twitter. I turn now to four of the games I learned to play, which I shall provisionally label 'gaming the algorithm', 'gathering the #facts', 'self-promoting' and 'killing time'.

In the weeks and months leading to the 15 May 2011 mobilizations across Spain, influential activists promoted certain slogans and ideas by means of Twitter's trending topics facility. Aware that the site's algorithm prioritizes novelty over volume when ranking the more popular topics (Cullum 2010), skilled players would constantly change the campaign keywords, asking their followers to share them widely so that they would trend. To find my own competitive advantage in this game, I developed a set of techniques such as using Google to search for recent news items in English on a Spanish trending topic, and then feeding the more valuable finds into the relevant thread, often copying the tweets (via the 'cc.' abbreviation) to influential Twitter users operating in specific niches such as online journalism or copyright law. I found this game to be rewarding both extrinsically – in that it boosted my 'name and fame' (Miller 2000) – and intrinsically, as a pleasurable activity in its own right, with instant psychological rewards (Warde 2005).

A second game that I played with Spanish activists and other field agents was 'gathering the #facts' – a sub-typè or variant of gaming the algorithm. This relatively new Twitter game is a modification of the now classic internet game that grew around the actor Chuck Norris, under the rubric 'Chuck Norris facts'. The original game consisted of sharing, tongue in cheek, made-up 'facts' portraying Norris as 'a tough, all-powerful super-being' (Wikipedia 2012). Since 2005, this subgenre has spawned countless variants around the world and been applied to many other public figures. The Twitter version of the game turns the phrase into a hashtag. For instance, in late December 2010 the Spanish pop star and tax exile Alejandro Sanz tweeted: 'Spanish politicians are such cowards, they're not going to vote for the new bill safeguarding intellectual property' (my translation). This tweet provoked an outcry that was channelled through the Spanglish hashtag #alejandrosanzfacts, with tweets ranging from the humorous to the factual via the outright insulting. Not surprisingly, Sanz's alleged tax evasion featured prominently in the discursive torrent. As this case shows, a transient Twitter public can instantly expand to swallow up an unsuspecting microblogger who is then hurled into a turbulent sphere of discursive action over which they have little or no control. (By the same token, these ephemeral publics will often contract and dissipate equally as fast.)

A third Twitter game I play regularly is 'self-promoting'. In common with other forms of online and offline self-promotion, the prefix 'self-' belies the thoroughly collective and reciprocal nature of this activity. Thus, seasoned Twitterers tacitly understand that retweeting a contact's self-promoting messages may be reciprocated in due course. As in other contexts, this game must not be overplayed. In other words, public scholars promoting their work on Twitter must also engage in activities of other kinds, such as sharing topical information on events or publications not directly related to their career achievements, or participating in both serious and light-hearted threads of conversation.

My final example is a game we may call 'killing time'. Not all Twitter activity can be devoted to the dogged pursuit of professional or political agendas. As in all social worlds, there are also times on Twitter for relaxation and conviviality. One common way of doing this is to join existing trending topics where the conversation is likely to be animated and the cognitive investment required low. The topics are usually steeped in popular culture but can vary widely in subject matter (e.g. sport, television, sex, health), longevity (from a few hours to a day), cultural framing (regional, national, global), and so on. For the anthropologist these seemingly banal threads can provide valuable glimpses into the state of 'the national conversation' at any given point in time. Over a period of months or years, recurrent themes and trends can be triangulated with other sources of data (the mainstream media, interviews, offline observation, etc.). My own participation in the game of killing time will vary from non-participant observation and replying to a particularly amusing tweet – often from a total stranger – to posting my own informal tweets.

Awkward Facebook

Boyd and Ellison (2007) have suggested that the term 'social network site' is a more accurate way of describing platforms such as Facebook or Myspace than the commonly used phrase 'social networking site'. This latter formulation, they argue, is more applicable to sites such as LinkedIn that are designed for the purpose of 'networking' for career or other instrumental ends. By contrast, Facebook and similar sites draw their sustenance from users' existing social networks.

However, this neologism – popular today among internet scholars – is itself problematic, for it conflates a fundamental distinction made by social network theorists since the 1960s between 'whole' and 'personal' networks (Knox, Savage and Harvey 2006). A personal (or ego-centred) network comprises an individual's set of ties – friendship, family, work, etc. Diagrammatically, this is represented by a central 'ego' connected through nodes and lines to a finite set of other individuals. In contrast, a whole (or socio-centric) network lacks an individual centre – or indeed, a centre of any kind. Examples of whole networks include organizations, cities and markets.

Personal networks are unique social formations in that they revolve around individuals without whom they cease to exist, normally after the individuals' biological death. Virtually all other social formations centre on a collectivity, not an individual. Therefore, from the perspective of its individual users, Facebook could be described as a *personal* network site. At the same time Facebook is a gigantic *whole* network comprising hundreds of millions of individual users and clusters of users (e.g. fans of a given football team, celebrity or cause). It is the dynamic interactions between the personal, group, and total logics of Facebook that lend this multitudinous site its unique character and attraction.

While a great deal of media and academic attention has been paid to issues such as privacy and collective action on Facebook (Liu et al. 2011), surprisingly little work has been done on the curious social morphology of this platform. Following ethnographic research in Trinidad, Miller (2011) writes: 'Facebook has all the contradictions found in a community. You simply can't have both closeness and privacy. You can't have support without claustrophobia. You can't have such a degree of friendship without the risk of explosive quarrelling. Either everything is more socially intense or none of it is'.

Leaving aside the problematic status of 'community' as an anthropological concept (Amit and Rapport 2002; Postill 2008), this passage highlights a crucial aspect of Facebook: its awkwardness as a social space. Facebook collapses the inner walls of our personal networks, bringing into close contact people from different times and regions of our life trajectories. This architecture results in a digitally mediated 'open plan' sociality, a quality of social intercourse in which formerly discrete facets of our lives are now within the purview of our wider network. Increasingly, Facebook brings into the semi-public personal spaces of ethnographers two sets of significant others, namely the researched and the non-researched, sometimes even blurring the distinction between the two. This is the stuff of scientific insight – and potential trouble.

For example, early in my Barcelona fieldwork I shared on Facebook a news item relating to the controversial Spanish judge Baltasar Garzon. Shortly after posting this item, a robust exchange took place between two of my Facebook friends holding diametrically opposed political views. Although privately sympathetic to the leftist, pro-Garzon position, I managed to defuse the tension by adopting a diplomatic stance. Because the exchange took place on my Facebook wall, I had no choice but to play the role of a congenial host mediating between two quarrelsome guests.

On another occasion, my Facebook wall was the setting for a rather more scholarly exchange about Spain's Indignados movement. Here I found it more difficult to remain impartial, as I had recently undergone something of a political conversion to the new movement (Postill, 2014). My exchanges with a Barcelona-based political scientist were particularly helpful in that they shed light on the chasm between emic and etic under-standings of the unfolding protests.

Intra- and Inter-platform Engagements

As we have just seen, each of the main media platforms that I use for my anthropological work is unique. This uniqueness compels me to behave in ways that I consider appropriate to that particular site. Compare, for instance, the relative sizes of the media anthropology mailing list versus Twitter. Whilst the listserv is a small bounded network of some 1,500 sub-scribers, Twitter is a huge aggregation of over 500 million registered users. Another key difference is the mode of communication. Mailing lists are designed to facilitate many-to-many exchanges, even if in practice some subscribers will of course be more prolific than others. By contrast, Twitter affords one-to-many exchanges – the 'many' varying greatly from a score to millions of followers. But arguably the most striking difference is the ab-sence of bounded groups within Twitter. Although efforts were made in the past to form Twitter 'tribes' (known as Twibes) around common interests such as art, golf or anthropology, these all foundered. Instead, Twitter has become the world's pre-eminent open market of news, commentary and discussion, with participants engaging with one another through ephem-eral threads, not sustainable groups. As a result, on Twitter the public scholar has no option but to engage with a far more heterogeneous pop-ulation of users and issues than is the case on a specialist forum such as the media anthropology list or a subject-specific blog like Savage Minds.

In my pre-social media research in suburban Malaysia in 2003–2004 (Postill 2011), I found that internet-savvy activists, politicians and others had to tread carefully when traversing the country's variegated online terrain. For instance, the influential activist Jeff Ooi developed a rugged 'networked individual' (Wellman 2001) persona when blogging – a stance that brought him accolades from fellow bloggers but made him run foul of the country's ruling elites. Yet despite his national prominence, Ooi had to mind his language when interacting online with fellow residents of the Kuala Lumpur suburb of Subang Jaya. Thus another resident once took him to task for bragging about his achievements on a residents' web forum devoted to discussing 'community' issues – ironically, a forum that Ooi himself had founded (Postill 2011: 77).

Similarly, public scholars must learn how to navigate the often treacherous waters of online discourse by developing an acute sensitivity to the specific ethos and 'netiquette' of each site. For example, some years ago a new subscriber of the media anthropology list used the list to loudly protest the four-post limit imposed on e-seminar participants, a rule intended to encourage wider participation. He regarded this rule to be contrary to the free spirit of the internet. This was a strange accusation coming from a seasoned anthropologist, who would have known that different social groups will develop their own rules and conventions over time – internet-based groups being no exception.

Of course, human agency always intervenes in the maintenance and transformation of socio-technical practices (Tenhunen 2008; Shove, Pantzar and Watson 2012). In my own public anthropology practice, I have learned how to exploit the limits and possibilities of different platforms, not in an ahistorical void but through the vagaries of both my life course and a changing media landscape. One ongoing area of learning is cross-platform participation in issues of public concern. Given the centrality of participant observation to the ethnographic approach, anthropologists are well placed to study the use of participatory media in public processes. As noted earlier, one remarkable feature of the Indignados movement was the pervasive, decentralized use of social media by hackers, students, pro-democracy activists and countless ordinary citizens to form a common front. Although a few fundamentalist hackers refused to use corporate platforms such as Facebook and Twitter, most campaigners I encountered justified their use of corporate social media on pragmatic grounds. For example, when the Barcelona chapter of the umbrella organization Real Democracy Now! (in Spanish, DRY) was created in March 2011, participants were encouraged to use both Facebook and a non-proprietary web forum to coordinate their activities. When it became apparent that Facebook was the preferred platform, the group's informal leaders readily went along with the majority.

Throughout the course of my research into the 15M movement, I took part in a range of collaborative activities across various online platforms. As a native English and Spanish speaker, part of my modest contribution to the movement was to act as an occasional translator and proofreader. Thus I once shared via Facebook what I regarded as an improved version of a passage taken from the English translation of the DRY manifesto. In a matter of minutes, another user replied with what we both agreed was a better translation, which I duly forwarded via email to the manifesto team. This example may seem pedestrian, but it captures neatly the sorts of micropolitical collaborations amongst strangers – including scholars – that social media, especially Facebook owing to its critical mass and popularity, enable on a much vaster scale than was possible even a few years ago.

Conclusion

It is exciting to look back at the digital progress that anthropologists have made since around 2005. Reluctantly at first, countless anthropologists (young and old) have acquired valuable digital skills and, perhaps more importantly, digital self-confidence in a matter of a few years. Let us not forget that Facebook only opened to the general public (us included) in September 2006, or that Twitter caught the world's attention a mere eight years ago, in 2007. I have no figures to hand, but personal experience suggests that a substantial proportion of anthropologists are now regular users of mailing lists and Facebook. This means that they are also likely to be, via other people's shared contents, indirect users of Twitter, YouTube, Instagram, Academia, and so on.

In this chapter I have argued that the practice of public anthropology is today caught up in three convergent global trends: the mainstreaming of nerd politics, a viralized media environment, and digitized public spaces. With their commitment to ethnographic methods, anthropologists are well equipped to contribute to the new public environment, characterized by its increasingly participatory and politically engaged nature. To support this argument, I drew from my own personal experience 'doing' public anthropology while researching and participating in momentous techno-political events unfolding in Spain and other countries on the receiving end of post-2008 'austerity' measures. Spain's protesters, like their counterparts in Greece, Turkey, Brazil and elsewhere, are collectively 'hacking' their country's representative democracy and demanding new forms of governance and social justice. In the process, they are ceaselessly forming and reforming new publics open to anthropological interventions of the kind discussed above.

Digital media are integral to these processes, but they are by no means the preserve of young 'digital natives'. While inequalities of class, race, gender and age will remain important, never before has access to personal and communitarian media been so wide. As mobile media continue to experience rapid growth across the global South, there is an urgent need for new forms of civic engagement and democratic reform, to which anthropologists can contribute their cross-cultural expertise. The omens are good for anthropologists wishing to conduct further incursions into uncharted digital territory – many of whom were happy until recently to leave Web content creation and sharing to others. These incursions could well include those outlets once known as the mainstream media.

John Postill is Vice-Chancellor's Senior Research Fellow at RMIT University, Melbourne, and Digital Anthropology Fellow at University College London (UCL). His publications include *Localizing the Internet* (2011), *Media and Nation Building* (2006) and the co-edited volume *Theorising Media and Practice* (2010, with Birgit Bräuchler). Currently he is conducting anthropological research on new forms of digital activism and civic engagement, with particular reference to Indonesia and Spain. He is also writing a book provisionally titled *Freedom Technologists*, and co-editing the volume *Theorising Media and Change* (with Elisenda Ardèvol and Sirpa Tenhunen).

Notes

Some parts of the section 'Intra- and inter-platform engagements' are taken from Postill (2012).
   1.   See http://en.wikipedia.org/wiki/Twitter

References

Amit, V., and N. Rapport. 2002. *The Trouble with Community*. London: Pluto.
Apprich, C. 2013. 'Remaking Media Practices – From Tactical Media to Post-Media', Mute, 14 February 2013. http://www.metamute.org/editorial/lab/remaking-media-practices-%E2%80%93-tactical-media-to-post-media
Barassi, V., and E. Treré. 2012. 'Does Web 3.0 come after Web 2.0? Deconstructing Theoretical Assumptions through Practice', *New Media & Society* 14(8): 1269–85.
Bolter, J., and R. Gursin. 1999. *Remediation: Understanding New Media.* Cambridge, MA: MIT Press.
Boyd, D.M., and N.B. Ellison. 2007. 'Social Network Sites: Definition, History, and Scholarship', *Journal of Computer-Mediated Communication* 13(1): Article 11.
Bräuchler, B., and J. Postill (eds). 2010. *Theorising Media and Practice.* Oxford: Berghahn Books.
Brooke, H. 2011. *The Revolution Will Be Digitised: Dispatches from the Information War.* London: William Heinemann.
Castells, M. 2001. *The Internet Galaxy.* Oxford: Oxford University Press.
Chadwick, A. 2011. 'The Hybrid Media System'. Paper to the European Consortium for Political Research General Conference, Reykjavik, Iceland, 25 August 2011. http://newpolcom .rhul.ac.uk/npcu-blog/2011/7/25/npcu-at-ecpr-2011-reykjavik.html

Corsin, A., and A. Estalella. 2011. '#spanishrevolution', *Anthropology Today* 27(4): 19–23.

Couldry, N. 2003. *Media Rituals: A Critical Approach*. London: Routledge.

———. 2010. 'Theorising Media as Practice', in B. Bräuchler and J. Postill (eds), *Theorising Media and Practice*. Oxford: Berghahn Books.

Cullum, B. 2010. 'What Makes a Twitter Hashtag Successful?' *Movements.org*, 17 December. http://www.movements.org/blog/entry/what-makes-a-twitter-hashtag-successful/

Doctorow, C. 2012. 'The Problem with Nerd Politics'. The *Guardian*, 15 May, http://www.guardian.co.uk/technology/2012/may/14/problem-nerd-politics

Estalella, A. 2011. 'Ensamblajes de esperanza: Un estudio antropológico del bloguear apasionado'. Unpublished Ph.D. thesis, Universitat Oberta de Catalunya, Barcelona.

@galapita and @hibai. 2011. *Maig del seixanta-tweet*, *Enfocant*, 21 June. http://enfocant.net/noticia/maig-del-seixanta-tweet

Juris, J. 2012. 'Reflections on #Occupy Everywhere: Social Media, Public Space, and Emerging Logics of Aggregation', *American Ethnologist* 39(2): 259–79.

Kelty, C. 2008. *Two Bits: The Cultural Significance of Free Software*. Durham, NC: Duke University Press.

Knox, H., M. Savage and P. Harvey. 2006. 'Social Networks and the Study of Relations: Networks as Method, Metaphor and Form', *Economy and Society* 35(1): 113–40.

Liu, Y., K. Gummadi, B. Krishnamurthy and A. Mislove. 2011. 'Analyzing Facebook Privacy Settings: User Expectations vs. Reality', in Proceedings of Internet Measurement Conference (IMC). Association for Computing Machinery.

Mao, I. 2008. 'Sharism: A Mind Revolution', in J. Ito (ed.), *Freesouls*. Tokyo: Freesouls.cc, pp. 115–18.

Marcus, G.E. 1995. 'Ethnography in/of the World System: The Emergence of Multi-sited Ethnography', *Annual Review of Anthropology* 24: 95–117.

Mason, P. 2013. *Why It's Still Kicking Off Everywhere: The New Global Revolutions*. London: Verso.

Miller, D. 2000. 'The Fame of Trinis: Websites as Traps', *Journal of Material Culture* 5(1): 5–24.

———. 2011. *Tales from Facebook*. Cambridge: Polity.

Naughton, J. 2011. 'Twitter's Five-Year Evolution from Ridicule to Dissidents' Tool', The *Observer*, 13 February.

Porta, D. della. 2011. 'The Road to Europe: Movements and Democracy', *Open Democracy*, 24 August 2011. http://www.opendemocracy.net/donatella-della-porta/road-to-europe-movements-and-democracy

Postill, J. 2008. 'Localising the Internet beyond Communities and Networks', *New Media and Society* 10(3): 413–31.

———. 2010. 'Researching the Internet', *Journal of the Royal Anthropological Institute* 16(3): 646–50.

———. 2011. *Localizing the Internet: An Anthropological Account*. Oxford and New York: Berghahn Books.

———. 2012. 'Digital Politics and Political Engagement', in H. Horst and D. Miller (eds), *Digital Anthropology*. Oxford: Berg.

———. 2014. 'Democracy in an Age of Viral Reality: A Media Epidemiography of Spain's Indignados Movement', *Ethnography* 15 (1): 50-68.

Postill, J., and S. Pink. 2012. 'Social Media Ethnography: The Digital Researcher in a Messy Web', *Media International Australia* 145: 123–34.

Shirky, C. 2008. *Here Comes Everybody: The Power of Organizing without Organizations*. New York: Penguin Press.

Shove, E., M. Pantzar and M. Watson. 2012. *The Dynamics of Social Practice: Everyday Life and How it Changes*. London: Sage.

Tenhunen, S. 2008. 'Mobile Technology in the Village: ICTs, Culture, and Social Logistics in India', *Journal of the Royal Anthropological Institute (N.S.)* 14: 515–34.

Treré, E. 2012. 'Social Movements as Information Ecologies: Exploring the Coevolution of Multiple Internet Technologies for Activism', *International Journal of Communication* 6(0). http://ijoc.org/ojs/index.php/ijoc/article/view/1681

Turkle, S. 1984. *The Second Self: Computers and the Human Spirit.* New York: Simon & Schuster.

Warde, A. 2005. 'Consumption and Theories of Practice', *Journal of Consumer Culture* 5: 131–53.

Wellman, B. 2001. 'Physical Place and Cyber Place: The Rise of Networked Individualism', *International Journal of Urban and Regional Research* 25(2) (June): 227–52.

Chapter 8

ANTHROPOLOGICAL PUBLICS AND THEIR ONLOOKERS
The Dynamics of Multiple Audiences
in the Blog 'Savage Minds'

———— ∞∞∞ ————

Alex Golub and Kerim Friedman

George Marcus once coined the phrase 'research imaginary' to describe 'the changing presuppositions, or sensibilities ... that inform the way research ideas are formulated and actual fieldwork projects are conceived' (Marcus 1998: 10). Marcus's goal was to examine the way the conditions of postmodernism and globalization had altered the nature of anthropological fieldwork. In this chapter we extend Marcus's work by describing the blog Savage Minds (www.savageminds.org) with reference to anthropology's 'professional imaginary'. By this we mean the way anthropologists imagine their professional and service work: what it is, what it can or could be, and how that might change. The internet has been a place where people have sought to radically rethink many aspects of our professional culture: online course material helps people to create DIY education projects; digital publications have allowed people to rethink the book as a genre; peer review is being rethought in light of search and social media; standards for tenure shift as online forums are weighed in the process; and finally, the meaning (and cost) of 'publishing' changes radically in the context of the internet. It seems futile today to describe the way scholarly communication in anthropology is changing. We now have public anthropology, collaborative anthropology, engaged anthropology, applied anthropology, and perhaps more. The media of anthropology seem equally in flux: media, new media, social media, blogs, Twitter, and a renewed culture of the book enlivened by print on demand technology. The question is not what has changed, but what has stayed the same; not how best to grasp the nettle of public engagement in the world of new media, but rather to determine what sort of task we seek to undertake in a landscape saturated in new forms of community.

From its founding, it became clear that Savage Minds filled an important niche, quickly drawing the attention of others in the academic blogosphere. In 2006, *Nature* ranked Savage Minds seventeenth out of the fifty top science blogs across all scientific disciplines (Nature.com 2006). In 2010, *American Anthropologist* called Savage Minds 'the central online site of the North American anthropological community', whose 'value is found in the quality of the posts by the site's central contributors, a cadre of bright, engaged, young anthropology professors' (Price 2010: 141). Through an analysis of our own involvement as co-founders and editors of Savage Minds, this chapter seeks to explore the reasons for our blog's success – not for the purpose of self-aggrandizement, but to better understand the as-yet-unfulfilled promise of online scholarly communication in anthropology, for which Savage Minds constitutes an initial public beta. To the extent our site is a successful example of public scholarship, it is so (we argue) because of the way it straddles, engages with, and transforms two key spaces of discourse: anthropology's 'professional imaginary' and 'public anthropology'. We argue that the goal of public anthropology is best served by the blog when it takes the form of 'doing anthropology in public' – embodying the professional imaginary on a public platform.

Savage Minds: Behind the Scenes

Founded in 2005, Savage Minds is a blog by and for people trained in anthropology that seeks to capture the 'excitement and engagement' that drew us to anthropology in the first place. In doing so, we were caught up in the spirit of academic blogging as described by Henry Farrell, a founding member of the political science blog Crooked Timber:

> Academic blogs offer the kind of intellectual excitement and engagement that attracted many scholars to the academic life in the first place, but which often get lost in the hustle to secure positions, grants, and disciplinary recognition … [they] provide a carnival of ideas, a lively and exciting interchange of argument and debate that makes many scholarly conversations seem drab and desiccated in comparison. (Farrell 2005a)

Crooked Timber, along with a number of other successful academic group blogs such as Language Log (http://languagelog.ldc.upenn.edu/nll/) for linguistics and Cliopatra (http://hnn.us/blogs/2.html) for history, had been founded two years earlier, in 2003, yet by 2005 there was still no similar site for anthropologists. The authors (Alex Golub and P. Kerim Friedman), together with Dustin Wax and Christopher Kelty, had all, as academics, experimented with blogging on their own, but their blogs were not 'academic blogs' in the sense of engaging online with the 'wider world [about] their academic or civilizational concerns' (Ahmed 2005).

Six years on, Savage Minds has attracted a sizable and steady community of readers, even if it remains small by internet standards. In 2011 it had 186,415 'unique visitors' (according to Google Analytics), or an average of just over 500 visitors per day. That number is deceptive, however, as traffic ebbed and flowed with the academic year and with the volume of new posts on the website. On 1st February, for instance, 2,206 people visited the site. One of the things we are proud of is the large percentage of people who return to the site. Of the 316,640 visits to the site last year, 133,629 (42 per cent) were returning visitors. The community comments section has been consistently lively and informed, with an average of eight comments per post, with some posts getting many more. Many of our users never visit the site directly, but access it via its subscription feed (aka 'RSS feed'). Currently there are 14,848 people (or robots) subscribed to that feed, but if we only count those who actually 'engage' (Google's term) with the feed (i.e. by clicking a link), the number is 228. An additional 791 people are subscribed to the Facebook page, and the Twitter account has 2,942 followers.[1]

The membership of Savage Minds is constantly changing, which has posed a problem for managing the site in a democratic fashion. Besides the authors, the current list of Savage Minds authors includes: Adam Fish, Christopher Kelty, Jay Sosa, Matthew Thompson, Dustin Wax, Ryan Anderson and Thomas Strong.[2] All of these are on a Google Groups mailing list where most of the backchannel decisions are made with regard to the management of the site. There is even a set of unofficial guidelines defining the responsibilities of these site 'editors'. These guidelines are mostly technical – reminding people, for instance, to use the 'more' tag if their post exceeds more than three paragraphs, so that a single post does not dominate the front page. There are also guidelines for comment moderation (each blogger is responsible for moderating the comments thread on their own posts), for nominating guest bloggers, which anyone can do (but they must give the other editors three to five days in which to support or veto the nomination if they so wish), and so on. Yet participation in these backchannel discussions, even membership on the editorial board itself, is largely determined by how regularly bloggers post to the site. The authors, who have each posted over five hundred posts on Savage

Minds since it was founded, tend to be the most vocal, while other founding members who now only post once or twice a year remain on board as editors but tend to be more hands-off. The number of posts by the other full-time members varies greatly; some (like Ryan Anderson) have only joined recently but have been very active, while others (like Dustin Wax) were founding members but no longer post as regularly as they once did. The number of posts from these other full-time members can range anywhere from about 30 to about 160.

The backchannel email list involves constant discussion about how to improve the site. This includes site layout, handling problems that emerge on the comments feed, finding new guest bloggers and trying to recruit new full-time bloggers, responding to requests to do book reviews, and posting announcements on the site (we usually turn down such offers for fear of becoming a bulletin board for the American Anthropology Association). We also organize special events, from blog posts on the anniversary of the Haiti earthquake to April Fools' Day hoaxes. And we organize informal real-world events at the annual meetings of the AAA. We are always looking for new full-time bloggers, but it is hard to find people who understand blogging as a genre distinct from academic writing who are also willing to make a long-term commitment to the site.

Like many anthropologists, we are mindful of diversity. Throughout the site's history we have sought to expand our list of full-time Savage Minds authors (what we call 'Minds') and to include perspectives from authors from a wide range of genders, ethnicities and sexual orientations. On the whole, however, we have not been very successful. Since more anthropology degrees have been awarded to women than men (Givens and Jablonski 2000), a discussion of gender diversity on our website might help to exemplify our struggles in these areas.

When we first launched the blog we thought it was important to have at least two women Minds, and so were very pleased to have Kathleen Lowrey and Nancy Leclerc. However, both left after a year of blogging, and since then we have struggled to maintain the gender balance we wanted, since it is hard to find anyone (male or female) willing to post regularly week-after-week, year-after-year, let alone anyone willing to take the added responsibility of helping to manage the site. Our solution has been to broaden the nature of participation in two ways: first, by creating accounts for 'guest bloggers' who are given posting privileges for one month and, second, by inviting 'occasional contributors' to write single posts that are published under someone else's account. In sum, we have had 30 occasional contributor posts, and 59 authors, including guest bloggers. Of these 59 guest bloggers, only 23 are women. While 38 per cent of our bloggers are women, far less than 38 per cent of our content is generated by them, since the vast majority of posts are written by just a small handful of people, and they are white American men.

We often invite guest bloggers to continue as full-time Minds, but few accept our invitation because of the time commitment that being a Mind requires. Full-time Minds are expected to post regularly (at least once or twice a month), to participate in the backchannel discussion, post to the Twitter and Facebook feeds, and help to find new guest bloggers. (Not all Minds currently meet those requirements, but because they have all done so for an extended period in the past, they remain on the masthead.) Not surprisingly, not too many academics voluntarily take on such extra responsibilities over and above those demanded by their department. It is possible that the problem is especially acute for women, who are often saddled with more than their fair share of 'service' jobs both at home and in the workplace. To accommodate this we have created a 'part-time Mind' category which grants all the privileges of being a Mind (i.e. the ability to post whenever they like) without any expectation of regular posting or participation in site management. We currently have two women who are part-timers: Zöe Wool and Maia Green. This solution is not entirely satisfactory as the lack of a female presence among the full-time Minds has made it harder to attract new female bloggers. But in the summer of 2012, we were able to recruit Carole McGranahan, although she joined on the understanding that she would not remain the sole female member for long.

Another issue which may have contributed to the perception of a male-centric atmosphere is the high number of comments from a small cadre of male readers. These comments are frequently confrontational in nature. Although tame by internet standards (we have a strict comments policy and remove comments that we find abusive), several women readers have cited these comments as a reason they do not contribute more. This is not a problem unique to Savage Minds. Yahoo! News correspondent Virginia Heffernan recently criticized the nastiness of the comments genre, especially as directed towards female writers, asking: 'Is there a way to comment without trolling, bullying or gas lighting?' (Heffernan 2013).

Unfortunately, there is only so much that can be done about this. A lot of our backchannel discussion involves how best to handle comments. We do not want to turn them off completely, although individual threads are sometimes shut down if they get out of hand. Because moderating comments is a lot of work, we ask each author (including guests) to moderate their own comments, although the full-time Minds sometimes step in to help out the guest bloggers if things get out of hand. Because each author has a different interpretation of how strictly the comment policy should be enforced, the nature of the comments varies quite a bit from author to author.

Since the blog began in 2005, our membership has changed as the authors have moved through various life stages. Most of the initial members were graduate students, and some have moved on to tenure-track positions in the course of blogging, while others have dropped out of the academy together. The result is a 'multigenerational' blog, with newer members who are in graduate school, more established members who are on the tenure-track, and one or two members or affiliates who are in senior positions. This spread means that the blog reflects a wide diversity of positions in anthropology, which we believe to be valuable.

While David Price may have been right in 2010 to call Savage Minds 'the central online site of the North American anthropological community' (Price 2010), it is less clear that this is the case today, when Savage Minds is just one among an increasingly large number of popular anthropology blogs. Savage Minds, because of its history and the large community of writers, may still have an important leadership role, but it would be a mistake to say that any single anthropology blog remains at the 'centre' of what is increasingly a decentralized web of anthropology blogs, including a number of blogs appearing in other countries and other languages, such as Guavanthropology (http://guavanthropology.tw/) in Taiwan. Indeed, we feel that one of Savage Minds' greatest successes has been its help to promote the development of an anthropological blogosphere in which we play an increasingly less important role. Neuroanthropology (http://blogs .plos.org/neuroanthropology/) – a subfield grown out of a blog! – is a good example of this.

Doing Anthropology in Public

In his piece on our blog, David Price wrote that 'blogs present vital opportunities to allow publicly engaged anthropologists to break through the often-narrow analysis of traditional corporate-media outlets' (Price 2010). We agree with this sentiment – indeed, it is an argument we have used in trying to attract guest bloggers. While we recognize that traditional media outlets still drive most online discussion, we believe that Savage Minds can and does function as an alternative op-ed page for this kind of publicity. However, we do not feel that Savage Minds does 'public anthropology', because it does not imitate the genres of existing forms of corporate media. Rather, we believe our impact is a result of our decision to do 'anthropology in public'. That is to say, by writing in anthropological genres for a global audience, we have avoided the sort of 'popularization' and simplification implied in the term 'public anthropology'. By not prejudging what our audience wants to read or is capable of understanding, we have built a community that keeps coming back, as well as sparking discussion with other blogs. Geertz once said that anthropologists 'read culture' over the shoulder of their informants (Lende 2012). On Savage Minds, it is the other way around.

Our conception of 'anthropology in public' is grounded on a different set of theoretical assumptions from those employed by exponents of 'public anthropology'. On the whole, proponents of public anthropology imagine that anthropologists know something that the public would benefit from knowing, if only anthropology were written in a style that suited the taste of the public. Such a position assumes that anthropologists have something the public wants, and that they know how the public wants to be told about it.

Such self-confidence in the power of anthropological knowledge – both of audience expectations and specialist knowledge – seems misplaced to us. Drawing on theorists such as Michael Warner (Warner 2005), we emphasize that publics are elicited through speech, not something that pre-exists it. We also emphasize that our own identities as bloggers are themselves shaped by the audience. As Markell puts it, 'identity … is not something over which agents themselves have control. Because we do not act in isolation but interact with others, who we become through action is not up to us; instead, it is the outcome of many intersecting and unpredictable sequences of action and response' (Markell 2009: 13). We do not assume that we know who will read our posts, or how they would prefer us to speak. We do not see ourselves as 'experts' speaking to a lay 'public'. Instead, our sense of who we are has been shaped by the way our audience defines us. At times this means accepting that non-academics know as much (if not more) than we as 'experts' do. At other times, it means speaking with authority to people who want to hear expert judgments, even if we are uneasy with such epistemological authority. We are willing, in sum, to recognize that others may know more about us than we do, and to forsake the privileges of institutionalized authority for 'the less grand and more tentative pleasure of potency – of simply having (and being carried along by) effects in the world, without necessarily being able to determine their trajectory' (ibid.: 133). We believe that in the long run, this has resulted in a wider readership for our blog and more responsive writing from our authors.

An example of this openness can be seen in our rethinking of academic norms. Doing anthropology in public has meant adhering to the genre standards of our professional imaginary, even as we use the medium of the internet to transform it. Academics communicate in a variety of different genres: face-to-face meetings for service, mentoring and research; newsletters of professional associations with a specific area or topical focus; journalistic coverage of academia in publications like the *Chronicle of Higher Education*; and of course peer-reviewed journals themselves. And this is not to mention innovations like email lists, blogs, and social media.

In each of these genres, there is considerable variation across two important dimensions: formal vs. informal discourse, and public vs. private audiences. Peer-reviewed journals, for instance, are extremely formal and (to subscribers) public loci for academic communication, whereas faculty meetings are informal and private. Digital media can also be analysed along these lines: email lists, for instance, can be public or private depending on whether the list requires a paid membership, whether you must be approved by the list administrator, whether posts are moderated, and so on. Over time, the communities that form on lists are often relatively informal. Websites are by definition public, and are often formally written. Here too, however, there is considerable variance, with some blogs having a more informal tone than others. This analysis can be extended to the comments policy, which can be more open or more tightly controlled depending on the management style of the blog.

Many writers have used the internet as an opportunity to fundamentally rethink these genres – for them, digital anthropology enables an irresistible transgression of established genres. This is partly because of the freedom one has online to write what one likes without censorship, and partly due to the modernist vision of progress that people bring to the internet, which is often discussed breathlessly as the location for the latest and most iconoclastic phase of global modernity.

In contrast to this, Savage Minds has self-consciously sought to tweak, rather than transgress, the genres of our discipline. At the broadest level, we have taken private, informal academic discourse and made it public without increasing its formality. Savage Minds, we like to say, does not strive to be an online version of an academic conference – it strives to be the hotel bar at the conference. This mix of old and new is reflected in our set-up: our posts are single-authored and relatively 'monologic' in Bakhtin's sense (Bakhtin 1981: 270), but the comments section of the site is active. Our policy is to censor disruptive commentators, even as we try to encourage a community of readers. We are not, in other words, rethinking epistemological authority or traditional formats of writing and authorial voice. Savage Minds, then, is not *hors de categorie*. No Mind has asked their department to count their contributions to the blog as publications (although we do list them as 'service'). We stick to a long, single-authored form rather than attempt to burst genres. We are not rethinking what it means to think, read or write. Uptake within the discipline, then, has been facilitated by the fact that our work is, as they say in the development literature, 'culturally appropriate'.

In what follows we substantiate this claim by examining three genres that our blog takes up while transforming: mentoring and professionalization, 'public anthropology' in the traditional sense of the term, and academic governance.

Case Study: Mentoring and Professionalization

One of the most significant genres of academic interaction is that of the private, informal meetings in which scholars are socialized into roles as graduate students, teaching assistants, junior professors, peer reviewers, and so forth. Much of this advice remains private. Indeed, while Biber notes that there has been an 'explosion of research on academic discourse' (Biber 2006: 6) in recent years, there has been relatively little on the 'spoken registers that are common in university life' (ibid.: 9) – the skinny, as it were, on how to be a professor. A main focus of Savage Minds is to take these private genres and make them public.

There are many reasons for this information remaining private. This cultural capital can make or break careers, and professors often hoard it; indeed, even opinions on which how-to book is the best are often closely guarded. Alternatively, some knowledge, such as the embarrassing amateurism of field methods, for instance, is often kept private to avoid the awkwardness that comes from revealing that the emperor has no clothes. Mostly, however, because academic socialization 'goes without saying because it comes without saying' (Bourdieu 1977: 167), most professors simply have not thought to address mentoring explicitly. One study of university office hours asserts that they 'are always (but not exclusively) task-oriented; with a view toward solving students' problems' (Limberg 2007: 223). The highly contextual, individual and task-oriented nature of these meetings means there is often little opportunity to provide more general advice on professionalization, based on the accumulated experience that professors gain from talking to numerous students.

We feel it is important that this information be available to all. As graduate students some of us struggled to reinvent the anthropological wheel. For others with pedigree training from the best universities, the inequalities between the haves and have-nots of cultural capital are appalling. Now as a tenured or tenure-track faculty, we often simply wish students had a place to read advice on graduate school so that we would not have to repeat it so often. As a result, a major part of our writing revolves around how to read, write, study and perform well as an anthropology graduate student. Because the Savage Minds bloggers are themselves graduate students and junior faculty, such advice has the added benefit of being in some ways more similar to advice from classmates than from professors, although many of these posts were written after the authors became academic advisers themselves.

These posts take a wide variety of forms. One of the more popular entries on the site, '(More) Advice on Graduate School Applications', was written by Alex to provide a basic overview about how to evaluate potential graduate schools, and then successfully apply to them. The post was written after his own experience serving on the graduate admissions committee of his department. The goal of the post is to help graduate students and schools to find the best fit, and to get potential graduate students up to speed on academics genres so that their applications will be judged on the merits of the students, not on their (in)ability to conform to the genre standards of the admissions game. Similar posts from Alex, such as 'How To Ask Someone To Be On Your Dissertation Committee', deal with straightforward but rarely discussed aspects of graduate life.

Another theme on the blog is reading and writing, and particularly how scholarly habits are changing in the age of digital publication. Kerim has written several articles on this topic under the 'Tools We Use' column. Sometimes these posts focus on recommendations for programmes, websites, and concrete workflow for processing digital documents – for instance, in his post 'Going Paperless'. At other times, posts simply describe (often critically!) our own habits of finding and using information online, and how our reading and writing practices are shaped by them. 'Reading Fast, Reading Slow', for instance, discusses how to balance browsing online sources with the work of actually reading what you find online.

But in fact there are a variety of posts related to professionalization. 'Wasting Away in Grantlandia' by Ryan Anderson is a personal reflection on how unpleasant it is to write grants for funding which takes its cue from the Jimmy Buffet song 'Margaritaville'. In the column 'Dead Wrong Scholars or Future Collaborators?', Adam Fish reports the advice of one of his mentors about the importance of befriending, rather than angering, the scholars you disagree with. Overall, the blog does not have a programmatic take on professionalization or mentoring, and entries are often written without extensive planning or footnoting – which is why, we believe, they are so widely read and helpful.

Case Study: Jared Diamond

While economics and political science blogs have no difficulty in finding stories in the mainstream media that fall squarely within their professional domain, even if they disagree with the mainstream take on their discipline, the same cannot be said for anthropology. There are many stories that touch on topics that anthropologists study, but they rarely take an anthropological approach or even interview anthropologists. Stories of 'uncontacted tribes' and new archaeological discoveries aside, anthropologists are rarely asked to comment on public events. One notable exception was the use of anthropological methods by the Human Terrain Teams in Afghanistan, a topic that was extensively covered by Savage Minds and Open Anthropology. As a result, a lot of discussions relating to what might be referred to as 'public anthropology' often end up in boundary disputes, as anthropologists must first stake a claim to the topic. When the object of critique is a popular one, these boundary disputes can be quite vicious, as happened when Savage Minds had the temerity to take on best-selling author Jared Diamond.

Scott Jaschik's 2005 write-up (Jaschik 2005) does an excellent job of summarizing the debate that had flared up surrounding the Savage Minds critique of Jared Diamond's *Guns, Germs, and Steel* and the subsequent attack from more established liberal bloggers. Attempts by several Savage Minds bloggers to question Diamond's methodology were attacked by Crooked Timber's Henry Farrell for exhibiting some 'underlying deformation of thinking' (Farrell 2005b). He was specifically referring to what he saw as an attempt to argue that 'certain kinds of reasoning are inherently racist and repugnant to right thinking people'. I do not want to recap those arguments here, but rather take this debate as an opportunity to examine more broadly why anthropological critique has a harder time establishing its legitimacy in the public sphere. That is, why a site like Savage Minds can never occupy the same place as Crooked Timber. When, after Jaschik's piece was written, Deborah Gewertz and Frederick Errington, experts on the country of Papua New Guinea where Diamond had done his primary research, wrote a series of guest posts on Savage Minds, it did not draw nearly as much attention. The *New York Times* did interview them about many of the issues they discussed in their posts for an article about Diamond's new book, *Collapse,* but the article made no mention of the blog (Johnson 2007). Nevertheless, this piece did get at one of the problems with anthropological critique:

> For the anthropologists, the exceptions were more important than the rules. Instead of seeking overarching laws, the call was to 'contextualize', 'complexify', 'relativize', 'particularize' and even 'problematize', a word that in their dialect was given an oddly positive spin. (Johnson 2007)

Indeed, this is what Gewertz and Errington did in their posts on Savage Minds.

We try not to depict Yali or other Papua New Guineans in an essentialized fashion. We do make clear in the book from which our posts are excerpted … that PNGuineans are thoroughly caught up in history and are not all alike – but differ considerably according to cultural group as well as social class. In addition, we discuss the fact that they engage with each other and with Europeans in a range of ways, including both gift exchange and commodity transactions.

Implicit in this approach, however, is an argument that certain kinds of simplifying grand-narratives are inherently problematic and even racist precisely because they overlook such particularity, because they take Yali out of his own context, making nonsense of his question. I would argue that this is what was so threatening to otherwise sympathetic political scientists and economists about the Savage Minds intervention in this debate. There was an implicit critique of the analytic tools of their own profession.

Case Study: Open Access

The third important way in which academic blogs can play an important role is in discussions over academic governance. Savage Minds has been at the forefront of an ongoing discussion over the extent to which the American Anthropological Association should embrace open access publishing models. The issue first arose in June 2006, when the AAA executive board wrote a letter to Senator Susan Collins (R-ME), Chair of the Senate Committee on Homeland Security & Government Affairs, expressing opposition to S. 2695, the Federal Research Public Access Act. This letter was written with no public discussion among the AAA member associations. For this reason, academic blogs became an important venue for public discussion of association policies, which did not necessarily represent the opinion of the membership as a whole. The intervening years have only made this truer. In January 2012, the AAA wrote yet another letter opposing government mandates that would expand public access to research through open access (Lende 2012). This time, Savage Minds was not even the first to respond, but a large number of Anthropology blogs reacted strongly to the news, and the AAA's official blog quickly back-pedalled, stating that they were not against all forms of open access, even though – as pointed out by Neuroanthropology (Lende 2012) – saying so is not the same thing as actively supporting open access.

Academic blogs and social media also became an important voice in the wake of a decision by the AAA to remove explicit mention of 'science' in its long-term planning statement. Using the #aaafail hashtag on Twitter, many archaeologists and biological anthropologists were particularly outspoken in their opposition to the changes, using it as an opportunity to voice underlying discontent relating to the status of their sub-disciplines within the AAA. This was less of a concern to the authors of Savage Minds, although we did use it as an excuse to talk about more general issues pertaining to science in anthropology. But the vocal nature of the more scientifically oriented sub-disciplines in the anthropology blogosphere is worth noting and helps to explain the strong reaction against the AAA's anti-open access policies. The 'hard' sciences have largely embraced open access already, but the humanities and social sciences have tended to be slower to embrace new publishing models.

Conclusion

In this article we have argued that there are two main reasons for Savage Minds's success. First, our blog accepts and builds upon anthropology's professional imaginary and the institutions of our discipline, using the internet as a space to transform that imaginary while still keeping it readily identifiable to readers as a relatively orthodox academic space. Second, we have argued that the blog is successful because of the way it appeals to audiences outside of the academy. This method, as the title of this volume suggests, has not been 'public anthropology' in the traditional sense. We have not attempted to explain specialized research to a general audience. Rather we have been successful in the way we have pursued 'anthropology in public', writing for ourselves and, perhaps, a general anthropological audience in a forum that is world-readable.

In conclusion, we might point to a few lessons that could be drawn from the example of Savage Minds. First, success requires the perseverance to write often, to write (relatively) well, and to do so day after day, month after month, year after year. Although some people see the internet as a place of breathless, rapid change, our experience has been that the most important virtue to have online is *sitzfleisch* (stamina). Second, although we present our blog as a success because of the traditional scholarly virtues we claim it incarnates, in fact Savage Minds has been only a modest success. We have not done the things that attract huge readerships or sought the fame that, frankly, it is not that hard to cultivate on the internet. To this extent, Savage Minds might be regarded as a failure by those who seek Margaret Mead-levels of fame and notoriety. Occasionally we meet people who imagine that we started Savage Minds out of a desire for attention or fame. Nothing could be further from the truth: in fact, we took over the internet by accident. Savage Minds has opted out of building a strong and engaged social media presence, making public declarations about current issues, and so forth. We feel ambivalent about the fame we have achieved. It is always nice to meet fans, and to have a stranger come up to you at a conference and shake your hand or have their picture taken with you. We also feel that anthropology's slightly paranoid ethos – that somewhere else, something important is happening in private – has given us, the purveyors of the inside scoop, a certain sort of indefinable soft power, both within our departments and more broadly.

A final point is related to issues of fame. Savage Minds is not an example of how to become a full-time blogger or a member of the digerati. It has always lived alongside other, more important things in our lives such as our academic careers, artistic endeavours, and family. It has always been, in other words, a junior partner in our work. Blogging is a stimulating and important part of our lives, but never the most important part of it. The deep concentration and intense commitment that it takes to create a book or documentary are far more satisfying to us than the transient fame afforded by the internet. In fact, writing for Savage Minds has made us look askance at more traditional forms of academic fame. We know that it is easy to get attention by inciting controversy or cultivating adherents, but we also know how transient that attention can be. Working on this blog has reaffirmed our belief that the work that is most worth doing is the work that we most want to do. Being in the limelight has taught us to look beyond it.

In the end, whether Savage Minds successfully 'makes anthropology public' is a judgement that each of our readers will have to make themselves. In this chapter we have tried to explain what it is we have undertaken in the blog, and why we are satisfied with our efforts. We hope that our readers are satisfied as well, and that we will have the opportunity to write more for them for many years to come.

Alex Golub is an associate professor of anthropology at the University of Hawai'i at Mānoa. A political anthropologist, his book *Leviathans at the Gold Mine* examines mining, corporations and indigeneity in Papua New Guinea. Dr. Golub also has a focus on American culture and the internet, and has conducted research on the online video game World of Warcraft. Dr Golub is also the founder of the anthropology blog Savage Minds (savageminds.org); he is an open access advocate, and has written popular pieces for The Appendix, Inside Higher Ed, and other websites.

P. Kerim Friedman is an associate professor in the Department of Ethnic Relations and Cultures at National Dong Hwa University in Taiwan. His research explores language revitalization efforts among Taiwanese Aborigines, looking at the relationship between language ideology, indigeneity, and political economy. An ethnographic filmmaker, he co-produced the Jean Rouch award-winning documentary *Please Don't Beat Me, Sir!*, which is about a street theatre troupe from one of India's Denotified and Nomadic Tribes (DNTs). He is also a founding member of the group anthropology blog Savage Minds.

Acknowledgement

Thanks to Carole McGranahan for her comments.

Notes

1. As we make the final revisions on this article in June of 2015, the user statistics for Savage Minds are dramatically different from what they were in 2011 when we wrote this piece; since this article represents a snapshot in time, we have decided to leave the numbers untouched. Based on the most recent numbers from Google, the site now averages around 911 unique visitors a day, of which 35.2 per cent are returning visitors. However, Google analytics rely on unreliable javascript. We now have much more accurate numbers from CloudFlare, which routes the site via their own DNS servers. These show Savage Minds as receiving approximately 3,410 unique visitors a day. Our Facebook page now has 6,143 "likes" and Twitter has 11,400 "followers." We do not currently have accurate usage numbers regarding our RSS feed.
2. The site has grown significantly since this paper was written. As of June 2015 the list of full time contributors to the site has grown from nine to twelve members, including four women (a number we continue to work on improving). In addition to those mentioned in the text, the current roster includes: Carole McGranahan, Dick Powis, Maia Green, Uzma Rizvi, and Zoë Wool. Jay Sosa and Thomas Strong have left the blog.

References

Ahmed, M. 2005. 'Ceci n'est pas une Blague'. Chapati Mystery. http://www.chapatimystery.com/archives/univercity/ceci_nest_pas_une_blague.html (accessed 14 April 2013).
Bakhtin, M. Mikhail Mikhailovich. 1981. 'The Dialogic Imagination: Four Essays' (Volume 1 of University of Texas Press Slavic Series). in J. Michael Holquist (ed.), *The Dialogic Imagination: Four Essays*. Austin: University of Texas Press.
Biber, D. 2006. *University Language: A Corpus-based Study of Spoken and Written Registers*. Amsterdam, NL: John Benjamins Publishing Company.
Bourdieu, P. 1977. *Outline of a Theory of Practice*. Cambridge and New York: Cambridge University Press.

Farrell, H. 2005a. 'The Blogosphere as a Carnival of Ideas', The Chronicle Review. http://chronicle.com/article/The-Blogosphere-as-a-Carnival/2674 (accessed 14 April 2013).

———. 2005b. 'Cultivating Ignorance'. Crooked Timber. http://crookedtimber.org/2005/07/28/cultivating-ignorance/ (accessed 27 April 2013).

Givens, D.B., and T. Jablonski. 2000. 'Survey of PhD Recipients'. American Anthropology Association. http://www.aaanet.org/resources/departments/SurveyofPhDs95.cfm (accessed 27 April 2013).

Heffernan, V. 2013. 'You will Hate this Article'. Yahoo! News. http://news.yahoo.com/comment-trolls-women-kogan-173842372.html (accessed 27 April 2013).

Jaschik, S. 2005. '*Guns, Germs and Steel* Reconsidered'. Inside Higher Ed. http://www.insidehighered.com/news/2005/08/03/ggs (accessed 27 April 2013).

Johnson, George. 2007. 'Question of Blame When Societies Fall'. The *New York Times*, 25 December.

Lende, D. 2012. 'American Anthropological Association Takes Public Stand against Open Access'. Neuroanthropology. http://blogs.plos.org/neuroanthropology/2012/01/31/american-anthropological-association-takes-public-stand-against-open-access/ (accessed 27 April 2013).

Limberg, H. 2007. 'Discourse Structure of Academic Talk in University Office Hour Interactions', *Discourse Studies* 9(2): 176–93.

Marcus, G.E. 1998. 'Introduction', in *Ethnography through Thick and Thin*. Princeton, NJ: Princeton University Press, pp. 3–30.

Markell, P. 2009. *Bound by Recognition*. Princeton, NJ: Princeton University Press.

Nature.com. 2006. '50 Popular Science Blogs (written by scientists)'. http://www.nature.com/news/2006/060703/multimedia/50_science_blogs.html (accessed 14 April 2013).

Price, D.H. 2010. 'Blogging Anthropology: Savage Minds, Zero Anthropology, and AAA Blogs', *American Anthropologist* 112(1): 140–42.

Warner, M. 2005. *Publics and Counterpublics*. Reprint. Zone Books.

Chapter 9

THE OPEN ANTHROPOLOGY COOPERATIVE
Towards an Online Public Anthropology

Francine Barone and Keith Hart

We attempt here to explore the relationship between anthropology, social media and public engagement through a web-based network that we helped to found and manage. We argue that obscure social and technical dynamics are at work here, but academic anthropology today also poses significant obstacles for this enterprise.

The Open Anthropology Cooperative (OAC) is an online organization for professionals, students and the general public with an interest in anthropology. It was founded in mid-2009. A small network of mostly young anthropologists raised the possibility of such an organization on Twitter, and then moved for a few days to a forum that allowed more extended discussion; shortly after, on 28 May, they formed the OAC as a social media platform. The response to the OAC's formation was explosive. Over one hundred members joined on the first day, seven hundred in the first month and one thousand in the first three months; by the end of 2014 it had eight thousand members around the world. The ad hoc, volunteer 'committee' that launched the OAC was taken by surprise and the initial months were turbulent. In the first year, some political crises had to be overcome, but eventually things settled down. The OAC is rather quiet now, punctuated by short bursts of activity around hot topics. A majority of the members appear to be dormant, but identifying active and engaged readers or tracing social media 'sharers' is always problematic on the internet. The promise of this social experiment is great, but we still have many problems to solve.

The OAC consistently receives, on average, five hundred visits a day. The top ten countries varies, but the United States accounts for almost a third of these visits with Britain a clear second, followed at the time of writing by India, Australia, Canada, Germany, France, Italy, Japan and Brazil. Visits are divided roughly as follows: United States 30 per cent, other Anglophone 30 per cent, Europe 30 per cent, Rest of the World 10 per cent. This distribution understates the remarkable geographical and social range of the OAC's membership, which is much broader. The OAC has over fifty members in each of twenty countries, and double-figure membership in over thirty more countries (see Appendix 1). Active participation through posting comments on the site, however, is skewed towards native English speakers, although the OAC early on hosted specialist groups operating in German, Norwegian, Italian, French, Russian, Portuguese, Spanish and Turkish. Yet despite this initial diversity and the OAC's worldwide reach, the trend is inexorably towards Anglophone dominance. The language issue is crucial for a site with global aspirations.

In practical terms, the OAC is a place of online interaction, with discussion forums, blogs, groups, messaging, a chat room, and facilities for sharing photos and videos, announcements, posting offers and making friends. It also serves as an archive with each member able to store photos, videos, music and texts on their home page and to post similar material around the site. This, along with its social media look, gives the OAC a Facebook feel. Interaction on the site is ego-centric for technical and cultural reasons, and despite the founders' collectivist aims, the result is a conglomerate of individually curated pockets of information. We also built up a repository of source materials and advice that might be of professional, educational and public value. There is an underused wiki for course outlines, reading lists and similar material. The OAC Press publishes working papers which are discussed in online seminars lasting a couple of weeks. We also republish classical papers and have a book reviews section. There is thus a balance between ephemeral and more durable contributions. Given our initial focus on openness and freedom, however, we underestimated what it would take for the OAC to become a viable social concern.

The world is going through a major transformation that is social, technological and cultural in scope. It has fundamental consequences for the human condition and hence for anthropology. The best way to learn about these developments is to take an active part in them (Hart 2009). There are analogies between the print revolution and today. For most of human history, information was hard to come by and had to be sought out. With printing, information became omnipresent and for the first time people had to learn how to select what to read. Once this became acceptable, the way was then open for the mass media. But the relationship between sender and receiver was still asymmetrical. The internet and especially social media, commonly referred to as 'Web 2.0' (O'Reilly 2005), have made a plethora of options available through easy-to-use tools that allow anyone to become a communicator in their own right (Barone 2010: 239–42). New social forms adequate for channelling this unprecedented freedom of self-expression are at best incipient. They are, moreover, compromised by a bureaucratic capitalism whose command-and-control system and intellectual property regime continually provoke vigorous demands for more open access to information and for the democratization of its production, distribution and consumption.

Activists too often envisage change through models shaped by what has been rather than what could be. Contemporary anthropology had its origins in the democratic revolutions of the eighteenth century, but has been reduced since to compiling passive descriptions of exotic phenomena or implementing bureaucratic imperatives rather than engaging with revolution. Few of us have received an education in revolutionary practice. Moreover, the universities are going through a crisis that gives many would-be anthropologists the choice of being medieval apprentices, precarious piece-rate workers or just unemployed (Kendzior 2012; Stoller 2012). This is the main constituency for something like the OAC, but their social predicament often conflicts with the liberation they aspire to. The new organizations we try to create are often hamstrung by the old intellectual equipment we bring to the task.[1] We unknowingly reproduce the dominant social forms in striving to resist them.

The Open Anthropology Cooperative's founders believed that they were launching a new social movement; and the heady first weeks reinforced that feeling. But the OAC was born as a short-term reaction to academic bureaucracy, and its leadership has been trying to catch up with events ever since. At present, the OAC lacks dynamism and a transparent identity. Building an open association as an antidote to a closed academy turned out to be more complicated than we realized, not least because the prisoners do not know what to do when they have been broken out of jail. The ethnographic detail, historical reflections and political commentary of this account of the experiment we launched may help others to plan similar initiatives in public anthropology with greater foresight than we brought to the task.

The shift from the OAC's charismatic launch to more routine issues of organization and development posed some hard questions. Its brief history bears on the new social media, anthropology, its public face and the dynamics of innovation. We first outline the circumstances of the OAC's formation, then the social and technical questions that arose in its early development and how the organization has changed in five years. We also identify our main concerns for its future. Finally, we draw some lessons from this public experiment on the relationship between anthropology and democracy.

Origins

The OAC was founded in a way unique to its time: via social media. Through blog comments and an exchange of tweets, a few individuals across several countries, most of whom had never met face-to-face, produced a new online anthropology forum with astounding ease. Back in May 2009, frustration with the American Anthropological Association's hostility towards open access led Savage Minds blogger P. Kerim Friedman to express his disappointment over the AAA's foot-dragging (Friedman 2009a). This is now once again a hot issue.[2] Kerim's initial post led to a heated exchange of comments by readers agreeing that the AAA's impenetrable bureaucracy had built a wall between those who govern it and its supposed beneficiaries. For instance, anthropologist Chris Kelty remarked that the professional organization mainly served the interests of its employees; it was a 'neurotic institution' run by non-university staff, made worse by academics' lack of interest in participating in its governance (Friedman 2009a).

This blog post resonated for anthropologists around the web. Responses revealed widespread frustration with the AAA's actions. Casual griping rapidly spread to Twitter, where a loose network of anthropologists had already formed. Before long, quasi-revolutionary suggestions were made to start a new, open, less bureaucratic and more inclusive worldwide community of anthropologists. The pool of participants in the early conversation on Twitter grew rapidly. Twitter was ideal for spreading the news and gaining momentum, but when the discussion turned to actually constructing a new network for anthropologists, more space and organization was needed. Keith Hart and Justin Shaffner set up a forum on Keith's website, 'The Memory Bank', to that end.

From 20 to 28 May, a small group of these Twitter friends, most of them Anglophone graduate students, plus a couple of senior academics and one interested outsider, committed to specifying a name and purpose for this collective undertaking. The key voices in this early exchange included: P. Kerim Friedman, Paul Wren, Keith Hart, Francine Barone, Carol Mc-Granahan, Jeremy Trombley, Steven Devijver, Cosimo Lupo, Olumide Abimbola, Àngels Trias i Valls and Justin Shaffner. This group shared an attachment to anthropology, an interest in new media and a commitment to open access. A consensus was soon reached to take advantage of the momentum before individual commitments waned. In the new forum we brainstormed two pressing issues: 'structure' and 'function'. What would a new organization look like and do?

Graduate student Jeremy Trombley suggested that 'we should begin by offering a structure that is open enough to allow it to become whatever it can down the road' (TMB forum). In contrast to the AAA's bureaucratic intransigence, Trombley proposed that 'every member [should] be able and willing to take an initiative. There's no need to get bogged down in unnecessary voting (like the AAA poll that started this discussion); if there's something you think needs to get done and you can do it, then go for it'. This philosophy, which most of us shared, was opposed to the AAA's perceived shortcomings, especially its predilection for top–down control and failure to support open access initiatives. The OAC's founders, relying only on digital tools, aspired to truly global scope, egalitarian ideals, and the abolition of academic hierarchy. Aiming to reach a far wider audience beyond the universities, its social and organizational model sought to negate academia's typical malfunctions. This antithetical framework proved to be both liberating and a handicap in the months ahead.

Naming the OAC

The name of the website was itself a response to the 'closed' and confining nature of the dominant professional associations – hence 'open anthropology'. Rejection of authoritarian control was axiomatic. Yet the term 'open' was difficult to pin down. As Paul Wren (later an administrator) pointed out: 'We should view "open" as having many faces – open access, open membership, open to new ideas, open to whatever the organization might do or become'. This approach was refreshing, especially for academics frustrated by the slow pace and restrictions of the universities.[3] It also made sense, at a time when open access was becoming a fashionable buzzword for change (Kelty et al. 2008), that the OAC's philosophy should harness the passion of geeks for open technology.

Defining openness became slippery and contradictory as the site grew. We soon learned that in order to keep some aspects of the OAC open, others had to be closed. This is analogous to freedom and its antithesis, necessity: you cannot be free in everything at once, but need to hold some things constant in order to be free in others. Freedom of movement requires fixed places like airports and train stations. We felt that an open community should accept anyone who signs up. But that let in the 'trolls' (people who bait their opponents in ways that undermine the aims of the site, its moral code and the comfort of its participants)[4] – not to mention the spammers. The administration team was occasionally called upon to discipline public offenders, but decisions to do so and communications with offenders were normally conducted in private. In retrospect, we could have avoided the information maze that the site became if we had imposed stricter standards on members opening new groups, but we encouraged the trend for new members to open one as soon as joining. Crucially, being 'open' made it harder to reach agreement on our common goals.

The dialectics of openness merit more serious consideration than they usually get in internet circles. If as anthropologists we aim to extend our public reach beyond the boundaries of academia, we should be aware of the pitfalls of treating the internet as an open medium. While information is instantly accessible to a wide audience, the quality, consistency and usefulness of that information may not match the site organizers' intentions. If there is no way to control the audience (given full public access), regulating members becomes essential – even if it contradicts the site's ethos.

The term 'Anthropology' should have been self-evident, but we did not want to just replicate institutionalized versions of the discipline. We hoped rather to revolutionize the field of anthropology, beginning with its presence on the web. Keith Hart spoke of an inter-disciplinary project involving 'whatever we need to know about humanity as a whole to make a better world; and anyone who wants to place their self-learning within the most inclusive framework of human history'. This broad scope inspired – and challenged – the OAC's new members to think outside established boundaries.

The last part of the name was trickier. Was this going to be a network, a community, a movement, a conversation, an organization, a platform or just a group? 'Cooperative', with its 'sense of action and movement in addition to the collaborative aspect' (Àngels Trias i Valls, TMB forum) had the right tone to encourage open interaction towards shared goals. It avoided the weasel word 'community' and put distance between the new project and the idea of being yet another professional 'association'. Such a cooperative would offer its members democratic involvement, be more inclusive and make better use of social media for transparent access within and beyond anthropology itself. As a label for a network of anthropologists, each part of the OAC's name had deliberate and recognizable meaning, but it was also subject to diverse interpretations and intense debate. Career anthropologists will find this unsurprising.

The issue of the name became more divisive once the site was launched, leading to quarrels between founding members, a site-wide referendum and eventually several departures from the core administration team. Bouts of bickering, in-fighting, relentless debate and disputed meanings and intentions chipped away at the upbeat mood of free-flowing consensus that launched our enterprise with such high aspirations. We inverted academic power relations, encouraging equal participation by students, teachers, researchers and outsiders alike, but this had unexpected consequences. This effacement of hierarchy turned out to be a social experiment in itself. At different times, new site hierarchies, factions and divisions formed. Where decisions had to be made, it was inevitably through 'cooperation' – the key pillar meant to hold up the OAC – and we often failed to follow through on them before attention faded. Is this symptomatic of online interaction (a tragedy of the digital commons) or does it just reflect anthropology's lack of an agreed core and the individualism of anthropologists?

New Media, New Possibilities

We certainly did not want to form another professional 'association', but this model did influence some of our members' aspirations, if only by negation. Kerim Friedman saw the OAC more as an anti-AAA[5] which nevertheless shared some of its goals, such as using 'a set of tools and platforms which allow people to accomplish the same things that associations have traditionally provided'. We aimed to build a global space for intellectual exchange, workshops and seminars, research publications, and a pooling of syllabi and teaching materials, while providing an attractive interface for relaxed conversation between students, amateurs and professionals. We also wanted blogging and messaging facilities; a repository of anthropological resources such as photos, videos and podcasts; and to offer practical advice concerning fieldwork and technical matters. Some of these features involve more programming knowledge than others. What we needed to put it all together was mostly available around the web in fragmented pockets, and offered endless possibilities. The same could be said of anthropology.

The OAC needed a permanent and fitting home. We had to build a platform quickly while interest was still fresh. Nine days after Kerim's initial blog post, Maximilian Forte joined the conversation and suggested that we might try setting up a site on Ning, a relatively new online service that allowed users to create their own Facebook-style social networks with many useful features (described below). On 28 May 2009, Keith Hart created a free Ning network as a base for the OAC with a few clicks of the mouse. Producing a 'Facebook for anthropologists' took no time at all, but making it work has been another matter.

The team that launched the OAC had only our own volunteer labour and no funds, so we naturally drew on whatever free and easy-to-use tools and applications could be found on the web. For most of us, being 'open' meant the freedom to be creative and free from proprietary control over our data. Pursuing our lofty goals and adhering to the egalitarian ideals represented in the OAC's name thus depended on the technological tools at our disposal in mid-2009. In short, the OAC piggybacked on the Web 2.0 revolution which had lowered the technical threshold and already captivated anthropologists who were sharing, publishing, promoting and interacting online. At best, we were striving for 'Anthropology 2.0' (Friedman 2009b).

There are now hundreds of anthropology bloggers and thousands of anthropologists with an active presence on the web. Students and academic anthropologists with varying levels of computer literacy use Tumblr, Blogger, Wordpress, Typepad, Drupal and other platforms. They share photos on Flickr, interact on Facebook, produce videos for YouTube and create wikis for teaching and research. Although there are still some active academic mailing lists, they are only a small fraction of the public conversations that anthropologists now engage with online. The OAC's founders came together as a result of one such conversation. Web projects are formed and abandoned all the time. The OAC has already lasted for six years.

The most useful lessons coming from the OAC experiment are pragmatic. The social web offers an ever-evolving selection of sites, apps and services, many of which are free or relatively low-cost. Innovation is rapid and open source is increasingly common. On the other hand, the speed of application launches and failures means that free[6] sites are not always stable over long periods. Most anthropologists know little of computer programming and often feel powerless in the face of technological change. New desktop software and web applications may not be tailored to academic needs, but they are often flexible enough, given basic technical knowledge, and a willingness to endure many bouts of trial and error can go a long way. One simply has to invest the time and energy to find out what works and what does not.

Even though the OAC's future is still as uncertain as it was in the beginning, we can offer some insights that may be relevant to similar projects. Use of social media has enabled a small group of strangers of varying technical ability to build a richly interactive network for thousands of anthropologists. Moreover, the OAC has a well-recognized presence and is an often-cited source of anthropological information on the web.

No Turning Back

Ning[7] distils the essence of Facebook (a fully featured social networking site) into a simple design template with a limited, but flexible, modular interface. It offers a fairly elegant solution for website development that requires no server maintenance and minimal knowledge of programming or web design. User profiles, discussion forums, groups, blogs, a chat room and multimedia uploads (photo- and video-sharing) are built in and ready to use, so that new members can just sign up and start adding content. User interactions, member contributions of all types and activity across the site are visible on the home page, which acts as both a landing platform and a navigation hub. Each site feature, from the public discussion forums to individual blog posts, allows other members to comment or reply, and may be followed by email subscription or RSS feed.

Founded in 2005, Ning was still undergoing changes in ownership and vision around the time of the OAC's launch. Its monetization features, such as advertisement and subscription services, proved popular with corporate brands, musicians and celebrity fan sites, but were less than ideal for an open quasi-academic network. From the beginning, we were challenged to make Ning work for us. Without any ready-made viable alternatives, it provided an ideal test for at least one key aspect of our global experiment: to see if our movement could sustain itself on 'free' technologies and volunteer efforts.

After the OAC's almost accidental launch, its membership grew exponentially with each passing day. Keith sent invitations to his professional email address book and this provided a catalyst for the OAC's growth, attracting hundreds of anthropologists in the first few days. Hundreds soon grew into thousands, much faster than anyone expected. We felt that if we were to back away from Ning we would lose momentum. This was decisive. The initial structure, including the benefits and limitations of the platform we had chosen at a whim, greatly shaped the OAC's development in form and function.

The site owner (or Network Creator, here Keith Hart) and a self-appointed team of administrators have access to a control panel of management functions, activity records and appearance settings. The network and its accumulated data are hosted and controlled centrally by Ning. Simple at first glance, the power and complexity of this system should not be underestimated. It took the administrators time to master navigation, control of certain features, privacy protocols and the more complex tasks of editing, organizing and keeping track of site and member information. Ironically, we had chosen this *proprietary* service as a platform for opening up anthropology to the online public. Ning's de facto ownership of network data (it has only recently offered backups and exporting) was always at odds with our open source ethos.

Members were quick to point out Ning's faults. Any structural changes made by Ning, downtime, glitches, or imperfect features directly affect the day-to-day running of the OAC. Its social features are similar to Facebook, which means that preconceived notions about communication there, including privacy concerns, turned some people off. Academic snobbery was reinforced by Facebook's emergence as the commercial antithesis of attempts to build a genuinely free and open internet. More significantly, the OAC's 'social network' appearance practically constrains how content may be displayed and arranged. Organizing and moderating the site is complicated by the fact that it only takes seconds to add and delete information. Before Ning provided a fix, members could inadvertently leave gaping holes or delete whole conversations by quitting the OAC. Spam was rampant before stronger controls on access to membership were put in place.

All of this contributed to a sense that it was easy to lose track of information for large portions of the site. The administrators have had to take on the roles of editor, sub-editor and curator of a site that rapidly passed the threshold of information overload. Web development left less time to focus on site culture, impact and productivity. A majority of our creative energies went into keeping the site functioning and clean rather than developing its social integrity. When the OAC was formed, questions of administrative function were never raised. Yet, however open the network was in conception, its vitality hinged on the few people who agreed to run it. An informal division of labour emerged between us, with Keith paying more attention to content and crowd control, while Francine focused on site development. But apart from routine decisions, the team as a whole pitched in as we could, given the constraints of our 'offline' lives.

By the end of the first year, we had more or less weathered the storm. Shortly after, Ning's new management team converted its free accounts to a paid, premium fee structure. By now we had amassed enough content for the OAC to be widely recognized as an invaluable repository. The possibility of moving the network to free, cheaper or more open alternatives was mooted in response to the new fees. Migration to a new server, however, required the time and dedication to learn a new platform all over again; and Ning's services made it easier for non-technical administrators to help to manage the site. We decided, therefore, to absorb the premium subscription costs. These were initially covered by Keith and later by member donations.

Governance

The task of site governance became a pressing problem for our new cooperative. The OAC was founded on principles opposed to elitism, bureaucracy and academic hierarchy; so we optimistically (or naively – probably both) set out to avoid centralized leadership and control. But what kind of leadership replaces hierarchy? Bureaucracy was originally intended to provide equal access to public resources, but in the twentieth century many came to see it as a means of impersonal domination. Resistance to state and corporate control made it difficult for some to see how self-organization and bureaucracy might be fruitfully combined. Calls for less bureaucracy could transmute into anti-bureaucratic slogans. It was against this background in academic anthropology that the OAC adopted a laissez-faire policy privileging self-regulation over firm 'rules'. This is like promoting the free market without rules of oversight. No one would try to build a community on free market principles; but in retrospect, this is just what we did. Liberals masquerading as consensual democrats were recruited as volunteer administrators. Minimal regulations limiting anti-social behaviour were drafted collaboratively. Writing a 'mission statement' proved to be too divisive and was deferred time and again, so that only a brief statement of our common objectives is on display for visitors to this day.

It seemed sensible then to make all major decisions on the OAC's governance, appearance and purposes available for review by the membership, and even occasionally for a vote. Everyone should have a say. Before long, however, it became impossible to sustain such an unwieldy decision-making chain even for simple matters. Opening every major site decision to public referendum – from rules and regulations to designing a site logo – extended each task and made a consensus hard to reach. Building our organization by an open committee was a mistake that we unwittingly borrowed from academic bureaucracy.

In the end, the administrators had to cut through the indecision. From the beginning we had kept a private back channel going by email, and resort to this became increasingly necessary to weed through the contradictory, even baffling, 'open' discussions that took place in the public forums. We were soon saddled with more formal governance and crowd control than with anthropological substance, although Keith still saw his main role as greeting members and contributing to forum discussions. It did not help that the administrators were effectively strangers who never met each other. What might have happened if we had a regular offline rendezvous?

There were some quite radical differences among administrators and members concerning how the site should be run. These were mainly over freedom and accountability, since if members were to be accountable they could not be free in any absolute sense. The membership struggled to come to terms with the site's commitment to transparency. There is a liberal tradition that considers anonymity to be the only guarantee of true internet freedom, since otherwise people might be held to account for transgressions against authority.[8] But this can also provide cover for anti-social behaviour, and we opted for insisting that members participate as who they 'really' were or how they were known elsewhere in their professional lives. We requested full personal names as a basic prerequisite for membership, and spent our time chasing members up on this before deciding to screen new applicants. We refused to delete content except in clear cases where privacy had been violated, and in instances of bullying. Some of our members indulged a propensity for antagonistic behaviour and extremist attitudes. We were slow to moderate applications for membership because it felt wrong to control entry to an 'open' network.

We had no way of requiring members to take greater responsibility for their actions and contributions to the OAC, even less to invest in its future. For instance, people are allowed to set up new groups on any topic. There were soon over a hundred. Most of them became moribund and their owners drifted away. The administration team's philosophy of non-intervention simply caused more tail-chasing in the long run. Without firm rules in place, abuse of the site's openness became rampant. This forced us to acknowledge that, in order to be 'open' to all, we had to install more bureaucracy of the type we had hoped to avoid. We were forced to acknowledge that some rules and tighter controls were required to keep the site civil and productive. To be responsibly open, we had to also keep some aspects of site governance closed.

The rocky moments in the OAC's development were interpersonal more than technical. This was usually a question of people talking past each other or succumbing to the norms characteristic of open exchange on the web. Unfortunately web-based discussion allows some people to regress to childish bickering. Perhaps less is at stake than in face-to-face situations. Left unchecked, this kind of behaviour can ruin the atmosphere and discourage many from participating. Our experiment attracted young and old, bullies and zealots, rebels and slackers. Novices were sometimes slow to learn the ropes. The majority of members undoubtedly lurk rather than expose themselves to the slings and arrows of internet discussion. Social media cannot sustain a revolution alone. Just because the tools are available does not mean that they will be used as expected.

When thousands of members descended upon the OAC, managing day-to-day tasks sapped our energies, diverting us from what motivated us in the first place. Before we could get around to purposeful collaboration, we found ourselves on the defensive and overwhelmed by trivia. In short, we have been preoccupied until now with duct-taping together a ramshackle vehicle for changing the scope of anthropology rather than with actively cooperating to effect such a change.

The original team expected to be temporary stewards for a term of six months each. Five years and eight thousand members later, only three were still on board (the third being Justin Shaffner) and no one has ever stepped up to take our place. Our level of commitment has slowly subsided. Several attempts have been made to reinvigorate site activity and to inspire a new burst of energy. We have asked more members to help us to look towards the future and to renew excitement over the OAC's achievements and prospects. There is usually a flurry of interest at first, but it does not last.

A Provisional Assessment of the OAC

The OAC is an online organization on a social networking website with forums and file storage open to anyone. Structurally, this is true. But we aspired to do something better than previous anthropological initiatives have achieved; and who knows, after this first stage, what we or others might achieve in the long run? The OAC places few restrictions on new members' initiatives. Perhaps people assume that the administrators wish to retain their powers of direction as a monopoly. It is not so, but equally we have not succeeded in harnessing fresh energies to develop the OAC. At least we have kept open many possibilities for the future.

For the majority of the OAC's members – semi-regular participants, lurkers and absentees – what we have outlined here will sound unfamiliar. First, only a tiny minority contribute to discussions on the OAC's purposes, or are committed to its organizational tasks. The site has remained more or less unchanged in appearance and practice since the 3,000-member mark. Second, even in periods of low participation, the OAC receives regular visitors. Links to OAC content are shared around Twitter, Facebook, Google+ and other sites daily. Our conversations are cited on popular anthropology blogs like Savage Minds[9] and Neuroanthropology.[10] OAC members have created offshoots like the Anthropologies Project[11] and PopAnth,[12] in part inspired by exchanges on the site. For the vast majority of our members today, the trials and tribulations detailed here are probably inconsequential.

Many members are apparently happy to visit regularly, share resources and personal stories, engage in vibrant discussions, debate anthropological theory and practice, and discover new media and interesting people. Anyone who browses the site will learn something new on every page. The number of members grows each day. Some are not formally trained anthropologists or even anthropologists at all. We have personally received thanks for creating the OAC, for keeping it alive and for giving anthropologists a place on the internet to come together in a more relaxed atmosphere. The social aspects of the site – personal user profiles, chat, blogging, forming 'weak ties' (Granovetter 1983) – should not be underestimated just because they are not easy to track or quantify. Informality reduces barriers for interaction between established anthropologists, students and interested amateurs. This is helpful to anyone finding their way in anthropology, and to part-time adjuncts, unemployed postdocs and retired senior faculty who feel disenfranchised from the academic mainstream.

Much of the internet is made up of fleeting encounters and hurried searches for information. Commitments change from one day to the next. These are the unavoidable limits of the online world, but the benefits of having a global communication network outweigh any of its disadvantages. The OAC experiment relies on borrowed energy and volunteer labour, with no promise of social reward beyond an opportunity to take anthropology somewhere it has not been before. The real challenge for web-based enterprises like ours lies in the *longue durée*.

Rob Borofsky (2011) asks, 'How do we transform anthropology into a more publicly engaged discipline in the sense discussed here – moving beyond talking the talk of change to making a real difference, as a discipline, in the broader world?' The OAC's founders proposed to do this through new media, open technology, cooperation, public outreach and a passion for anthropology. If the old way was not working, we would try something different. We hoped to establish a universal medium capable of expressing the unlimited potential of an anthropology that ought to be universal, but often is not. What concerns us now is not that we have failed to revolutionize anthropology, but that we may have plateaued and fallen into the same lethargy that is afflicting anthropology in universities. Have we, too, simply reverted to the anthropologists' safe zone: observing, participating, collecting more and more data, but not putting it to any useful purpose? Almost six years on, it is hard to judge where to place the OAC within the wider movement for creating a more engaged anthropology, since such a project is at best incipient.

Between Social Networks and Academia: Anthropology Online

Participation in the technological revolution today is both passive and active. We are all affected by the internet's impact on academic life, whether we choose to join in the change every day or only occasionally, or even to ignore it. The internet and social media are powerful tools for growth precisely because anyone with access can take some kind of action with little effort. This chapter grows out of a serendipitous online meeting between two academics at opposite stages in their careers, which would not have happened without Twitter. Yet blogging, communicating via social media and producing freely accessible publications online is still relegated by universities to the status of an academic hobby, and not seen as significant work. This is a serious impediment to moving the OAC forward as long as the majority of our members frame their participation by an academic career.

We have both been active in the use of information technology in teaching and research: Francine as an alumna of Britain's most computer-sensitive anthropology department, Keith as the head of the relevant university committee at Cambridge. Departments of anthropology vary in the speed and commitment with which they adopt new technologies and, with the exception in Britain of University College London's programme in digital anthropology, do not usually train their students to make the best of the technological revolution. This is sad for a discipline as global in its reach as anthropology. It also leaves great gaps in technical capacity between people of various ages and backgrounds. The profession has been slow to recognize promising developments in the new media, such as online publishing and blogging, because they do not fit traditional models of academic achievement.

The OAC has shown us that anthropologists can be adaptable *bricoleurs* online, piecing together various communication technologies for chatting, learning, teaching and sharing. The sheer volume of its contributions is difficult to keep up with. Yet the OAC's participants struggle to break through established academic prejudices about online publication and interaction. Regular contributors make up a tiny fraction of our membership. Some still hesitate to participate openly in our forums since the OAC bans the use of pseudonyms and everything is indexed by Google's web crawlers. Many are reluctant to give up control over how they appear online. Anthropologists do not easily let their guard down. Perhaps our formation as apprentice fieldworkers encourages self-protective behaviour. If so, it is inconsistent with opening anthropology to the public to cherry-pick only the best parts. The OAC's online seminar series most closely recreates an acceptable academic mode of production and its value system. This is also our most popular feature, drawing the most traffic from members and online visitors. It seems that we can only draw participants if we reproduce the academic values that the OAC was founded to escape from.

The OAC aspires to be a transparent academic community, so we encourage informal chat alongside formal debate with other anthropologists and across disciplines. This makes the experience hard to categorize, especially given the universities' dominance in our membership. The network is an anomaly in an otherwise tidy classification system, a sad reflection on anthropology as an exclusively academic practice, where online and academic conversations are treated as being mutually exclusive. The OAC is a compromised public island that seeks to avoid the formal restrictions of university life, yet is largely populated by its denizens.

How then do non-academics find a place among us? How effectively do anthropologists use technology, even those of us who acknowledge its usefulness, not just for teaching, but as a way of changing the public face of anthropology? How accessible are anthropologists? Why are we so rarely approached by the outside world? As a discipline, we are only comfortable talking amongst ourselves. Perhaps we do not know what anthropologists really have to say. These questions point to a direct parallel between where anthropology is today and why the OAC keeps hitting a wall. We started out focusing on the social and technical constraints of the platform and soon confronted the cultural intransigence of the network's object, anthropology.

There are significant differences between social networks and academic networks concerning return on time investment, volunteer labour and long-term objectives, not to mention power relations and status hierarchies that carry over online from the academic world. Much activity on the social web need not concern itself with aims, intentions or long-term goals. It keeps ticking over until boredom or newness force change – whichever comes first. Academic networks do not work the same way. The OAC mixes them together, which may be one source of its current identity crisis.

Playing around on Twitter or keeping in touch on Facebook are not the same as what goes on at the OAC. Twitter is fleeting and impermanent, while Facebook is an intimate meeting point for friends and family. Being an active member of the OAC takes more time commitment, at least some critical thought, and involves the shared expectation of some kind of pointed exchange or response. We have tried to add site features that lower the barrier to participation (such as share buttons, a Twitter tab and RSS feeds), but the returns on this are quite low. Content that is uploaded without any expectation of reciprocity or a response (e.g. sharing a video, 'liking' something, listing an event) has only a marginal place on the OAC.

The more significant products of the OAC's concerted efforts require investments of time and energy. Among these, the OAC Press stands out. It produces online publications in html, pdf and epub formats with a Creative Commons licence. There is no restriction on further use. Working papers by old hands and novices alike are each discussed in OAC online seminars, as already mentioned; but we also republish classic articles by distinguished authors and review articles on newly issued texts. Before long, we expect to publish longer manuscripts. These activities have a clear end-product and fit long-standing models of academic value; but they also break new ground in form, content and authorship. We may think that new modes of communication make a difference to how we live and work, but academics change slowly. This is why email has not yet imploded as the main means for transmitting academic information. Mailing lists are still popular because they are semi-closed/private and simple. They do one useful thing well enough to stick around. In the OAC's early days, Twitter was a big deal, a real paradigm shift that led to our developing a new medium. Today, few in our circle are bothered to engage on Twitter. Perhaps it no longer occupies the communicative niche it once did. We have recently developed an OAC Facebook page, which has acquired ten thousand members in two years, many of them South Asians. There is not much interaction between the two sites.

A plethora of content prevents adequate use and navigation of the OAC. Hence our future plans for site development always involve streamlining access to the most interesting content. Instead of hoping for some new impetus to what we started, we should probably concentrate on making better use of what we have already produced. Not much more can be done without wider and more engaged interest for more members. In short, it is one thing to propose a strong, free and public-facing anthropology online, but achieving it in practice is another.

On Models for Change and Social Movements

Our report has so far replicated the ethnographic model that dominates contemporary social anthropology. But that model was never intended to inform a movement to change the world. We stumbled into writing this chapter without an active plan for what we hoped to achieve with it. Both of us relate to the site in a very different way. Francine has written an extended reflection on the social impact of the internet in her Ph.D. thesis (Barone 2010), and Keith has published a short memoir of his own experience of the world revolution in communications (Hart 2009). We have provided the ethnography. All we need now is the anthropology or, breathe it softly, a dose of social theory.

Contemporary anthropology (or social science more generally) reflects the world, but is not designed to change it. Anthropologists are conservative. After all, we spent the last century – a century of urbanization, war and the break-up of empires – seeking out isolated places to study as if they were outside modern history. Then, having realized that we are part of a world unified by transnational capitalism, we spend our time bemoaning the fate of the universities and our own irrelevance to public discourse. The internet's growth has generated a strong counter-movement to the status quo that a few anthropologists are taking seriously (Coleman 2013).[13] The years 2011–12 saw some dramatic political responses to the world economic crisis in which the new media have played a marked role. Even anthropology may be affected by this development. The OAC can as yet claim only to have played a flawed part in such a process.

The OAC was born as a reaction more than a movement. Its slogan of being 'open' turned out to be contradictory. The leadership we mustered to implement an abstract rejection of hierarchy became merely managerial and half-hearted. We preferred to maximize membership at the expense of making rules that might exclude people. People left anyway. We were always catching up, never ahead of the game. We failed to identify ideas that some members could believe in and work for, preferring to let a thousand flowers bloom, except that they did not. The contradictory hybrid that is Ning hardly sustained revolutionary zeal; graduate students were a majority of the team, and writing a thesis left little time for building an alternative. It is disheartening, but not unexpected, that a cooperative of eight thousand people yields no volunteers to help in its development. Perhaps Web 2.0 makes it so easy to do your own thing that few see the point in joining other people's initiatives.

It is remarkable that we have hardly used anthropology or social theory – old or new – to address the problems we face. We point here to just a couple of examples that might have helped. Max Weber's notion of 'the routinization of charisma' (1978: 246–49) certainly gets at some of these problems. The OAC leadership was never charismatic and we rejected the notion of leadership in the first place. But we did aspire to a sort of collective charisma aimed at putting the boundaries of traditional authority at risk. We saw ourselves as a revolutionary movement. Weber argued that the power of a revolutionary challenge inevitably subsides. By 'routinization' he meant that charismatic authority is replaced by bureaucracy or at least by a mixture of bureaucracy and traditional authority. Weber developed this typology because he was interested in understanding power with a view to using it.

But why stick with the classics? Perhaps anthropologists should be more open to the reflections and even concepts of the people who currently shape social media. Most progressive intellectuals have a twentieth-century baggage that inhibits learning from the successful exponents of Web 2.0. To take one example, Seth Godin is a mega-blogger whose self-promoting excess would make most of us cringe. He has a little book called

Tribes: We Need You to Lead Us (2008). Anthropologists may not have noticed that many people out there use our traditional label (which we have largely abandoned) to describe the social forms that they see emerging online. Here are some extracts from that book:

> A tribe is a group of people connected to one another, to a leader and to an idea. A group needs two things to be a tribe: a shared interest and a way to communicate. Tribes need leadership. Sometimes one person leads, sometimes more. People want connection and growth and something new. They want change. You can't have a tribe without a leader. A movement is the work of many people, all connected, all seeking something better. The new tools of the Net make it easier than ever to make a movement. Tribes need faith, belief in an idea and a community. Management is about manipulating resources to get a known job done. Leadership is about creating a change you believe in. A tribe grows by transforming a shared interest into a passionate goal and desire for change, by providing tools to tighten communications between members [and] by gaining new members. The first two are more important than the last. [We] need a story of who we are and what future we are building, connections between leaders and the tribe, and something for members to do with each other. A crowd is a tribe without leaders or communication. Participating isn't leading. Leaders are generous. (Godin 2008: several pages)

Most academic anthropologists would dismiss this as muddled hype, a misappropriation of 'our' concepts. But something important is happening to how leaders and followers are conceived and portrayed in society today; and this is not limited to the genre of business sales, education or self-promotion. When the Latins decided it did not pay to be a disorganized rabble, they formed themselves into 'tribes', three named groups, killed a cow and 'dis*trib*uted' the meat among themselves in a ritual (Hart 2003). They then made ad hoc alliances with neighbours for mutual protection and called each of them *socius* (an ally), the whole thing *societas*. These words share the o-grade root of *sekw-*, meaning to follow (as in *second* and *sign*). Whoever was attacked would assume de facto leadership and the rest would follow them, but such leadership was temporary and contingent. The idea of society as a bounded hierarchy synonymous with a state was a medieval French invention. If we are now living in the 'network society' (Castells 2000), it seems to be one in which 'followers' and 'friends' play a major part. These relations are often ephemeral. Maybe we should think a bit more about the implications of all this for anthropology and the academy.

Anthropologists, it seems, suffer from an inability to catch up with a changing world, at the same time as they meticulously document it. Meanwhile, we are losing control of our master-concepts like 'culture' to other disciplines, and even to web moguls who are not afraid to engage with popular media.[14] Anthropologists do have something to offer the general public. It is just that we are terrible at communicating it. We all know this, and perhaps this volume as a whole will help us to understand why.

This very real PR problem carries over to the OAC, where we have had difficulty formulating a clear identity or public face. This is reflected, for instance, in our failure to post a coherent site-wide statement of purpose. More often than not, anthropologists are confounded when interacting with the world outside academia. The OAC has failed to reverse this trend, and reinforces it by producing little that might attract general audiences. Fear of marketing our expertise, of 'branding' anthropology or seeking out media attention could fatally undermine an innovative project that once promised so much. Our web-based activities closely resemble office-based politics in this respect. The OAC began as a public-facing anthropological experiment and became a self-serving exercise by academics and for academics, subject to similar prejudices and hierarchical constraints to those of anthropology in the universities.

Conclusion: Anthropology and Democracy

Our story began with some friends meeting on Twitter and ending up on Ning. A chaotic explosion of collective action was followed by slow quiescence. The principles and limitations of the social media have undoubtedly shaped our attempt to expand anthropology's horizons to a global level, yet we have not been able to draw on our own discipline to help us fulfil the OAC's promise.

Anthropology was born in the eighteenth century as a tool for making a democratic revolution. The liberal philosophers asked what it is that human beings have in common (their 'human nature') that might be the basis of a truly democratic constitution. This tradition was revived in the twentieth century by the ethnographic turn, as a result of which, for the first time, a segment of the academy left the ivory tower to join the people where they live, and to find out what they do, think and want. We all know what has happened since. At the beginning of the twenty-first century, corporatized universities produce young anthropologists in droves with scant prospect of ever plying their trade there; and academic writing is confined to formats dictated by publishing monopolies.

A visitor to our site from America's leading anthropology blog once wrote that he did not 'get' the idea of the OAC. For many the point of a public anthropology is to project one's ideas onto a more general plane than the introverted professional circle with which we are familiar. Intellectuals generate 'ideas' and would like the public to be aware of them. But ideas are cheap. Everyone has ideas. The real challenge is to develop new social forms capable of expressing our ideas more effectively. C.L.R. James concluded that democracy has two facets: the freedom to be a fully developed, creative, individual personality, and to be part of a community based on principles conducive to that aim.[15] This was the unity of private interest and public spirit that de Tocqueville found in the early American democracy.[16] Today it has become a universal goal with the emergence of the people of Latin America, Africa and the Middle East as potent symbols of the collective force of humanity in its opposition to the forces of unequal society.

It is no simple thing to create new social forms, and the most radical ideas are often subverted by unconscious retention of old social forms. The OAC is a genuinely new social form. For example, it allows female Asian graduate students to express themselves more freely than in any other serious forum; it encourages all types of anthropology students to network with academics well beyond their departments; and it enables those without institutional affiliations to have access to information, publications and discussions that are normally locked behind university doors or journal pay walls. Of course it still lacks a big idea, and old social forms lurk beneath the surface ready to suck the life out of its capacity to support invention and self-expression. But we would claim to have contributed to public anthropology by providing a genuinely global and largely status-free medium for exploring anthropology's potential to change the world. Humanity has recently discovered universal media, but we are still searching for a genuine democracy. The OAC is, more self-consciously than most initiatives of its kind, part of that search.

Appendix 1

OAC members by country on 17 June 2012 (Total 6,300)

USA	1,594	25%
UK	855	14%
Canada	260	4%
India	258	4%
Portugal	247	4%
Germany	192	3%
Italy	169	2%
Brazil	167	2%
Australia	154	2%

Norway	135	2%
Netherlands	117	2%
France	108	2%

Denmark 97, Spain 88, Romania 84, Turkey 79, Greece 74, Sweden 64, Poland 60, South Africa 51

Slovenia 46, Mexico 44, Belgium 43, Ireland 39, Nigeria 37, New Zealand 37, Russia 36, Finland 36, Georgia 34, Pakistan 33, Japan 32

Israel 29, Iceland 29, Taiwan 27, Czech Rep 26, Argentina 25, Kenya 22, China 22, Croatia 22, Bangladesh 21, Peru 21, Slovakia 20

Serbia 19, Hungary 19, South Korea 18, Chile 18, Colombia 17, Bulgaria 15, Iran 15, Philippines 14, Egypt 14, Ethiopia 11, Singapore 10.

Europe	45%
North America	30%
Asia	10%
Latin America	5%
Oceania	3%
Africa	2%
Under 10 and NA	5%

Francine Barone is a social anthropologist and internet researcher. Her work is primarily aimed at understanding people's everyday computing practices, interactions and activities on the web, social media and mobile devices. As an urban ethnographer, she emphasizes place and locality in her analyses of technological change and the socio-cultural impacts of the digital age. She is a founding member of the Open Anthropology Cooperative.

Keith Hart is currently international director of the Human Economy Programme in the Centre for the Advancement of Scholarship at the University of Pretoria, and centennial professor of Economic Anthropology at the London School of Economics. An anthropologist by training, he contributed the concept of the informal economy to development studies and has written at length on money, including the collapse of the twentieth century's dominant form, national capitalism. He has taught in more than a dozen universities around the world, especially Cambridge University where he was director of the African Studies Centre. He runs a website – thememorybank.co.uk – and is a founder and member of the Open Anthropology Cooperative. His recent books include *The Human Economy: A Citizen's*

Guide (2010), *Economic Anthropology: History, Ethnography, Critique* (2011), *People, Money and Power in the Economic Crisis: Perspectives from the Global South* (2014).

Acknowledgments

We are grateful to Ryan Anderson, Jürgen Schraten and Simone Abram for their helpful comments.

Notes

1. For a related discussion, see Hawks 2011.
2. See Thompson 2012; Anderson 2012a, 2012b, 2012c.
3. See Taylor (2012) for a impassioned discussion launched at the OAC by Erin Taylor, 'Producing academic scholarship: If universities are failing, where else do we go?'
4. See Herring et al. 2002; Shin 2008; Hardaker 2010.
5. Keith Hart formed an anti-AAA in the 1990s called the *amateur anthropological association* (motto: 'Amateurs do it for love') known as the *small-triple-a*.
6. As in zero-price (*gratis*) and with few or no restrictions on use (*libre*).
7. http://ning.com
8. As in the subversive hackers' network, Anonymous – see Coleman 2012.
9. http://savageminds.org
10. http://blogs.plos.org/neuroanthropology/
11. http://anthropologiesproject.org/
12. http://popanth.com
13. When Gabriella Coleman, who holds a Chair in Scientific and Technological Literacy at McGill University, decided to study the free software movement, she was told not to expect a job in academic anthropology – a prophecy that has so far proved to be correct.
14. See Breidenbach and Nyiri 2009.
15. James 1993.
16. Tocqueville 1840.

References

Anderson, R. 2012a. 'Opening Our Anthropological Conversations: An Interview with Tom Boellstorff'. Savage Minds. http://savageminds.org/2012/08/29/opening-our-anthropolog ical-conversations-an-interview-with-tom-boellstorff/ (accessed 19 December 2012).
———. 2012b. 'Anthropologies of Access'. Anthropologies. http://www.anthropologiesproj ect.org/2012/03/introduction-anthropologies-of-access.html (accessed 19 December 2012).

———. 2012c. 'News: AAA Response about Public Access to Scholarly Publications'. Savage Minds. http://savageminds.org/2012/01/31/news-aaa-response-about-public-access-to-scholarly-publications/ (accessed 1 February 2012).

Barone, F. 2010. *Urban Firewalls: Place, Space and New Technologies in Figueres, Catalonia.* Ph.D. dissertation. Canterbury, UK: University of Kent.

Borofsky, R. 2011. 'Defining Public Anthropology'. Center for a Public Anthropology. http://www.publicanthropology.org/public-anthropology (accessed 25 January 2012).

Breidenbach, J., and P. Nyiri. 2009. *Seeing Culture Everywhere: From Genocide to Consumer Habits.* Seattle: University of Washington Press.

Castells, M. 2000. *The Rise of the Network Society.* New York: John Wiley & Sons.

Coleman, G. 2012. '"Our Weirdness is Free". The Logic of Anonymous – Online Army, Agent of Chaos and Seeker of Justice', *Triple Canopy* 15 (13 January). http://canopycanopycan opy.com/15/our_weirdness_is_free (accessed 10 December 2012).

———. 2013. *Coding Freedom: The Aesthetics and the Ethics of Hacking.* Princeton, NJ: Princeton University Press.

Friedman, K. 2009a. 'Dear AAA, can I have my $$$ back?'. Savage Minds. http://savagemi nds.org/2009/05/19/dear-aaa-can-i-have-my-back/ (accessed 13 February 2012).

———. 2009b. 'Anthropology 2.0: For Real?'. Savage Minds. http://savageminds.org/2009/06/27/anthropology-20-for-real/ (accessed 13 February 2012).

Godin, S. 2008. *Tribes: We Need You to Lead Us.* New York: Portfolio.

Granovetter, M. 1983. 'The Strength of Weak Ties: A Network Theory Revisited', *Sociological Theory* 1: 201–33.

Hardaker, C. 2010. 'Trolling in Asynchronous Computer-mediated Communication: From User Discussions to Academic Definitions', *Journal of Politeness Research: Language, Behaviour, Culture* 6. http://www.degruyter.com/view/j/jplr.2010.6.issue-2/jplr.2010.011/jplr .2010.011.xml (accessed 21 March 2013).

Hart, K. 2003. 'Studying World Society as a Vocation', Goldsmiths Anthropology Research Paper No. 9. http://thememorybank.co.uk/2010/01/11/studying-world-society-as-a-voca tion/ (accessed 10 December 2012).

———. 2009. 'An Anthropologist in the World Revolution', Anthropology Today 25(6): 24–25.

Hawks, J. 2011. 'What's Wrong with Anthropology?' *Anthropologies.* http://www.anthropolo giesproject.org/2011/10/whats-wrong-with-anthropology.html (accessed 21 March 2013).

Herring, S., K. Job-Sluder, R. Scheckler and S. Barab. 2002. 'Searching for Safety Online: Managing "Trolling" in a Feminist Forum', *The Information Society* 18: 371–84.

James, C.L.R. 1993. *American Civilization* (A. Grimshaw and K. Hart, eds). Oxford: Blackwell.

Kelty, C.M., et al. 2008. 'Anthropology of/in Circulation: The Future of Open Access and Scholarly Societies', *Cultural Anthropology* 23: 559–88.

Kendzior, S. 2012. 'The Closing of American Academia'. *Al Jazeera,* 20 August. http://www .aljazeera.com/indepth/opinion/2012/08/2012820102749246453.html (accessed 21 March 2013).

O'Reilly, T. 2005. 'What is Web 2.0?: Design Patterns and Business Models for the Next Generation of Software'. http://www.oreillynet.com/pub/a/oreilly/tim/news/2005/09/30/what-is-web-20.html (accessed 21 March 2013).

Shin, J. 2008. 'Morality and Internet Behavior: A Study of the Internet Troll and its Relation with Morality on the Internet'. Proceedings of Society for Information Technology & Teacher Education International Conference 2008, pp. 2834–40.

Stoller, P. 2012. 'Changing Culture in Higher Education'. *Huffington Post.* http://www.huffing tonpost.com/paul-stoller/changing-culture-in-highe_b_2155954.html (accessed 21 March 2013).

Taylor, E. 2012. 'Producing academic scholarship: If universities are failing, where else do we go?' http://openanthcoop.ning.com/group/theanthropologyofanthropology/forum/topics/producing-academic-scholarship-if-universities-are-failing-where/ (accessed 18 December 2012).

Thompson, M. 2012. 'Digital Anthropology Group Is Happening Now'. Savage Minds. http://savageminds.org/2012/03/22/digital-anthropology-group-is-happening-now/ (accessed 11 April 2012).

Tocqueville, A. de. (1840) 2003. *Democracy in America*. London: Penguin.

Weber, M. 1978. *Economy and Society* (2 vols, edited by G. Roth and C. Wittich). Berkeley: University of California.

The Memory Bank Forum: http://api.ning.com/files/wIUqLpuYa*vXXp3mwN3B0X3rDbXu JcMrbddW74oJjGwtcr*B*IrSonpDfD8kBz-pJGSCJ6OOjFxXhbTNCysci*eiHVszOpdU/ SS2.png

INDEX

.

www.ingramcontent.com/pod-product-compliance
Lightning Source LLC
Chambersburg PA
CBHW070922030426
42336CB00014BA/2503